REBIRTH
OF BRITAIN

A symposium of essays
by eighteen writers

A PAN ORIGINAL

PAN BOOKS LTD : LONDON
in association with
THE INSTITUTE OF ECONOMIC AFFAIRS

First published 1964 by
PAN BOOKS LTD
8 Headfort Place, London S.W.1

'I should like to thank Hamish Gray
for assistance in editing the essays and
clothing them in book form, a task
which often seemed that of the coach-
man drawn by 17 headstrong thorough-
breds.'

A.S.

July, 1964

PRINTED IN ENGLAND BY
HAZELL WATSON AND VINEY LTD
AYLESBURY, BUCKS

£1-5
ND

6/-

The Institute of Economic Affairs is a non-party group of economists, held together by a common interest in the working of free economic institutions.

The idea for this book sprang from a special issue of *Encounter* magazine, published in July 1963. Under the editorship of Arthur Koestler, sixteen writers wrote on economic planning, education, the Welfare State and other issues. The cure for Britain's supposed ills was greater direction of the economy from the top and greater uniformity in education, most of them urged.

To a number of economists and writers associated with The Institute of Economic Affairs, much of this reasoning seemed wide of the mark. Their analysis of Britain's needs led them to opposite conclusions and remedies. For too long, they saw, the inherent skill, energy and adventure of the British had been bottled up by state uniformity and all kinds of 'restrictive practices'. What was needed was to unleash these energies, by creating the conditions for maximum competition. The law against monopoly and other restrictive practices should be strengthened. Inflation should be ended. Taxation should be reduced by drastic pruning of unnecessary state welfare services. The Institute's researches showed that, 'the whole machinery of the Welfare State is becoming to a large extent a vast engine for carrying coals to Newcastle'.

The classic example of prosperity, several contributors to this book believe, is Western Germany. As long ago as 1948, Professor Erhard, then Minister of Economic Affairs, saw that what was needed to rebuild his country was to scrap all economic controls except those designed to eliminate monopolies, and then to let people get on with building their own, and thereby the nation's, prosperity. Each man should make the best of his own brains, brawn and material resources. This, most of our present writers suggest, is even now the way ahead for Britain.

CONTENTS

THE OSTRICHES AND THE LION

The statesman, who should attempt to direct private people in what manner they ought to employ their capitals, would not only load himself with a most unnecessary attention, but assume an authority which could safely be trusted, not only to no single person, but to no council or senate whatever, and which would nowhere be so dangerous as in the hands of a man who had folly and presumption enough to fancy himself fit to exercise it.

Adam Smith (1776)

The idea of a co-ordination of human activities by means of a system of impersonal rules, within which what spontaneous relations arise are conducive to mutual benefit, is a conception at least as subtle, at least as ambitious, as the conception of prescribing positively each action or type of action by a central planning authority.

Lord Robbins (1937)

It was supposed, until our time, that despotism was odious, under whatever form it appeared. But it is a discovery of modern days that there are such things as legitimate tyranny and holy injustice, provided they are exercised in the name of the people.

Alexis de Tocqueville (1835)

INTRODUCTION

THE OSTRICHES AND THE LION

THE 1950s and 1960s have brought a new faith in old devices based on state initiative, regulation, or direction. 'Co-ordination' and rationalisation for transport, marketing boards for agriculture, aid for 'special' areas, import controls, subsidies, national economic 'planning' in one form or another; they all enthrone authority and degrade individual spontaneity. Nor is this thinking original; it may seem new to younger people but it was all heard in the 1930s or earlier: even 'social cost/benefit analysis', now called in aid by 'planners', is a distorted version of Professor A. C. Pigou's 'private/social net product' theory of 1912.[1]

For a time the war and post-war siege economy of rationing, controls and licensing taught the British people the dangers of central authority: monopoly, despotism, waste, corruption. Post-war nationalisation in fuel, energy and transport confirmed the lessons. It solved nothing: it postponed decisions until large-scale surgery had to replace gradual adjustment to change. For a time spontaneity reigned in the 1950s. But lack of nerve, lack of faith, lack of patience, lack of respect for the consumer, the citizen, the tax-payer, restored faith in authority. It is now back in full cry by politicians of all parties, business men, trade union leaders, social scientists, journalists.

In particular the method of authority has been favoured by British intellectuals. The advocates of authority largely dominate the theatre, broadcasting, the so-called 'quality' press, the literary journals, the universities. They write profusely for the consumption of the 'average' reader. They

[1] See Brunner, p. 39, and Wiseman, pp. 87–90.

were, for example, in force in the July 1963 number of
Encounter, 'Suicide of a Nation?', in which they combined
to create the impression that the British economy was run
largely by amateurs, the products of public schools and class
privilege, who kept down the rate of economic growth, and
that stagnation, decay and doom awaited us unless the state
further increased its authority over the economy, education
and society. The editor, Mr Arthur Koestler, argued that
'the average Englishman' was a lion in crises but an ostrich
between them. Not all the contributors sounded the sepul-
chral note of death and destruction but the general sense
was clear : Messrs. Goronwy Rees, Michael Shanks, Andrew
Shonfield, Austen Albu, John Vaizey, Mrs Elizabeth Young
and others made the reader feel that Britain was, or seemed,
incapable of saving itself from suicide.

It is to examine the new post-war faith in authority that
this symposium has been assembled. It was inspired by the
July 1963 *Encounter* but the 18 writers range over the main
trends in economic and social thought in post-war Britain
and quote a wide selection of writers to illustrate the arguments. They discuss not only the errors in the debate on
economic 'growth' and the demand for more central authority but also the significant omissions—anti-monopoly
legislation, agriculture, taxation, state welfare, local government, nationalisation, import restrictions. They do not
merely exhort; they propose specific measures to rebuild,
reform and perfect the legal, institutional and fiscal
framework of society to allow, educate and encourage people
to exercise their inherited or acquired qualities to the full in
voluntary exchange with one other. In contrast to the paternalistic Authoritarian Society they present a vision of a
Spontaneous Society.

They dissect the great paradox of our day : that we are
more capable economically, socially, educationally and
politically of making decisions as individuals without direction, yet we acquiesce in more power for authority to make
them for us. And they make the reader ask : who is the lion
and who the ostrich? Is not the lion the man who is free

to produce wealth? And the ostrich the intellectual who will not learn from experience: from post-war Russia and China, from war-time and pre-war Britain, from pre-war Germany and Italy, from the Hapsburgs and the Romanoffs and Louis XIV, from medieval mercantilism, from ancient Rome and Sparta and Byzantium?

The authors of these essays range from academic economists in the universities to professional writers interested in economic affairs; some were at public schools, most at state schools; their ages range from the middle thirties to the early sixties; they do not write in a partisan spirit although they include sympathisers at one time or other with all three political parties. They write as individuals and do not necessarily share one another's views, and indeed differ on some, but they share doubt about the fashionable faith in central authority as the key to economic progress.

This book was devised in the summer of 1963 and the essays were written in March and April of this year before the date of the General Election was known. It may now be published during the pre-election period when party slogans will diminish the hearing for non-party analysis of principles, but it is intended as a work of long-term interest to be pondered when the tumult and the shouting have died down. For the principles it discusses will be ignored by future governments, whatever their political label, at our peril.

A. S.

April 1964.

PART ONE

FADS AND FANCIES

There are valuable human activities which require the motive of money-making and the environment of private wealth-ownership for their full fruition.
. . . dangerous human proclivities can be canalised into comparatively harmless channels by the existence of opportunities for money-making and private wealth, which, if they cannot be satisfied in this way, may find their outlet in cruelty, the reckless pursuit of personal power and authority, and other forms of self-aggrandisement.
It is better that a man should tyrannise over his bank balance than over his fellow-citizens . . .

Lord Keynes (1936)

I think that democratic communities have a natural taste for freedom: left to themselves, they will seek it, cherish it, and view any privation of it with regret. But for equality, their passion is ardent, insatiable, incessant, invincible: they call for equality in freedom; and if they cannot obtain that, they still call for equality in slavery.

Alexis de Tocqueville (1835)

. . . the doctrine of self-reliance and self-denial, which is the foundation of political economy, was written as legibly in *The New Testament* as in *The Wealth of Nations*.

Lord Acton (1907)

GRAHAM HUTTON

I was born in the rural Britain of 1904. The war and the peace thrust me into evening classes in economics while I mutinously served five years in a family East India merchants' office, whence freedom was won for study at the London School of Economics. There, in the shadow of the General Strike of 1926, I became a Socialist and New Fabian, with Dalton and Robbins as my tutors. Later we – Gilbert Walker, Colin Clark, Hugh Gaitskell, Bob Fraser, Honor Croome, *et al* – were critically trained by Laski, Gregory, Tawney, Eileen Power, Hobhouse, Malinowski, Ginsberg, Hayek, etc. Two great men, Beveridge and Layton, made me teach (at the LSE) and write (in *The Economist*) in the 1930s till the Foreign Office swept me up in 1939 for two years here and four in the USA. After the Second World War consultancy gave me freedom from commuting and car-driving, and permitted indulgence in parish churches, Mexico, the Middle West of America, productivity, inflation, and planning. I get much fun from a circus of multi-national friends, a pretty patient (pretty *and* patient, I mean) American wife, three grown-up daughters, and as many of other folks' children and animals as I can get. A Liberal for the past 30 years, a barrister for 32 years, I'd say I was a radical reactionary: I want more people to have more choice and freedom, even if they make mistakes, as that's the only way children become adult.

1: THE RUIN IN THE NATION

GRAHAM HUTTON *opens with a general review of the weaknesses of the British economy but concludes hopefully that they are not inevitable, and outlines what needs to be done — mainly to improve the use of our manpower. And if it is achieved he holds out a bright vision of doubling living standards in ten or even five years.*

DOWNRIGHT Dr. Johnson upset Boswell by declaring that the finest prospect a Scotsman ever sees is the high road into England. In revenge 'Bozzy' prevailed on 'The Great Cham' to quit England for 'A Tour of Scotland and the Hebrides', during which they made the acquaintance of the Professor of Moral Philosophy at Glasgow, 'Mr' (as he put on his visiting cards, not valuing his honorary doctorate) Adam Smith, author of *The Wealth of Nations* and father of economics. When the other honorary doctor, Johnson, flatly said that a certain policy would prove the ruin of the nation, Mr Smith replied, 'Sir, there is a *deal* of ruin in a nation!' For once, the dogmatic English dictionary-maker was floored.

100 years' ruin in Europe

It is not yet a century since Bismarck's Prussia, after defeating France in 1871, imposed an unprecedentedly heavy indemnity in gold and goods on the young Third Republic, born in that war. All the world thought France crippled for the foreseeable future; which was, indeed, the Prussian militarists' intent, though not Bismarck's. Yet so quick and thoroughgoing was the French recovery that the indemnity was paid off in a few years.

The reparations imposed by the Allies on Germany after 1918 were ridiculed by the great Cambridge economist, J. M. (later Lord) Keynes, in that famous work *The Economic Consequences of the Peace* (1920). Keynes's main point was that, to be able to secure enough of the other currencies (or gold) to pay the reparations, the Weimar Republic of Germany would either have to be granted enormous 'recovery loans' from the victorious Allies themselves, or gain enough trade from them. He was right: the inter-allied Dawes Loan shored Germany up until America, Western Europe and the trading world ran into the Great Depression of 1930 to 1933. Everyone raised tariffs against everybody else's goods; trade declined; banks and currencies crashed; unemployment soared; and moratoria on German reparations and other international monetary obligations had to be agreed. Yet within five years the 'ruined' Germany launched the Second World War with the unprovoked assault on Poland in 1939, overran Europe and nearly defeated a solitary Britain.

Japan, a little less 'ruined' than Germany in 1931, and also with no gold in the kitty, had launched her war on China in Manchukuo. Mussolini's Fascisti had not escaped the general economic 'ruin'; yet they launched their unprovoked assault on Haile Selassie's Ethiopia in 1935. The Spanish Civil War was inflicted upon an economic organism recognised for 250 years as sick. It racked that country – economically enfeebled even in the 19th century and by-passed by industrialism – from 1936 until 1939.

Prosperity out of prostration

Finally, amid examples of vast national waste and economic ruin, from which (indeed, often *on* which) swift and astounding material recoveries or military achievements were made, let us remember two others.

First, the United States when war broke out in Europe in 1939 still had over 11 million unemployed and roughly 25 per cent of industrial capacity was idle. In the Depression its national income had been halved, and one worker in three had been unemployed : 'ruin in a nation'. It was lucky for Britain and the Allied cause that such a reserve of productive capacity existed in safety across the Atlantic; for between 1939 and the end of 1942 it was cranked-up to full output. Yet, even in America, people feared the effect of victory and 'peace breaking out', gloomily prophesying widespread unemployment. President Roosevelt and the former Vice-President Henry Wallace predicted during the 'fourth term' campaign in 1944 '60 million jobs' in the foreseeable peace-time economy; they were laughed out of court.

I well remember my friend the late-lamented John Strachey assuring me in his mother's house in the autumn of 1945 that 'America will be on her knees to us to take her surpluses of foodstuffs, and to give her orders for manufactures, now that President Truman has stopped Lend-Lease'. But the *working* population of the US steadily rose, passing the 60 million mark by 1947, before the great General Marshall launched his imaginative Plan for European Recovery; and although American unemployment had re-emerged at its 'normal' higher percentage figure than that of other industrial countries by 1957, American employment steadily went on rising to the present record of over 67 million in work out of 72 million available, despite the ending of the European Recovery Programme and the reduction of American economic, military and other foreign aid. Voices telling of 'ruin to come' in the great American Republic are still raised, inside and outside; yet in its 1964 Budget it substantially reduced taxes on companies as well as on individuals, while maintaining a defence effort costing more than the total national output of Britain or Western Germany.

This great Republic still contrives to turn out – for a very rapidly rising population of over 190 million – an average material standard of living over double that of the highest average in Western Europe, for an average working week *less by one whole working day* than that of the most favoured West European working people. And by methods that the critics of the free economy still fail to understand.

The second example is Western Germany after 1945. To

one who (like me) saw the *real* 'ruin' of the Ruhr and Hamburg and most of the great cities of Western Germany after war ended – people living in 'caves of the earth' and cellars in the light of a candle, under tents of sacks or in shacks of beaten tin cans, girls selling themselves for a cigarette or a little soap, wizened children of more-wizened mothers – what was accomplished after 1948 in Western Germany, upon a 'ruin' hardly conceivable even amid the economic ravages of the Great Depression of 1931–34, truly merits the name of 'miracle'.

In every other department of its economic life Western Germany quickly revived and led Western Europe by the deliberate introduction of an economic system based on sound currency, free markets, private enterprise, freedom to make profits and distribute them as dividends. Dr Erhard took the exactly contrary course to the British Labour Party – he put a heavier tax on profits retained or 'ploughed back' in a business, thus powerfully helping to increase savings and investments and to stimulate innovations and modernisation. Within 15 years of 1948 Western Germany had the second biggest reserve of gold and hard currency in the world after the USA, was still running a large export surplus, keeping her selling prices down (despite the cessation of refugees from Eastern Germany), bearing a defence burden equal to that of Britain or France, and affording her people a higher average standard of living if we take account of the shorter working week. History affords no more striking example of recovery from ruin than the emergence of Western Germany after 1948 as the leading trading power of Europe, and second only (to the USA) in the world of 1963.

Poor old us

How did Britain fare after 1945? Despite the sale to Americans in the main of most of her investments abroad to buy munitions, by 1960 Britain had rebuilt their capital value (though not their annual yield) out of current trade and UK companies' savings.

In addition to the burden of sterling debt and the American loans, she set about earning the necessary gold and hard currencies for interest and had to pay as she went for *all* her necessary imports (before 1939 invisible income from past investments had paid one-quarter of the bill). Nevertheless, at home wages and the lower salaries were pushed faster and further upwards in money, as unions armed with power to resist depressions exploited the inflationary possibilities of full employment. Meanwhile the most severely 'progressive taxation' in the western world redistributed the national income from the so-called 'unearned' incomes (from saving) and from the higher earners to the lower earners and by way of 'the welfare state'. The wartime controls on consumption, rationing, raw materials, lasted till Mr Harold Wilson's 'bonfire of controls' in 1950. But it took the Conservatives after 1951 another five years to complete the demolition of rations and controls. Even today one-fifth of Britain's homes are rent-controlled, and Britons resident here can still not transfer their savings out of sterling except for minimal amounts and at high penalty.

British taxation cramps growth

Britain's version of an 'economic miracle' has been peculiar. It started by making British businesses and the minority of Britons earning the highest incomes pay for universal education, medical care and pensions, irrespective of the ability of recipients to provide for themselves or their families. For over 15 post-war years since 1948, two-fifths to one-half of the entire annual Budget has gone to plug widening gaps in the finances of 'the welfare state'. As these gaps have widened, taxes have been quietly stepped up and passed on to 'beneficiaries' who increasingly pay by direct and especially indirect taxation for the 'free' services.

The state's 'grab' at the citizen's earnings bites ever deeper since, if we confiscated all incomes over £2000 a year, including 'household income' over £40 gross a week, we should draw in less than an extra £500 (once only) million in a budget exceeding £6000 million. Taxes, levies and tolls on initiative and responsibility are so penally heavy that the wonder is British managements from foremen and supervisors up are as good as they are.

British inflation cramps growth

Other nations have rows, civil strife, sharply differing policies of differing parties. But our politicians, journalists, broadcasters and other publicists agree on the desirability of the economic and social policies which produce overfull employment, the upward wage-push by trade unions, the parallel upward wages-drift and the recurrent British economic crisis known as 'over-heating of the economy' or 'inflation'.

The trouble Britain has had will continue until some British government (no matter what party) stops following and starts leading, and plainly tells the British people that *they* are their own worst enemies; that *they* work the 'ruin' in their nation; that *theirs* are the old-fashioned restrictive, 'work-making,' 'work-sharing' practices which impose a terrible toll of waste on the country's richest and almost its only natural resource – human skills – and keep modern equipment under-employed, making it not worth-while to junk the old and modernise; that *theirs* are the cosy cowardly 'runs for cover' whenever a cool, competitive economic breeze gets up; that *theirs* have been the whining, in unison, from 'leaders' of the employers and trade unions in industry after industry for subsidies or other cocooning at public expense. If they now lack good rail and bus services, highways, schools, hospitals, universities, etc.; if their scientists emigrate to the USA and elsewhere, and their managements of state and private concerns are poor, they caused it by the suppression of competition, the growth of political 'management' and the consequent penal taxation of even modest and middling professional and managerial incomes, merely to subsidise rents, health services, farming, shipbuilding, etc.

Politicians and intellectuals

It isn't the amateurs in politics and business who have failed Britain. It is the professional politicians and intellectuals in most of its press, the B.B.C. and I.T.V. who have gutlessly echoed the out-of-date slogans and deadly platitudes of the least thinking mass. This is the real treason of the self-appointed intellectuals. False prophets, they have only prophesied unto the people smooth things, toadying to popular illusions.

At last, all parties, and even the pundits, now agree that Britain's regular post-war economic crises have shown two things in common : that they were brought on by inflationary overheating of the economy; and that the subsequent cooling-off measures by successive governments led to a spasmodic, hiccupping, alternating 'Go-stop' (more accurate than 'Stop-go') stretching over a three-year cycle, which worked against any steady long-term programming of new investment by private enterprises. The National Economic Development Council ('Neddy') in its report *Conditions Favourable to Faster Growth* in April, 1963, echoed what 'the three wise men' on the Cohen Committee on Prices and Incomes had put in their first report six years before : that the total of money incomes in Britain (of which wages and lower salaries account for four-fifths) had steadily risen faster than output. Consequently, despite the devaluation of the pound (from $4 to $2.8) in 1949, Britain's costs and prices have risen so far as to wipe out the advantages. Wage costs per unit of output in manufacturing rose on average about three per cent a year faster than in our competitors between 1953 and 1961. That process went on in 1962 and 1963, albeit more slowly.

But today, when even 'the almighty dollar' has become a bit suspect, no one in his senses can advocate another sterling devaluation and expect other countries to acquiesce in it, or even expect that the sterling area could survive it. No; Britain must look for her growth to her own efforts.

'A little inflation'?

The pundits who advocate 'a little inflation' all the time and 'according to plan' to secure full employment of our resources base their arguments on the overriding need to avoid unemployment of men and machines. But they have failed to make clear :

(a) how to avoid the recurrence of *general* inflationary 'overheating' without causing *some* unemployment (or under-employment) *somewhere* (as in 'special areas');

(b) how to avoid keeping inefficient businesses in existence by inflationary 'profits', thus hindering the transfers of skilled men and capital from old trades to new ones; and so

(c) how to redistribute the country's limited resources to the best economic advantage, for example, in trades, industries and businesses whose managements *can* keep unit costs down to compete both at home and abroad.

In 1962 Mr Reginald Maudling reversed the Selwyn Lloyd 'stop' signals. The inflationists, the 'Goes', have had it. Yet there has gradually emerged one feature rather discomfiting to Messrs 'Go'. One of their strongest arguments for 'a steady inflation' is that it tends to lower unit costs, especially the cost of labour, by luring businessmen to run to full capacity, replace plant and equipment more quickly, and offset rising labour costs by more output per worker. Yet over and over again, as 1963 and 1964 saw, the boom brings out 'the old familiar faces' of wage-push inflation and wage-drift, the 'Goes' were forced to admit that productivity per worker was growing no faster than in the last boom ('Go') period in 1959. The rapid fall in the unemployment figure was not countered by a proportionate rise in the value of Britain's output or by her exports, though imports flooded in to rebuild industry's stocks and to supply consumers. Consequently the nastiest 'old familiar face' re-emerged. British labour costs rising faster than those of foreign competitors. While no one dared mention a 'Stop' policy, little 'Stop' signals were put out : Bank rate went up from 4 to 5 per cent in February 1964; and even the 'Go' school shouted that extra taxation ought to be imposed in the April Budget – but only on private profit, private enterprises, and 'the rich'. All this was only too depressingly familiar. *Why* are the bearings of the British economy so given to overheating?

How to frustrate growth

The real ruin in the British nation is the organised, deliberate waste of its most precious natural resource, skilled labour. In no other western industrialised country are labour and skills so prodigally wasted. Even the communists are offering, in the teeth of the drab appeals for more equality, larger rewards and incentives to managers and supervisors to economise labour and set free human skills for new productive purposes.

Double the skilled men are needed to service one nationally-owned British Overseas Airways airliner per 1,000 miles flown than are required by private enterprise in America. The skills of British workers are first-class, and American manufacturers rejoice to get hold of any. Yet since the war British managements have been forced by trade unions to employ the same numbers of British trade unionists on more productive machines as were employed on less productive equipment; and in the state railways, airlines, tele-communications, docks and harbours, electricity and gas undertakings, hospital and other state or local authorities' buildings' maintenance, as well as over the whole range of private enterprises which secure virtually all Britain's vital exports. This prodigious 'ruin' explains the lag of British productivity behind that of every other industrial country since the war.

It explains more, too. The subsidising of mass consumption by successive governments means high and rising taxes on enterprise, profitability, experiment, innovation. It explains the continuous rise in prices. It means encouraging imports by making profits easier at home than in export markets. In spite of investment and other allowances penal taxes (and rates) combine with the unions' restrictive practices to stop managements from junking old equipment quickly. Why should they, if the new equipment cannot quickly pay for its high cost by being used 'full out' on two, three or even four shifts a day as in America? Modern science and technology advance so fast that a new machine may be technically out-dated in a year or so. You must flog it on shifts to make enough profit and depreciation to replace it speedily, as do the Japanese, Americans and Germans. But their taxes on companies' profits come down, while ours go up, because our state does more and more for people, instead of letting them do more and more for themselves with their rising incomes. Instead we watch the state demonstrate the obvious, that it is never as efficient, economical, creative and productive as a lot of private or personal enterprises in competition with each other, each pursuing its own judgment and so spreading the risks and avoiding the monolithic miscalculations we have suffered from in coal, atomic energy, roads, the costs of the social services, and so on.

Successive British governments, following the fashionable intellectuals rather than leading a newly-affluent mass-electorate, have tried to provide more universal services from taxpayers' money just when such a policy has been made more irrelevant by rising incomes. The *average* weekly earnings of men over 21 in British industry are now nearing £1,000 p.a. In the names of efficiency, humanity, equity, 'growth', and common sense there is everything to be said for restricting state subsidies to those still in need, to basic education, and to poorer farmers for a defined period to enable them to improve, combine or give up.

The reasons for stagnation

The reasons why our economy has lagged in the international growth stakes are few and clear. First, our governments have penalised the profits and rewards of exceptional enterprise, initiative and innovation more than any industrialised country except Norway, if you take all compulsory taxes, tolls and levies into account.

Secondly, the best professional managers are not allowed by the unions to get the best out of the firm's capital equipment or its employees. What Britain has afforded too much and too long is the 'concealed unemployment' which a few able observers have put at between 20 and 30 per cent of British industrial population.

Thirdly, government policies for 'full employment' of all resources all the time and at all costs including the consequent, periodic crises have robbed managements of much of the responsibility and the ability to manage labour and capital equipment properly. Policies of inflationary 'full employment' have concealed this waste of labour. Unemployment has been only two-thirds of the *average* long-term amount advocated by Lord Beveridge and his advisers. It has except for the fuel crisis winter of 1946 to 1947 *averaged* below 2 per cent each year since 1946, of which virtually half represents unemployables or untrainables. As a result, the state's unemployment funds are bursting at the seams. It would have paid us handsomely to winnow-out the redundant workpeople now classified as 'fully employed', and re-train them for other jobs, or re-deploy them over the 2-, 3-, and in some places the 4-shifts day. This re-deployment of *all* British labour by shifts, mainly in industry but also in shops, and even banks and offices, is a crying need. We need it to use our human resources more productively, on shorter working weeks, eliminating most of the inflated 'overtime', and letting automation come in with the least shocks. We need re-deployment to set labour free for multitudes of new products, skills and processes (as well as for more of the older skills, like the engineering crafts, building, printing, entry into which is still tightly restricted by the unions to preserve the *status quo* for existing incumbents). We need it because, by marrying the most economical use of human skill to the most intensive use of machines, we could cut our costs and prices, push up exports to pay for more imports, and pay our workpeople more for shorter working weeks.

Instead, we have repeatedly had to suffer such nonsense as demands for higher pay and shorter 'basic' working weeks, but without more productive or economical use of our labour and capital equipment. New machines, buses, trains, apparatus are never run at their higher capacities, but must only turn out in a week roughly what the old ones did in order that more 'overtime' still, at overtime rates, should be 'earned' after the shorter 'basic' working week has been 'idled up to' (as one union friend of mine put it). Small wonder that costs often don't come down.

After all, new equipment is costly and soon superseded; so if labour costs per unit do not fall, total unit costs will rise. If we were only to work our capital equipment intensively, instead of cossetting it on long single shifts so that it stays good as new after 20 years, if workers were re-deployed over multiple shifts to knock productive Hell out of it, they could have higher pay, shorter *real* working weeks (not short 'basic' weeks, dishonoured by long overtime), and a far higher standard of living. It is not ill-will, it is ignorance or indifference against which we need to struggle.

That is the failure of organised labour – the ordinary, decent, British workers – misled by a few official or unofficial mis-leaders into being loyal to outmoded irrelevant slogans. Faithful to economic nonsense cunningly presented to them, devoted to meaningless political myths, protected by the majesty of out-of-date trade union laws granting them monopoly powers and privileges which no employers have ever claimed or practised, our trade unionists continually demonstrate the finest British qualities on behalf of the worst causes.

Contrasts and consequences

All this waste and frustration stems from the old-time, uncritically accepted, traditional British hatred of work, of 'the bosses', and of profits throughout most of the professional trade union 'leaders'. An American trade unionist will leave a firm whose profits are falling. He looks for a job in a firm making *more* than average profits, because he reckons it is properly run and can pay better wages. The typical British trade unionist doesn't move. He thinks his firm's rising profits are a scandal (unions often demand *all* the extra profit arising from the introduction of new equipment and methods).

This attitude results in ruinous waste which damages everyone employed, unemployed, pensioners, the nation's ability to earn more by exports, enterprising firms and whole industries, and not least the state's revenues to pay for state services. Yet this pattern of behaviour throughout British organised labour persists today : more of the cotton trade, coal trade, rail transport, bus network, electricity supply and other services could have been preserved for consumers if only labour had agreed to some orderly, equitably compensated streamlining, and to some redeployment of jobs among the employed remainder. The cotton trade was finally and drastically forced into most severe 'rationalisation' (reduction of capacity); shipbuilding is slowly being forced along the same road, like coalmining. God alone knows what will eventually happen in Britain's docks, or with Londoners' buses (which get fewer, and offer worse services, for higher fares, each time their crews get more pay, roughly once a year). No one seems to want change, movement, adaptation, new ways and attitudes; yet everyone demands more pay.

And so the silly story goes on incessantly, in industry after industry.

The quiet life

This frustration of British managements by organised labour is reinforced by waste of executive, managerial and administrative skills. Partly this is due to managerial cosiness : the effects of penally high taxation plus protection by tariffs or subsidies or other shields for inefficiency and uncompetitiveness. To tackle the unions' local leaders or shop-stewards, to inculcate new attitudes for new rewards, to change from top to bottom the way of running a factory or business – this means hard work and high skills for managers. It is easier to let things slide on as they always have done : to cover high costs by inflation and protective devices, and pass the buck to consumers or even to taxpayers if subsidies or public contracts are available. Since 1959, when the Conservative Minister of Labour asked the employers' representatives to report on waste of skills and other labour in their plants, dusty answers have been returned time after time : most employers obviously did not want to bring the wastes their managers tolerated out into the light. They did not want their managerial incompetence, inefficiency or easy-goingness to be made plain for what it is — the aiding and abetting of trade unionists' restrictive and labour-wasting practices, in favour of a quiet life all round. This is one reason why it is hard to document the wastes and restrictive practices which maim British industry and the state's nationalised services.

Happily there are exceptions. Some British managements and union leaders have worked out agreements for pay, compensation against possible redundancy, pensions (and their transferability if the employee voluntarily moves), retraining in new skills, and even the transfer of skilled craftsmen in one union to do jobs deemed the monopoly of members of another. These few leading British managements and their local union leaders have put up record growth, productivity, and profit figures. Naturally they also pay better wages. They show that things necessary in British industry can be done. Unfortunately most British trade unions are heavily centred on London or other old-established cities, and their decisions and agreements tend to be nation-wide, general, and not local. Hence jealousy and envy prevent the occasional, successful, local agreement from becoming general. At least the exceptions illuminate the dark backwoods of British industrial relations, and show what prizes await those in politics, industry or unions who wake up to the need for leadership.

Ruin or reserve?

'The ruin in the nation' is therefore easy to eliminate. It requires two things : thinking and changing traditional attitudes. If the overwhelming mass of our people were to think logically about what they want in economic terms, one half of the problems would melt away. Further, if the majority of the British people were at the same time coolly to consider changing their attitudes to the hours of work in the day or week, to the profitability of British enterprise (state and private), and to economy and efficiency of high-quality production (*i.e.* productivity), the other half of the nation's recurrent economic problems could be swiftly solved.

In the upshot of these solutions, hours worked in a week could be reduced for everyone; costs and prices could be cut; exports could sharply rise, to provide more imports and develop resources overseas; and the real earnings of employees could go up. The biggest problems would be the release, re-training and re-employment of temporarily redundant employees, possibly in new homes and workplaces. But the scale of Britain's economic problems is really not large. Informed leadership would not need courage of heroic proportions. Spread, for example, over only five years, re-training and redeployment of as many as 2 million employees out of some 16 million in industry, mining, transport, distribution and other services, could be brought about in orderly fashion at an annual cost of £150 million. And that cost could be charged to the unemployment fund as a non-recurrent item, or met by modest increases in contributions on the cards of the majority left in work. Such a 'national growth plan' would include arrangements for transferring the re-trained workpeople to different places and homes. Yet we have wasted thousands of millions of pounds to no productive purposes; and we coped admirably with infinitely more cumbrous transfers of persons – from children to troops – in the war. Moreover, from the investment in the re-training we should get back an economic yield in new and better work. Our whole economy would be streamlined. We would have converted the ruin into a reserve.

I calculated 12 years ago that all of Britain's economic crises till then could have been solved if only we had turned out 2½ per cent extra national output for the same input: one-fortieth bit more from wasted efforts, materials, fuel and power, etc., by more efficiency, not by harder or longer work. That calculation is even sounder today, for industrial output has after all, and albeit more slowly than those of other nations, gone up by 70 per cent in the intervening years. Extra productivity of $2\frac{1}{2}$ per cent p.a. would net an extra £625 million worth of goods and services which we could divide between exports and home trade, between investments in new lines for our future and present consumption. If such 'manna from Heaven' can so easily be secured, how much more could we secure by doing the 'modernisation of Britain' job properly : by streamlining our firms and industries, our agriculture and communications; by reforming and revising our taxes and laws and rules and practices, our out-moded attitudes to profits, to how managers (and trade union leaders) should be selected, trained and paid. If we secured all these reforms, we could double our national output in five to ten years.

Other countries have done it

America, Western Germany, Japan have shown how fast standards of living can be raised if only governments set free individual initiative and competitive enterprise. Russia, Poland, Hungary, Czechoslovakia have also realised, and more recently have shown, that standards of living rise faster that way than by monolithic state enterprises, rigid state plans and detailed state controls over everyone and everything. Britain will not escape her persistent inflationary crises, her recurrent 'Go–Stop' spasms, by a National Economic Development Council, or 'an incomes policy', or any other exhortatory expedient. She will not achieve Neddy's 4 per cent per annum rate of steady growth year in and year out, unless and until her leaders show a majority of her people how much 'ruin' they are tolerating, and *then* insist on stopping it by reforms.

In these long-overdue reforms will be, first and foremost, a re-casting of the law about trade unions, to bring them and their members and officers back from the almost extra-legal position of privileged monopoly as a feudal Estate of the Realm, beyond public control and beyond responsibility and beyond accountability to the majority of their fellow-citizens who are not trade unionists. From that reform onwards,

nation-wide and general wage-agreements could be superseded by a national minimum wage plus locally negotiated
supplements differing between industries, firms and regions.

Then we must no longer cosset highly-protected industries
and their tariff-cushioned managements, highly-protected
retailers (too many buttressed by resale price maintenance)
highly-protected and highly-subsidised farmers (far too
many of them for the era of large-scale farming). We ought
not to need an American management consultant, William
W. Allen, to tell us that we could produce our present
national output with *one-half* of our present work-force.
Some of us were saying so in the late 1940's, let alone the
1950's and 1960's. Who listens to whom in this land of cosy
ruin? As a nation, we organise and afford a waste of resources to a degree which no other nation – at least this side
of the Communist Curtain – can parallel. If governments,
parties, managements, trade unions cut the cackle if we
really agreed on and carried out a national plan to eliminate
the waste from our economic body we wouldn't 'grow' at
'Neddy's' poor 4 per cent per annum rate. We could *double*
our standard of living in five years: ten at most. But it would
necessitate changes in attitudes, methods and equipment: not
more hours work in a week, but fewer; not more work,
but better.

Whatever happens from now on, under whatever kind of
government in this country, one thing ought to be crystal-
clear. Our lack of growth, our lagging economic development (slowly up, or else down or sideways), any spasms and
seizures, any continuation of our 'pull-Devil, pull-baker'
industrial tensions, any persistence of our remorseless inflation, any of this in future should be recognised by *all* our
people for what it is : a deliberate, organised, familiar, preferred or tolerated way of wasting their time and effort, their
capital assets and their other national resources. And it need
not be.

JOHN BRUNNER

I was born on the glorious first of June 1927 and formally educated in the suburbs of Windsor and Cowley. From 1950 to 1953
I was with Political and Economic Planning (sic) and from 1953
to 1958 at the BBC where I had a modest behind-the-scenes part
in a number of comparatively early essays in national introspec-
tion/disparagement. Subsequent disenchantment with inverted
patriotism might be put down to a three-year spell in the
Economic Section of the Treasury, from which I certainly emerged
with a surprising degree of respect for a much maligned institution (the principal scapegoat for our national and intellectual
impotence?). But I doubt whether it really had much of an
influence. For one thing the Treasury, like other monastic orders,
can only mould its novitiates properly if it gets them for longer
and at a more impressionable age. I would prefer to attribute my
misgivings to the heretic's instinctive reaction to orthodoxy – even
to yesterday's heresy turned orthodoxy. Since 1961 I have been on
the management of the *Observer*, and of one's present employers,
like the dead, *nil nisi bonum*.

2: THE NEW IDOLATRY

JOHN BRUNNER *questions some of the nostra currently fashionable in politico-economic circles suggesting that at best they are merely fatuous, at worst highly authoritarian in their implications. And whatever else they may be, they are certainly not modern.*

ONE of the most cherished of our contemporary illusions is the notion that ours is a tough-minded sceptical generation, imbued with the scientific spirit and disrespectful of all authority. We contrast our scientific selves with our poor benighted ancestors sunk as they were in religion, superstition and all irrationalism, and most of us find the comparison rather flattering.

But is it, or have we merely substituted one set of symbols for another? Is our present deference to economists and other experts who think they can identify 'the public interest' with the aid of the computer so very different from the deference of the ancient Greeks to the priests and acolytes who interpreted the word of the oracle for the populace to learn the will of the gods? One sees at work the same very human motivations, the same craving for certainty and the resolution of conflict, the same gullibility in face of those who claim to know the answers.

The present consensus on what is wrong with Britain is really rather remarkable. The great 'soft centre' now seems to embrace everyone from the so-called left wing leader of the Labour party to the so-called right wing press who vie with each other in taking credit for the conversion of their ostensible opponents.

The gist of their diagnosis can I think be fairly summarised in terms of 3 Ps, the need for more Professionals, more Planning and a sense of National Purpose. There are obviously differences of emphasis here and there, but these three ingredients, closely related as they are, seem to be common to almost all current recipes for national revival. Just how far does this diagnosis stand up? How relevant are the proposed remedies to the shortcomings, real and imaginary, they are supposed to cure? How much scientific evidence is there to support an analysis put forward in the name of science?

The pitfalls of professionalism

Take for a start this question of professionals. Now it is easy to sympathise with the emotional revulsion against the gentlemen *v.* players mentality, against the grotesque social divisions that still afflict us, and against the nepotism that continues in so many sectors of our society and economy. (These affronts could well be tackled by a wealth tax or, if this is too much for the Inland Revenue, a capital levy, measures that the Labour party apparently eschews as much as the Conservatives.) But to pretend merely because we dislike these injustices that more professionals are the answer to our problems, and more specifically, the key to a higher rate of economic growth, is a most disingenuous rationalisation. A moment's reflection on the situation of the US which, for all its much-vaunted schools of business and institutes of technology, is one of the few comparable nations with a lower rate of growth per head than ours, should be enough to make us hesitate before ascribing too many magical attributes to professionalism.

In fact, of course, virtually no attempt has been made to show just how more professionals would galvanise our economy. The imprecise manner in which the word 'professional' is being used is evidence of the totally unscientific nature of the argument. Those who bandy the word about cannot conceivably mean us to model ourselves on the learned professions who, whatever their other merits, can hardly be regarded seriously as the spearhead of the drive to get Britain moving when they themselves are among its most unregenerate elements. Nor is the word 'professional'

being used to describe anyone with a good general or scientific training, since so many of the most dynamic of our
entrepreneurs (Sir Isaac Wolfson, John James, Kenneth
Wood, John Bloom, Harry Rael-Brook) had only the most
rudimentary formal education. Nor again can 'professional'
be meant to indicate someone who has specialised at his job,
since the two blue-eyed boys of the cult of professionalism
are Dr Richard Beeching and Lord Robens, and in no sense
can they be described as professional railwaymen or miners.
(When this point was put to perhaps the most influential of
all contemporary anatomists, he changed the euphemism to
'technocrat', but this word too of course is quite inappropri-
ate as a description of Lord Robens, ex trade union official
and politician as he is.)

Another equally absurd aspect of the current reverence
for the professional is the idea that recognition of his role is
in some way the mark of a modern and scientific attitude.
We are lectured on how the vast sum of human knowledge
makes it impossible for any individual to remain proficient
in more than one subject. We are continually being reminded
of the virtues of specialisation. Somehow it all seems vaguely
familiar, until suddenly one remembers where one heard it
all before. It is of course one's first year economics all over
again, only then it was called the division of labour and
credited to that old square Adam Smith. Who says it's only
practical men who are the slaves of some defunct economist?

This new-found respect for Adam Smith comes at a time
when many people less emotionally embattled on this question are beginning to have serious doubts about the merits
of the division of labour in a dynamic economy. Men who
received a specialised training in their youth are all too
liable in the rapidly changing economic conditions of today
to find that their skills are outdated long before the end of
their working lives. They are thus obliged to adopt Luddite-
like tactics to defend their jobs and thereby constitute a
serious obstacle to growth.

In trying to counter this and other arguments for a rather
more qualified support for specialists, the devotees of pro-

fessionalism have confused the issue still further. In their efforts to knock the specialists they dislike without detriment to the good name of the expert, they have tied themselves up in the most incredible knots. For instance we have Professor Brian Chapman in his fashionable tract *British Government Observed* being forced to distinguish between good specialists, technical civil servants, and bad specialists because too specialised (sic), the administrative class. And Mr Anthony Wedgwood Benn, M.P., in a recent *Guardian* article ended an astonishingly tortuous attempt to square the circle with a stirring appeal to 'generalise professionally'.

From all this it would seem reasonable to conclude that words like professional and expert have lost all useful meaning in the mouths of their partisans, and are being used simply to distinguish the good guys from the bad.

The pretensions of planning

If this were no more than a quibble about the meaning of words, the time might be coming to say joke over, but no great harm would have been done. There are, however, dangers in encouraging too credulous a belief in professionals, for it is a cause, as well as being to some extent a symptom, of something that is rather disturbing. We seem to be excessively prone to believe in objective solutions to problems which, particularly in public policy, are not capable of such solution. The inflated reputation of economists and a correspondingly exaggerated faith in their ability to plan is a case in point.

That the economist should be treated as a contemporary saviour is not altogether surprising. Our national shortcomings are seen so much in economic terms – growth leagues and so on – that their solution is felt to be peculiarly the affair of the economist. Hence the virtually unanimous demand by all analysts of our discontents for the recruitment of more economists, a demand which economists have not gone out of their way to discourage. (Like other specialists, economists tend to believe in the employment of their fellows, their belief in the law of diminishing returns being

conveniently suspended in this instance!) But how far is faith
in economists and thus in economic planning justified?

Economic planning as the term is generally understood
has two essential elements – prediction and prescription. To
plan effectively one has to be able to take a view of the future,
of what will happen in the absence of the plan. The quality
of a plan depends to a large extent therefore on the accuracy
of the forecast on which it is based. How far then are
economists competent to predict the course of economic
events?

The record frankly is not very impressive. Despite some
immensely sophisticated model-building involving the use of
econometrics, computers and all the other fashionable tools
of contemporary economics, the accuracy of forecasts shows
little improvement. And the reason is simple. Human behaviour cannot be predicted in the way that natural
phenomena can be because history cannot be relied on to
repeat itself. The assumption that history does repeat itself
– or at any rate that past trends can be safely supposed to
continue – which is implicit in so much economic crystal-
gazing has no more validity in practice than the reliance on
'form' in other fields where the forecasting of human behaviour is involved, e.g. football results, elections, population changes, stock exchange prices. ('Invest in failure' seems
to be at least as good a working rule as 'invest in success'.)

But if form is an inadequate guide to the economic future,
what then? Judgement is clearly called for to guess in what
way the future will depart from the past, and judgement is a
quality with which economists do not appear to be very much
better endowed than other members of the community,
which is only to be expected. For the causes of economic
phenomena are often found well outside the province of the
economist. Economic changes may arise from technological
breakthroughs, political upsets, shifts in tastes, events abroad,
none of them matters on which economists can talk with any
particular authority.

Most economic practitioners would I think admit this,
though many would claim that it is early days yet and that

anyhow it is better to spell out the numerical implications of forecasts if only for consistency's sake rather than operate on mere intuition. (As Sir Robert Hall once said 'If intuition were given the "scientific" name of "non-statistical inference", no one would look down his nose at it'.) There is undoubtedly something in this claim, though elaborate projections can introduce their own causes of error.

Preoccupation with the refinements tends to distract attention from the assumptions, which are of course a much more potent source of error. Similarly, too great a delight in expressing trends and influences in the form of figures tends to introduce a subtle bias in favour of the measurables at the expense of the often crucial intangibles. This is not only true of 'macro-economic models' used for forecasting changes in total income, production etc. in the economy as a whole;[1] it is also in evidence in industry where big efforts are being made, quite properly, to improve on traditional methods employed by accountants for calculating the return on new investment. So carried away are the disciples of the new enlightenment with the elegance of their models that they are apt to forget that faulty techniques of appraisal remain a small source of error compared with the sales and costs forecasts which they take as more or less given.

One wonders how far the present vogue for planning would survive a closer public scrutiny of the record of economists in predicting the future. But even if they were much better than they are at saying what *will* happen, by what criteria are economists to say what *should* happen?

The search for the economist's stone – the formula defining the proper objectives of economic policy – has engaged the attention of economists at least since the time of Bentham. The so-called science of welfare economics which developed out of the attempts of the utilitarians to maximise happiness, and was refined at such length by Marshall, Pigou and others, received what should have been a death blow from

[1] Interested readers may like to see *Macro-Economic Models: Nature, Purpose and Limitations*, by Dr Malcolm Fisher, Eaton Paper 2, Institute of Economic Affairs, 1963. – Ed.

Mr Ian Little's *Critique of Welfare Economics* in which he conclusively demonstrated the inevitable part played by value-judgements in all such discussions. And indeed welfare economics as such has never really recovered from Mr. Little's strictures, although it occasionally flickers to life in the columns of the learned journals. What has happened, though, is that it has arisen in a new form, the phoenix in question going by the name of cost-benefit analysis'.[1]

This concept which is essentially an attempt to set monetary values on goods and services for which no market exists, has its uses, but the role of judgement remains paramount. Those who doubt this view might care to consult Appendix 2 to the Buchanan Report, *Traffic in Towns*, where the technique is employed to evaluate the cost-benefit ratios from three different redevelopment schemes at Newbury, the benefits being defined as improvements to the environment and greater accessibility. Even its advocates had to admit that 'this system relies on : enumerating particular aspects of the scheme; allocating an arbitrary number of points to each and thereby weighting them for importance; and 'measuring' the quality of the scheme under each heading by the subjective allocation of points.' Cost-benefit analysis at the most offers a helpful method of choosing between alternative means; it is no guide whatever to the desirability of ends.

And this goes for economics in general. Economists cannot properly be asked what to do, only how to do it, and even here – and this is especially so in the realm of public policy – political bias cannot be altogether excluded. This should of course be obvious from the very varied policy recommendations of different economists on how to deal with a clearly defined problem. Whether in combating inflation an economist is a deflator, devaluer or incomes policy man is largely a matter of political bent and temperament.

The hocus-pocus of 'the public interest'

I have discussed the limitations of economics and economists at some length, not by way of a gratuitous attack

[1] See Wiseman, pp. 87–90.

but because economists are after all regarded as the experts *par excellence* when it comes to allocating the nation's resources. If they turn out to be fallible, this is less of a criticism of them than it is of the layman who expects too much of them. Why should this be so? Why should we persist in believing there is such a thing as 'the public interest' which experts can identify for us?

The concept of the public interest so widely accepted at present is entirely devoid of serious content, at any rate in domestic policy. It is immeasurable, indefinable and purely subjective. As Mr David Riesman has observed (in his new collection of essays, *Abundance for What?*) about a similar concept fashionable in the US, it 'tends to crumble when one asks in whose interest within the country are the various definitions of the national interest'. Why then do we cling to it? No doubt partly from our yearning for revelation, but also I fear from impatience with our plural society.

Thus we have Professor Colin Buchanan, the intellectual folk-hero of our time with his vision of the public interest, pure and undefiled, under continual attack from 'powerful commercial and vested interests'. (He is also much given to lauding amenity in general while deploring particular manifestations of it such as cafés and garages with a similar lack of philosophical scruple.) Or again we have Professor Chapman, whose book I make no apology for returning to when people such as Mr Richard Crossman can seriously regard it as 'the most important book I have read since *The Affluent Society* :'[1] 'Most important of all,' writes Professor Chapman, 'is the genuine lack of doctrinal significance attached to the concept of public service in Britain. There is no sentiment that public office should involve public responsibility, or that public power should involve the exercise of dispassionate and disinterested judgement. All the evidence indicates that public policy is simply equated with finding the least controversial course between the conflicting interests of vociferous private groups. It is not a doctrine of government : it is a doctrine of subordination'.

[1] In the *Guardian*, 6th September, 1963.

The myth of the public interest, like so much else about the current zeitgeist, is really little more than a throwback to an earlier age. It can in fact be directly traced back to Delphi via Rousseau's general will and Lycurgus' constitution for Sparta. Rousseau betrays the same naïve belief in our ability to achieve detachment, the same distaste for pressure groups. 'It is therefore essential, if the general will is to express itself, that there should be no partial society within the State and that each citizen should think his own thoughts : which was indeed the sublime and unique system established by the great Lycurgus.' *Plus ca change, plus c'est la même mythologie.*

What is at stake here is the proper role of government. Either one believes that government is a matter of asking supposedly disinterested experts to tell us what to do and acting accordingly (what Professor Chapman calls 'the rational apportioning of resources and responsibilities between public authorities'), or one sees it largely as a process of adjudication between the various interested parties on the basis of the acceptability to the electorate of a particular policy. This does not mean to say that the government should always try to avoid incurring short-term unpopularity – with five-year parliaments a government can and must think more of a long-term approval – but it can never be altogether insensitive to political repercussions. Between those who see sensitivity to opinion as the mark of democratic government and those who see it as a defect the divide is apparently as deep as ever.

The one-track mind

As if to emphasise the point further the representatives of the new enlightenment stress the need for 'a sense of national purpose'. On the face of it this seems an innocent enough plea, but on closer scrutiny it appears as either merely fatuous or decidedly unhealthy. For under what circumstances will people start thinking more in terms of the public weal and less of their own hopes and ambitions, more of their loyalty to the state and less of their responsibilities to family, friends and immediate associations (those 'partial societies' at which Rousseau and his new-found disciples sneer)? I know of no case of democracies achieving sustained bursts of patriotism except at times of war, coronation or other national emergency. Which of these fates are we being asked to look forward to?

Our sort of democracy is an untidy business. It encourages wastes, publicises conflicts and tolerates a multiplicity of purposes. But are the alternatives any more preferable? If I might quote once more from the infinitely wise essay by Mr Riesman : 'Not even an institution, let alone a country can survive and prosper over any considerable period of time by serving only a single goal or purpose. If individuals try to purify their own lives to dedicate them to a single purpose only, they become fanatics. If they use their occupations and callings to define their purposes, even as artists and thinkers, they run the danger of becoming over-professionalised and less than fully human. And if in relative default of group and individual purposes, we use the nation to absorb the surplus, the chances are that we shall become more nationalistic – and in a world where others are doing the same, threaten the very goal (the relaxation of world tension) we seem to cherish.'

That the Americans should also be preoccupied with a quest for national purpose throws some light, I think, on why this monolithic mood should be so prevalent in Britain at the moment. As I have tried to show, the totalitarian or 'holist' urge is something that is always latent (like we understand other forms of cancer). It only becomes rampant when the body politic is seriously disturbed. The most likely disturbance in this case would seem to be the need that both countries have recently been experiencing to adjust to a more dependent status in the world. This, strangely enough, seems to have affected our intellectuals worse than the ex-colonial officials, tea planters and others who have suffered directly from the demise of our empire. But some soul-searching and hankering after a new identity is only to be expected where nations, which have got used to pushing others around, find almost overnight that their freedom of manoeuvre has been seriously restricted.

Another common feature of Britain and the US since the war has of course been their relatively low rate of economic growth, and it would appear quite plausible that a yearning for national purpose stems in part from a low rate of expansion. Similarly, a high rate of growth in so far as it widens individual horizons is likely to be destructive of patriotic fervour.

There is finally the all important influence of fashion, or what Marx would have called the dialectic of history. To some extent both here and in the United States we are witnessing the inevitable swing of fashion against climates of opinion and governments in the 1950s that (according to taste) were comparatively permissive or *laissez faire*. We are also in the rationalistic phase of the intellectual fashion cycle. After the war, with the memory of Hiroshima and Buchenwald fresh in our minds, it was difficult to believe in man's claim to be a rational creature. Books were written deploring the 'Retreat from Reason' and the rationalists were thrown on the defensive. Now as memories of the war are fading, rationalism and the idea of progress is becoming respectable again. Hence our renewed faith in experts, planning and harmony among men.

As a believer in the force of fashion in a world that puts such a premium on the appearance of novelty, I would not expect this phase of the cycle to outlive another Labour government (even allowing for the vast vested interests being built up in expertise and planning by the growing army of experts and planners). When the pendulum swings back, it may be an exaggeration to talk about the rebirth of Britain, but only because it will then become clear that we never committed suicide.

COLIN WELCH

Born in 1924 at Ickleton in Cambridgeshire and educated at Stowe and Peterhouse, Cambridge, (major history scholar and degree). In service in the Royal Warwickshire Regiment from 1942 to 1945, was twice wounded, but not by fellow officer Brigadier J. Enoch Powell (q.v.). Spent a year with the *Glasgow Herald* in 1950 and has since been writing leaders for the *Daily Telegraph* with an interval as half Peter Simple: deputy editor, 1964.

3: POLICIES AND PARLIAMENT

COLIN WELCH, *a close observer of Parliament, discusses the difficulties that politicians have in framing and applying economic policies in the interest of the country as a whole. He argues that in recent years Conservatives have been led into increasing state controls and that politicians generally are tempted to enlarge their powers to show that they can yield public good. He believes Parliament has suffered by being caught up in details at the expense of general principles and regards this tendency as dangerous for Parliamentary institutions since the expectations from the use of state powers cannot always be fulfilled. He notes the clamour that pensions and health be 'taken out of politics' as evidence that state services have not satisfied the public and concludes with the principles on which he thinks policies should be based.*

DE TOCQUEVILLE noted that Louis XIV's government in Canada adopted none of the great principles by which a country is rendered populous and prosperous; it had recourse by contrast to all kinds of trifling artificial processes and petty tyrannical regulations, ordering its subjects not merely to cultivate but what, how and where. 'We find ourselves,' he continued, 'face to face with an administration almost as numerous as the population, preponderant, interfering, regulating, restricting, insisting upon foreseeing everything, controlling everything and understanding the interests of those under its control better than they do themselves; in short, in a constant state of barren activity....'

Watching Parliament as on and off I do, I find these words coming again and again unbidden to mind. Against much barren activity I must in fairness set at least two recent decisions which – right or wrong – were courageously based on principles that de Tocqueville would have recognised as great. One was the decision to apply for membership of the Common Market, the other to abolish resale price maintenance; the one belated and abortive, the other belated and still as I write struggling towards the Statute Book; both based on the general principles that competition and freedom of choice are desirable in the public interest, where possible to be quickened, fostered and extended (though of course the Common Market had much more to it than this).

In many other fields the words and deeds of our rulers seem to be based on no recognisable principles whatever. They have rather the air of being improvised or reflex reactions to the conflicting stimuli of various interests, pressures and crises, real or imagined. Any principles which do operate in this welter are not great principles but little ones. They are also generally unstated and must therefore be deduced from what actually happens. After some thought I would state (or perhaps caricature) them thus : that nothing desirable can be achieved except by the direct action of the state, and nothing undesirable prevented; that everything good about our society must in consequence be the result of state intervention, everything bad the result of some failure to intervene; that whatever happens naturally and spontaneously is probably to be deplored and if possible prevented by the state, whatever does not happen to be initiated at once.

It is only to be expected that Socialists should act on these little principles with rather more ease and coherence than Conservatives can manage; for, after all, they are more or less their own principles, the basis of their penny catechism, to be adopted voluntarily on initiation. That Conservatives should act on them at all is surprising. Conservatives indeed would hotly deny that they do, and I must concede at once that they have embraced them piecemeal, reluctantly, involuntarily or even unconsciously, forced on despite themselves by a logic which they seem unable wholly to control or deny.

Among others, three powerful factors have assisted this

logic. One is the sort of Britain which the Conservatives inherited; another is their own much-vaunted pragmatism; a third is the natural vanity which they share with all other beings placed in any sort of authority.

Dirigisme or chaos

The Britain which they inherited was – and remains – roughly half-socialised and half not. Vast sectors of the national economy had been removed wholly or partly from the disciplines of the free market and placed under state management, control or influence. No-one but a lunatic can have expected the Conservatives to undo all that had been done, with, for logical consequence, the possibility that half the economy would be alternately socialised and de-socialised every five years. What they actually engaged to do was to take over the socialised sectors of the economy – the steel industry apart – and to run them in a more efficient, flexible and less doctrinaire way. More efficiently these sectors could perhaps be run, but quite differently – no. Centralised or decentralised, organised or re-organised, pulled or pushed this way or that, run by this man or that, they remained what they were – socialised undertakings, to be run in a socialist way or in no way. *Dirigisme* or chaos : this is the choice facing any Conservative put into a Socialist's shoes.

Institutions shape those who direct them. Those in charge of socialist institutions must become socialists themselves – socialists *pro tem.*, if you like, socialists *ex officio*. Even Mr Enoch Powell looked for a time, as director of the National Health Service, a socialist, though he was not one before and is not one now; and quite a formidable socialist he appeared, in whom even the Webbs might have taken a rueful pride.

Appoint the most zealous advocate of a free economy Minister responsible for some socialised service. The temptation cynically to vindicate his theories by presiding over predicted disasters may cross his mind; the impulse to success overwhelms it. His own back-benchers, themselves also perhaps in other circumstances friendly to a free economy, goad him on, as they are goaded in turn by their constituents. Furiously thus he plans and co-ordinates, regulates and controls, appoints committees, extends and intensifies his own activities, pursues success by all the means which he has in the past declared incapable of attaining it. He has become a socialist *malgré lui*; to this extent the Conservatives have become socialists *malgré eux*.

Nor does the matter stop there. A mixed economy is not in fact divided into two independent compartments, one public, one private. The non-economic activities of the public sector powerfully influence and are influenced by the operations of the private sector, which supplies what it needs and consumes what it produces. At every moment parts of one sector or the other are threatened with chaos as a result of the success or failure of some part of the other sector or of competition from it. Thus those charged with ensuring the success of the public sector are almost doomed to seek powers to regulate the private sector, even though every instinct in them may rebel against their doing so.

All planners now

It is possible to argue, moreover, that in the Britain inherited by the Conservatives the area of state control and intervention was so preponderant that the so-called free sector could not operate successfully in the very narrow space left to it. Too many of its decisions, perhaps, were nullified or rendered foolish by the unpredictable, arbitrary and non-economic decisions of the state; its incentives and rewards may have been set too low, or guaranteed by some sort of protection against the nemesis which should overtake incompetence.

Be that as it may, the Conservatives did for some years leave the free sector so far as they could to its own devices. The results seem to have disappointed them. A dull, sluggish economy mocked their slogan, 'Conservative freedom works'. In consequence they are all – or almost all – planners now.

Nor is there anything fundamental in their philosophy to prevent them from becoming planners. They pride themselves on their pragmatism. They have no built-in Hayek-[1] mechanism which sets against the direct advantages undoubtedly often to be secured by state intervention all the indirect, often delayed, disadvantages which will probably flow from it and eventually outweigh it. Thus they intervene once; the consequent disadvantages they correct by further interventions; and so *ad infinitum*.

And who in his heart can blame them? Does not each one of us have something particularly dear which he wants the state to look after for him? Only a government of inflexible doctrinaires could arrest and throw back the advancing tide of state intervention. And where now are such doctrinaires to be found? Where are the iron men who, in deference to the most austere Manchester principles, will allow known hardships to go unrelieved, orchestras to founder, old buildings to be swept away? And thus out of the sum of our most amiable weaknesses is the present *dirigiste* chaos formed.

Political vanity

A sort of vanity also urges Conservatives on to ever-wider interventions. When all goes well, governments naturally arrogate to themselves rather more of the credit than is their due. Nothing nice can be allowed to happen spontaneously; all must be attributed to the foresight, planning and wise management of the government. Then the times go sour, and bouquets turn to brickbats. It must be hard for any politician at any time to stand up before an angry electorate and confess or assert that there are parts of life over which he has no control whatever. It is quite impossible for him to do so if he has already taken the credit for whatever went well in the very sector for which he would now like to disclaim all responsibility. His empty boast must now be made real. Unless he is to look ridiculous, he must now willy-nilly equip himself with powers he has pretended already to possess and

[1] Professor F. A. Hayek, author of works on economic theory and political economy, including *The Road to Serfdom* and *The Constitution of Liberty* (in which the Postscript was entitled 'Why I am not a Conservative.') – Ed.

more, to have exercised with skill and success; powers which he may know in his heart are ill-designed for their ends or likely to make bad worse.

So the parts of life for which the government is held directly responsible are continuously enlarged. The expectations, hopes and fears of the entire population are thus increasingly focused on the government alone – development which may be more dangerous to our free institutions than any other of our time. More than anything else, it has already brought about the widely-noted and lamented decline in the quality of Parliamentary discussion. Every Member feels himself charged with the urgent task of furthering the particular interests, which might otherwise be overlooked, of his constituency, class, sex or calling. Thus preoccupied, he has little time or wit to spare for the great general issues which were once thought the proper business of Parliament.

Ministers also find themselves burdened in consequence with a mass of ridiculous detail. They look fools if they do not know about things which only fools in their position would know about – the contents of a meat pie, the siting of a urinal, a fallen telegraph pole.

Thus the concentration of expectations on the government produces inefficiency and folly. It may end by producing something worse : for, where all expectations are focused, there also will find its mark all the anger aroused by expectations unfulfilled – as some must surely be.

Using the profit motive

Conservatives have surely shown remarkably little initiative in diverting these expectations away from themselves. Poor Mr Marples, for instance, has built roads with an energy which may be insufficient but is certainly unprecedented. And what is his reward? 'Marples must go !' Instead of going, why on earth does he not invite others to help him? Why must he personally build whatever roads are built? Why does he not allow toll roads to be built by private enterprise for private profit? That is what he is supposed to believe in – indeed, to have prospered by. No profit? He could guarantee it, if necessary, by subsidy : there are precedents enough, as we know to our cost. Would chaos and vandalism result? Why should they? Mr Marples could still ensure uniformity of signs and safety standards; the planning authorities could ensure that the roads were well sited. (Why, incidentally, does Mr Marples not charge tolls for his own motorways? He might find the Treasury less tiresome and niggardly if it had some hope of return.)

In other fields, such as pensions and health, Conservatives have shown almost as little zeal to shed responsibilities. Here too they have on the whole maintained for themselves the right to take decisions, to take the credit or bear the odium as it may be. Yet they have not in fact succeeded in running these or other services so well as to silence a general and understandable clamour that they should be 'taken out of politics'.

There are two ways in which this might be done. One is to hand back the services to private hands, with subsidies to the consumer in order to make market discipline tolerable. The other would be to hand them over to some quasi-autonomous authority like the BBC, theoretically 'above politics', subject to no clear discipline at all and thus liable to impose upon the exchequer increasing burdens without let or hindrance. So far have things gone that no-one can still be certain which alternative Conservatives would choose if a choice had to be made.

Far from diverting expectations, Conservatives have seemed at times to concentrate them on themselves gratuitously. Take their incomes policy, for instance. They have in fact no incomes policy; if they had machinery capable of determining in each case what is a 'fair' or 'just' reward, they would still lack the means of ensuring that everyone got it. Such means are not compatible with a free society, unlikely to be acceptable, indeed, in any society. Yet Conservatives continually claim to have an incomes policy : thus they dignify their habit of imploring us all to put up more or less with what we have – fair or unfair as we may think it plus some arbitrarily-determined annual increase.

By such pretences the Government has managed – if anything – to make itself a party to every wage dispute (albeit often an ineffective party, without real means of pressing its case) and to attract to itself much of the wrath which, if justified at all, should be directed rather at mean employers or stupid trade unions or at the facts of economic life itself. Thus it advances, hesitantly and as it were backwards, into yet another field : first pretending to regulate; then perhaps being forced to regulate in fact; forced on then step by step towards the total regimentation of the economy.

Immigration and internal migration

Let us now watch our little principles operating in a number of controversies which have recently stirred Parliament. Firstly, two population questions – immigration, and the drift away from the old industrial areas towards the south-east. Notice how, in dealing with immigration, the Government assumed at once (perhaps rightly – I do not scoff) that there were no natural checks on the inflow upon which any reliance could be placed. If brakes were necessary, the Government itself had to supply them; and did so.

The old-fashioned Manchester reaction to such developments as the drift southwards would be to let it rip, relying on the spontaneous forces of a free society to effect the necessary adjustments. With their paternalist traditions, Conservatives might legitimately go further. They might first strive to find out who wants to move and where they want to go; then, by planning ahead, they might hope to ensure that the movement was as painless as possible, causing the least possible damage to family life and social cohesion.

What they are actually doing – though not with enough energy to satisfy the Socialists – is the reverse of this. The pattern of public social investment is being consciously distorted in order to give more to the declining areas, less to the rising, more especially to the north-east and to central Scotland, less to south-east England. As a result, houses, schools, hospitals and roads will be built less where they are most needed than where they are perhaps least needed. In an increasingly competitive world, moreover, new factories are being sited less on economic than on welfare grounds. By an extension of the same logic, coal mines might have been sunk in Wiltshire 100 years ago, cotton mills established at Kersey, the number of MPs from Old Sarum possibly increased.

The purpose of all this distortion is, of course, to arrest a drift which may have the same profound validity as the movement northwards 100 and more years ago. The result, as so often when governments pit themselves against great spontaneous forces, may well be merely more waste and dislocation than was strictly necessary.

Housing policy worsened unemployment

As the Government's intentions became clear, of course, MPs of all parties surged shamelessly forward, each hymning the exceptional miseries and deficiencies of his own area, till one might have thought Britain as a whole reduced to the state of Ireland during the famine. In selecting the appropriate areas for special treatment, the Government in fact relied primarily on the local incidence of unemployment. In this context, it would be interesting to know to what extent unemployment figures are swollen by mistaken housing policies. (One way of finding out, incidentally, would be to transfer the housing subsidy from the house to the tenant, so that he could take it with him when he moves, and see what happens.) A well-paid job in the south can have little power to attract if it means shifting from a subsidised council house into expensive lodgings; the difference in rent may far outweigh the rise in income.

In their rent policies, the Conservatives made a bold dash for freedom and then stopped halfway. They thought the spot shrewdly chosen; in fact they enjoy here the worst of two worlds and are exposed to attacks from all sides at once.

Advocates of a free market in housing, with consumers subsidised as necessary, must have been prepared for an initial period of turmoil while the accumulated distortions of 40 years of rent control sorted themselves out. In return they could promise a saner distribution of existing housing, fresh energies released to build new housing, an end to shortage : *per ardua ad astra*. They have been abashed and silenced by the existing compromise – half free, half not, with all manner of Rachmanite mayhem on the borderline – not, let it be noted, in the free sector. If extended, the free market could be expected to cure the very abuses which discredit it. These abuses have instead been used as an excuse not to extend it.

They also supply Labour's housing spokesman, Mr Michael Stewart, with endless material for his denunciations of landlords, who seem to be for him what the Jews were to Julius Streicher. Far from being in a position to deplore and refute these attacks, successive Conservative Ministers, Mr Henry Brooke and Sir Keith Joseph, have been forced presumably by their own defective policies to condone or even echo them, supplementing Mr Stewart's invective with threats and strictures of their own, with a frenzy of state regulation and activity. Of all that they have recently said and done, Mr Stewart was able to suggest that it was only what his own party has been urging for years : and alas, there was some truth in his suggestion.

In this field, as in others, half-freedom has produced results probably less satisfactory than either freedom or unfreedom undiluted. By their timid mistrust of freedom, Conservatives are inclined to dilute it heavily; and when the resultant compromise does not work, they tend to fall back in panic on authority. This they did, for instance, in allotting the third television channel to the BBC.

Broadcasting half-free

No-one can have expected the full fruits of unfettered competition to spring from the establishment of ITV, by which one strictly regulated commercial monopoly was permitted to compete with the BBC. Optimists thought it a step in the right direction. Pessimists feared that ITV would be impelled by its own monopolistic nature towards catering predominantly for the widest and lowest mass market, and that its consequent vices would be used to discredit the idea of competition itself.

The pessimists were right. Every disinterested argument in favour of the establishment of ITV envisaged it as the first of several competing independent services, catering eventually for most heights of brow and for many minority tastes and interests. Appalled by its first fruits, Conservatives shrank back in horror, from their own logic, thankful now for the existence of the very state monopoly they had set out half-heartedly to break. What sort of a press would we have now, we may wonder, how subservient, how dependent on the state, had people of this kidney been able to regulate its development from Gutenberg[1] on?

Uncritical acceptance of Robbins

Among the attractions of state initiative in any field is the fact that it can be rapid and comprehensive. Among its great disadvantages is that it destroys the forces of continuous and spontaneous improvement and correction which are always at work in a free society, no matter how slowly and inconspicuously. Wherever this has taken place, we may expect first some dramatic state initiative, like the Butler Education Act of 1944; then a period of torpor, in which the ingredients of crisis accumulate unremarked; then the crisis itself, calling, so it seems, for some fresh dramatic intervention by the state. This is the logic which underlies the wholly uncritical acceptance by most Conservatives of the Robbins report : this and one other factor, which is electoral.

There are those who advocate a fundamental reform of our educational system, by which the state would restore powers of decision, choice and control to private hands, to the individual and the family.[2] Now that the state has shown its inadequacy as an educator, they might expect a fair hear-

---

[1] The inventor of the printing press in the 15th century.

[2] Barker, p. 187; Seldon, p. 153; West, p. 171. See also *Education for Democrats*, by Professors A. T. Peacock and Jack Wiseman, Hobart Paper 25, Institute of Economic Affairs, 1964.

ing from Conservatives – but for these considerations : that their proposals would take time; that there would be much unscrambling to do; that no results could be expected at once; that things might get worse before they got better; that the whole operation might in consequence be torpedoed by misrepresentation before it produced any good fruit whatever.

Against this Robbins offers quick, spectacular, certain, predictable, once-for-all results, instant education – just dissolve the powder and shake. It is the old choice between a lump sum now (Robbins) and the prospect of infinite riches slowly accumulating in the future. What politician answerable to the electorate every five years can afford to wait?

What a tragedy it is : that nothing worthwhile can be accomplished in a moment; and that politicians, who insist on accomplishing everything for us, can accomplish nothing which takes more than a moment to do!

Yet if socialism we are to have there are perhaps some advantages in having it administered by convinced Socialists – that is to say, by people who may be supposed to have considered the problems involved and who know (if anyone can know) what they are doing.

Historical processes have conferred on the Conservatives the duty of representing at least two great and wholly legitimate traditions – one the Tory paternalist tradition represented by Disraeli, Shaftesbury and, more recently, Macmillan; the other the Whig or liberal tradition represented in different ways at different times by Burke and Adam Smith, by Cobden and Gladstone, by Hayek and Enoch Powell. In recent years the Whigs have had a very thin time of it indeed.

Many paternalist Conservatives are deeply worried to find where their own doctrines seem to be taking them. They do what they do because they can do no other : but they detest the results. In their predicament, they must recognise that only Whigs of a fairly doctrinaire kind can help them. Only Whigs can tell them how the tide of state intervention can

be first arrested and then rolled back, how the areas of freedom can be enlarged and secured, how private energies
seemingly stifled by state activity can be revived so that
people can do well for themselves what the state has on the
whole done so badly for them.

PART TWO

PRINCIPLES FOR GROWTH

Consumption is the sole end and purpose of all production; and the interest of the producer ought to be attended to, only so far as it is necessary for promoting that of the consumer.

Adam Smith (1776)

A productive system worked in this way may, therefore, be conceived as a process of response to a continuous general election on the principle of proportionate representation. The entrepreneur may, so to speak, put up the candidates; he may attempt to sway the election by propaganda and persuasion; but the ultimate decision lies with those who spend – with what is sometimes called the sovereignty of the consumer.

Lord Robbins (1963)

If the presumption of the modern mind, which will not respect anything that is not consciously controlled by individual reason, does not learn in time where to stop, we may, as Edmund Burke warned us, 'be well assured that everything about us will dwindle by degrees, until at length our concerns are shrunk to the dimensions of our minds'.

Friedrich von Hayek (1949)

JOHN JEWKES

I was born in the early years of the 20th century when, for a
decade or more, it was still to benefit from the stability, the respect
for law and the restraint in government authority it inherited from
the liberal capitalism of the 19th century. From Barrow Grammar
School I went to Manchester University. Apart from a spell with
the Manchester Chamber of Commerce my life has been in the
academic world with some years in public service. I was succes-
sively lecturer in economics, Professor of Social Economics and
Professor of Political Economy at the University of Manchester
from 1926 to 1948. During the war I was for a time Director of
the Economic Section of the War Cabinet Secretariat and in other
government departments. Since 1948 I have been Professor of
Economic Organisation at the University of Oxford and Fellow
of Merton College.

My academic life has also been supplemented by membership of
Royal Commissions and Committees on fuel, the cotton industry,
gambling, betting and lotteries, and on doctor's and dentists'
remuneration.

My teacher was George Unwin. Much that he taught me was
epitomised in his favourite quotation drawn from one of the letters
of William James:

As for me my bed is made: I am against bigness and greatness
in all their forms, and with the invisible molecular moral forces
that work from individual to individual, stealing in through the
crannies of the world like so many soft rootlets, or like the
capillary oozing of water, and yet rendering the hardest monu-
ments of man's pride if you give them time. The bigger the unit
you deal with, the hollower, the more brutal, and the more
mendacious is the life displayed.

So I am against all big organisations as such, national ones first
and foremost; against all big successes and big results; and in
favour of the eternal forces of truth which always work in the
individual and immediately unsuccessful way, underdogs always,
until history comes after they are long dead and puts them on
the top.

4: NO INDUSTRY WITHOUT ENTERPRISE

JOHN JEWKES *discusses the ways in which monopoly in the British economy impedes enterprise and expansion and discusses the legal rules required to prevent restrictive practices, mergers and other devices tending to monopoly in order to create as much scope as possible for competition. He concludes with a comment on the businessman's responsibility to play the rules of the game.*

IT comes as a pleasing surprise, after so much recent talk about the short cuts to economic progress, that quite old-fashioned ideas are beginning to appeal to some of the very writers who have helped to create the modern doctrines that prosperity can be guaranteed so long as the government pulls the right levers – a delicate push here, a deft restraint there.

One recipe now being resurrected is that competition is a great economic powerhouse in itself. The latter-day converts are, indeed, not always consistent. Thus Mr Michael Shanks, in an essay in *Encounter* (July 1963) is anxious that British industry should be more competitive. Yet as editor of a symposium on nationalisation, *Lessons in Public Enterprise*, he claimed that 'There is a powerful case for further selective extension of public ownership'. But the case for nationalisation is the case for monopoly, and public monopoly is just as likely to stifle enterprise as is private monopoly. Or again in *Encounter*, Mr Andrew Shonfield obviously has a grievance against British medical services : 'In a British hospital I am sometimes reminded of Whitehall'. But he discusses British medical facilities without mentioning that there is such a thing as a British National Health Service, that it is a monopoly, and that its monolithic nature accounts for some of its failings.

'Planning' destroys competition

If this revived interest in competition is not to prove merely another passing British economic fad, it is important to recognise what it implies and what are the merits of a competitive system. To start with, it must be accepted that competition and central economic planning make bad bedfellows. The more competitive the system, the more unpredictable is the outcome of the interplay of a thousand uncertainties. The more unpredictable the future, the less meaning and purpose central economic planning can possess. When the Labour Party, for instance, opposed the entry of Britain into the European Common Market on the score that the extension of the area of competition in Europe would defeat their planning designs for Great Britain, their logic was impeccable.

Again it is not true that British industry is less competitive than it was fifteen years ago. Since 1948 the Monopolies Commission and the Restrictive Practices Court have been set up. It may be that the Commission should have operated more energetically and on a more extensive scale, particularly since the passage of the Restrictive Trade Practices Act of 1956, and that its conclusions and recommendations should have been acted upon more vigorously by the Board of Trade. Or it may be that, after a flying start in some of its early opinions, the Restrictive Practices Court in some later decisions has lost itself in irrelevant issues and failed to check monopoly activities where they were clearly discernible. In my opinion, however, the post-war legislation has made a real contribution in bringing to light monopoly practices, in checking them in many instances, in challenging and, at least partly, reversing the strongly monopolistic trend of thinking which was so widely found in British industry before the war. And, apart from any public action, there is now more competition than formerly in British industry in the sense that more firms are seriously up against foreign competition, and are having to meet at home the challenge of new products and novel processes. Competition is what widens the range of choice of the consumer; no one can really doubt that increasingly there are more products and services making a bid for the money in the consumer's pocket.

State intervention represses competition

Again, it is not true that in the absence of public intervention there will be no competition. The simplest proof is that all over the world public and private authorities continue to devote much effort to the repression of competition. Governments employ tens of thousands of customs officials to block foreign competition; or seek to confer absolute monopolies upon nationalised industries. Private cartels continue to hunt out competitors in the hope of blocking their activities. Would all this effort to keep it down be necessary if competition did not have a continuing vitality of its own?

There is, and will continue to be, a great deal of competition in Western industrial systems. The only question is whether there ought to be more and, if so, whether it can be engineered through Government action which will do more good than harm.

It has to be confessed forthwith that one cannot *prove*, beyond a doubt, that competition is preferable to monopoly or that any particular shift in the balance between the two is incontrovertibly in the public interest. There is a *presumption* that in a competitive system economic resources will be more rationally distributed than under other conditions. There is a *presumption* that competition is more likely to make for improvement, innovation and initiative than monopoly although this view is not universally held by experts. When the economist has said all that he is qualified to say, a proper decision on public policy can only be reached by applying commonsense to some very broad social issues. The test might be put this way. What truth is there in the doctrine laid down by the great American judge, Mr Justice Hands, in the well-known Aluminum Case :

> Possession of unchallenged economic power deadens initiative, discourages thrift and depresses energy; immunity from competition is a narcotic, and rivalry a stimulant to industrial progress; the spur of constant stress is necessary to counteract an inevitable disposition to let well alone.

Or how far is one prepared to accept the verdict of Edward Gibbon in *The Decline and Fall of the Roman Empire* :

> The spirit of monopolists is narrow, lazy and oppressive; their work is more costly and less productive than that of independent artists; and the new improvements so eagerly grasped by the competition of freedom, are admitted with slow and sullen reluctance in those proud corporations, above the fear of a rival and below the confession of an error.

How monopoly impoverishes

If this, indeed, is the way of the world it is sensible to try to widen the area of competition. It is difficult to give chapter and verse for benefits which have flowed from monopoly; it is easy enough to pick out cases where monopoly has impeded and impoverished Western communities. I give three illustrations.

One of the strongest monopolies in the post-war world has been the International Air Transport Association, the power of which fortunately now seems to be on the wane. One consequence of its activities has been the maintenance of very high fares for international travel, especially across the Atlantic. In that way it has prevented a revolutionary form of transport from being used to the full for binding together the Western world. Or take the National Coal Board, upon which the British Government has granted a monopoly of coal-mining. This industry survives at its present size only because the importation of cheaper foreign coal is prohibited and a high duty is placed upon competing fuel oil. In consequence, British industry suffers from higher fuel costs than it need have had. Or, to move to private industry, the reports of the Monopolies Commission have revealed cases (as, for example, in the sale of motor car tyres, the manufacture of electric lamps, oxygen, motor car accessories and wallpaper) where the consumer has suffered from the rigging of the market and monopolies have been defended by methods sometimes resembling those of a Star Chamber.

Although I do not believe that it would be an utter disaster if Britain had no anti-monopoly legislation, I submit that more competition would now bring substantial economic advantages. But public policy must be properly designed. The overriding condition is that the nation must have a robust enough belief in competition to accept thoroughgoing measures to foster it. Half-hearted policies may well be worse than nothing. If some forms of monopoly are curbed and others left untouched, if the methods of regulation adopted inevitably involve long delays, if the legal and administrative bodies charged with the duties of investigation and control are left without firm guidance from above and are free to go back to first principles then inevitably inconsistencies and inequities will lead to disillusionment among the people and tempt business men to try to outsmart a code of control which appears to them both irrational and ineffective.

British 'trust-busting'

In 1948 Britain started virtually from scratch to build up a system of anti-monopoly regulation. It has not been a failure. But, inevitably, mistakes have been made which call for remedy if we are serious about fostering competition. The history is well known. The Act of 1948 set up a Monopolies Commission which produced many first-class reports but it has never been clear how energetically their findings and recommendations have been followed up by Government Departments. The Restrictive Trade Practices Act of 1956 gave expression to the right sentiments but embodied the compromises and hesitations which have bedevilled Conservative Party policy in this matter. The Act, while toughening up the law relating to Resale Price Maintenance in some directions, weakened it in others – a compromise which has led to much trouble since. It truncated the Monopolies Commision and its functions just at the time when there was a case for strengthening them. It set up a Restrictive Practices Court – in itself a courageous and imaginative measure – but the procedures laid down have been so complicated, the 'gateways' through which business interests could seek to pass in order to justify their restrictive practices so numerous and wide, that the Court, after making an encouraging start, has not so far been successful in building up a corpus of consistent doctrine and precedent. In its early days, with the help of the sharp eye and keen brain of a Devlin, the Court seemed to be hammering out a body of doctrine which made economic sense. But in later decisions the Court, with no precise guidance from the Act and perhaps confused by the conflicting evidence of University economists who have done much to darken counsel, has often wandered about erratically and handed down conclusions which, in my opinion, have let the case for competition go by default.

All the time, in the past fifteen years, a vigorous merger movement has been going on which, one suspects, has resulted in great changes in the structure of industry but which the Government has never thoroughly investigated (or if it has, has not deigned to report upon to the public) and which, in any event, it possessed no legal powers to check or control.

In March 1964 the government took steps to move the balance further in favour of competition. Although it is early to judge, the split of opinion within the Conservative Party and the almost pathological anxiety of the British to do nothing which hurts any minority even if it benefits the vast majority, may once again endanger the purpose of the new proposals.

A policy for competition

What steps should be followed by a Government determined to create a more competitive system? First, of course, it should refrain from creating new monopolies of its own through nationalisation. But beyond that? It has always surprised me that in these matters Great Britain has not been prepared to take more advantage of the experience and methods followed in the United States. In other directions we have in recent years become assiduous imitators of other countries. One of the principal reasons why we engaged in central economic planning was apparently because France was doing it (though what France has done exactly in this connection still remains a bit of a mystery). One of the big arguments in favour of our training many more scientists and technologists was that Russia was doing it. In some quarters it is strongly recommended that we should drastically reform trade unions because that is what Sweden has done. Or radically reorganise our civil service so that it could operate more nearly as does the French civil service. Or train our businessmen in great Schools of Business because that is what happens at Harvard or our technologists in separate Schools of Technology because that is what happens at the the Massachusetts Institute of Technology.

I am a little suspicious of these hasty and naïve international comparisons, which are often little more than shallow judgements based upon the belief that there are short cuts to economic success. But the experience of America in the control of monopoly is of a different kind. After all, there is in the United States a fully documented record going back eighty years of a continuously pursued intention to foster competition. This policy has had its failures as well as its successes but it has undoubtedly left its mark on the American economy. American industry is more competitive (and more productive) than that in any other country in the world and if this cannot be explained, in significant degree, by the operation of anti-monopoly policies it is difficult to know how it can be explained.

What has the United States to teach us about effective methods of maintaining competition? First, there seems to be a strong case in Great Britain for more '*per se*' legislation, that is, for laws which define and legally forbid certain practices. The Courts would then concern themselves not

with the hazy task of deciding whether 'on balance' such
practices are in the public interest but whether, in fact, such
practices exist, in which case they must be discontinued.
Whatever failure or success may be attributed to other
branches of American anti-monopoly policy, I think there
can be little doubt that '*per se*' legislation has virtually
stamped out agreements for fixing prices or restricting output. If in Britain we believe that the overwhelming proportion of price and output associations do operate contrary
to public interest (and if we do not so believe we should
drop anti-monopoly legislation altogether) then they ought
to be banned. It would be foolish to go to great pains to
preserve the few monopolies which might perhaps do more
good than harm, and thereby run the risk of letting slip
through the net more numerous monopolies which do more
harm than good.

It is more difficult to see what should be done about
monopoly that arises through the very size of firms. What if
a firm, by sheer efficiency and without any designs on
cornering the market, drives out competitors, has 'monopoly
thrust upon it'? Or if an industry comes to consist of a few
big firms which watch each other closely and, without formal
agreement, follow each other's actions? Here American
policy has not been, and perhaps could never be wholly suc-
cesful. But some of their moves are worth examining. One
good rule is to put up hurdles against an industrial merger
until a court or administrative tribunal has satisfied itself
that the merger is not likely to create undue control of the
market. If omelettes cannot be unscrambled, it may be possible to prevent too many eggs being broken for the purpose
of frying undesirable omelettes. Beyond that, where one or
a few large firms already dominate an industry, a Monopolies Commission with larger resources and working with
a greater sense of urgency than our present Commission,
should carry out studies periodically. In Britain there are
still firms dominating single industries, such as glass manufacture, which have not been investigated. The evidence
suggests that firms only rarely have monopoly 'thrust upon

them' through superior efficiency solely and without using unfair or intimidating tactics against competitors.

Whether a policy of fostering competition proves possible or not will in part depend upon other general economic conditions over which Governments can exercise an influence. A highly protectionist country (and we do well to remind ourselves that Britain is still such) will find it all the more difficult to maintain competition in the domestic market. It seems to me highly significant that the country with the most efficient industrial system in the world, the United States, although externally protectionist has a vast internal free trade area, and is also the country where small manufacturing firms play a most active part, where such firms are given the greatest possible public encouragement, where the individual innovator has a good chance of disposing of his ideas to advantage. None of these things in these days can be said to be true of Great Britain.

The business man and the rules of the game

In my opinion, however, we have one advantage which, firmly grasped, should make it comparatively easy for Britain to exploit to the full the economic benefits of competition. No complex, civilised community can exist unless every important group within it conforms to certain rules and restraints which are hardly ever written down, much less effectively enforced, as law. Each group must refrain from exploiting to the last degree the powers it possesses of exacting tolls upon the rest of the community. Wage earners by calling a General Strike could in fact bring the community to a standstill and thus enforce their demands; prolonged withdrawal of their services by any one professional group – teachers, lawyers, police, doctors – would be equally, even if less swiftly, crippling; any substantial group which chose to protest against real or imagined grievances by passive resistance in blocking traffic or throwing sudden unexpected demands upon public services and so on could create hopeless chaos for the rest of the community. Stable, organised society goes on just because these things do not happen.

These extra-legal and uncodifiable obligations accepted by the citizen have this feature in common : they throw upon him in the short run sacrifices which are made, and are recognised as being made, for the larger, long-period gains for which social cohesion is a condition precedent. A system as a whole is accepted because of its general benefits although its immediate, direct impact upon any one person may be disagreeable.

So with a competitive system. Within it the business man finds life more exacting than where he controls the market. He pays more heavily for his mistakes. He enjoys the chances of larger profits but also faces the risk of larger losses. He will be compelled more frequently to change his mind and the direction of his efforts. He will be less comfortable. It is precisely this state of affairs that the intensifying of competition is designed to bring about.

Now I cannot believe that, in the last resort, a thoroughly effective competitive system stands much chance of survival or that anti-monopoly legislation is likely to be worth the candle unless business men themselves believe in and accept the rules of the competitive game however sharp may be its barbs and arrows. It may seem to be a small matter to expect of the business man that he should sincerely favour private enterprise. It is in fact not so. He is being asked to do much more than make speeches which claim virtues for 'free enterprise' and are critical of government operation of industry. He is being expected deliberately to refrain from agreements to fix prices or output; to recognise, however galling it may appear to him, that when his organisation reaches a certain size or commands a certain proportion of the market, then the public has a direct interest in what he and his company are doing; to co-operate positively with the Government in accepting (and even, dare one say it, in devising and improving) rules for keeping industry lively and resilient through the perpetual rivalry of competitors.

As I say, this is a lot to accept. But, in the long run, sufficient imagination and courage on the part of the business man to do so is probably a condition of his survival. It is, after all, ideas which rule the world. The system of free markets and competition has been one of the most brilliant institutional inventions of the Western world; without it the world would be much poorer not only materially but in nearly ever other sense. The system has in recent years been attacked by one group of social scientists who seem to suffer from an irresistible itch always to gnaw at and undermine any institutional framework in which they happen to find themselves. But fortunately the system has also had its brilliant and robust defenders, scholars and thinkers of our time who, to my mind, are wiser about the laws determining the wealth of nations and about the institutions through which justice and compassion between men can best be nurtured. Private enterprise under competition can be defended intellectually, monopolistic private enterprise cannot. That is why I shall go on hoping that British business men will think out carefully the implications of their own broad belief in competition and act upon them, thereby making it easy for those egg-heads who also believe in competition to defend the case with confidence.

PAUL BAREAU

I came to England in 1914, a refugee from 'Kaiser Bill's' invasion of Belgium which left me with an undying hatred of despotism in all its forms, of aggressive nationalism, of all attempts by 'authority' to suppress human freedom. It has also left me with a deep respect for the country which received me as a small boy and of which I have become a citizen.

I was at the London School of Economics in the days of Beveridge, Laski and Dalton, and looking back on those years in the 1920s I appreciate Briand's remark: 'The man who is not a socialist at twenty has no heart' – though I am also inclined to agree with the second half of the quotation, 'but if he is still a socialist at forty he has no head'.

Much of my journalistic career was spent working on the *News Chronicle* with the late Sir Oscar Hobson, a man of passionate integrity, of superb skill as a journalist, a ruthless detector and exposer of anything that rang false. During part of the war I was seconded to the Treasury and for a time worked closely with Lord Keynes who has had more impact on economic thinking and policy than any other economist. He taught that money should be the servant and not the master of mankind. But any good servant must be honest. As Editor of the *Statist* I do my best to apply a philosophy forged in a full life and influenced by good tutors. 'Humanitarian radical' is how I would describe myself.

5: WANTED: COMPETITION
FROM ABROAD

PAUL BAREAU *looks at the external reasons why British industry is not as enterprising and as competitive as it can be. He criticises the numerous exchange controls and restrictions on the entry of competing goods and services by tariffs, quotas and other devices.*

Dr HJALMAR SCHACHT, onetime president of the German Reichsbank, and architect of much of the economic system that sustained Nazi Germany, once remarked that if he had to make do with one economic control, and one only, he would choose control of the foreign exchange market.

The choice is in no way surprising. The ultimate self-defence of a citizen against the tyranny of his government is to take himself and his family out of the tyrant's clutches to emigrate to a land of greater freedom. Every tyranny has produced its crop of pilgrims and emigrants who have gone forth to seek freedom elsewhere. One of the ways in which the escape route can be blocked is to prevent the individual taking his savings with him. Exchange control, if it is effective (and in Nazi Germany it had behind it the sanctions of the firing squad) is one way in which to keep the resident a prisoner in his own country by depriving him of the financial means to move to another country. Exchange control is an essential weapon in the armoury of tyranny.

It is also an effective means of controlling wide segments of the economy, extending well beyond the sphere of foreign exchanges and international payments. Through the appropriate manipulation of exchange control, the direction of export and import trade can be influenced. Most restrictions of imports are operated through exchange control, and this is therefore the way in which competition from abroad can be excluded. Exchange control is an essential accompaniment of any system of really penal taxation, since it closes the escape routes to capital. It is also a pre-requisite of any artificial manipulation of interest rates and of domestic capital markets since it is through exchange control that interest rates can be insulated from the outside world. It is through exchange control that a currency can escape the self-regulatory discipline of an international standard of value and of payments.

Exchange control necessary for state planning

It is not only tyranny that requires restrictions against the freedom of payments between the country in which it is established and the outside world. Exchange control also serves its purpose in an economy in which the inevitable mixture between private enterprise and the intrusion of the state tilts the balance in favour of the latter. The powerful intrusion of the state in the running of the economy can be inhibited and hampered by freedom of exchanges and by the admission of some external discipline. Conversely, exchange control is the inevitable, inescapable corollary of any attempt to direct, guide and control the economy through a central government planning authority. Every communist bloc country is hemmed around by the harshest wire fence of exchange control. That obstacle to payments freedom with the outside world is as essential a part of the system as the physical, electrified wire fences which prevent freedom of personal movement with the outside world. The two are complementary. They belong to the same repugnant model.

The case for complete convertibility should not be spoilt by being overstated. The essence of the Keynesian revolution in economic thinking and policy – a revolution which consciously or not has been accepted in almost all countries – was that money should be the servant, not the master of economic policy. (A good servant, may I interject, should be stable). One can recall instances when regard for the pound sterling trod heavily and damagingly on the British economy. The return to the gold standard after the First World War was a case in point. It was done for the sake of sterling and out of honourable regard for the sanctity of sterling obligations, but with insufficient concern for, or understanding of its consequences for British industry. To say this, however, is not a condemnation of freedom of payments and convertibility, but of the artificial parity which on that occasion was chosen as the basis for the return to gold. It was the overvaluation of sterling, not its convertibility or the freedom with which it could be exchanged for other currencies, which did the damage between 1925 and 1931 – when sterling severed its link with gold.

It is needless to labour the fact that exchange control is an inevitable and wholly justifiable attendant demon on the horrors of war. One of the many freedoms that had to be sacrificed in the two world wars was the convertibility of the currency whether in gold or other currencies. When the cause of mere survival leaps to the top of a nation's list of priorities, other objectives have to make way. Mobilisation becomes the order of the day and must apply to capital as well as to the citizens who own that capital. In total war the gold reserve is as much part of the country's means of defence and attack as the factories making munitions, the ships bringing in food and materials. In those circumstances control of foreign exchanges, imports and shipping is necessary and in practice has been applied and accepted without question.

But there is a dangerous tendency for these limitations on personal, political and economic freedom to outlast the emergency for which they were devised and in which they found their justification. The restrictions cannot, for obvious reasons, end on the morrow of hostilities. Time has to be allowed for economic as well as military demobilisation. An instructive object-lesson on the dangers of too much haste was provided in the immediate postwar years. In 1947 we were pushed too rapidly and against many people's better judgement into full convertibility of sterling as one of the conditions of the agreement by which Britain secured a post-war loan from the United States. This premature rehabilitation of convertible sterling lasted precisely six weeks, cost the gold and dollar reserve tens of millions of pounds and had to be abjectly abandoned after obtaining the necessary 'by your leave' of the US Government. This episode was doubly unfortunate for it tended to confirm the suspicions of those who feared freedom and whose prejudices favoured the continuation of exchange and other controls.

Sterling and the City

The memory of this affair dies hard. It is responsible for the suspicion with which the role that Britain still plays in international finance is regarded in some academic and political quarters. When a move is made towards more freedom of payments with other countries, or when interest rates are raised to defend the value of sterling, you may depend on hearing yells of dismay from people whose thinking stopped in the 1930s and who suspect that once again British industry is being sacrificed to the golden calf of sterling and the City of London. What utter rubbish this is in the context of the 1960s, of a set of declared Government economic objectives in which full employment takes unquestioned precedence. Among the more sophisticated purveyors of this view is Mr Andrew Shonfield who argued in 1957 in *Encounter* (1) that we would be well advised to use more of our capital resources to cultivate our own garden, rather than sow them in the soil of the underdeveloped countries and (2) that the role of sterling as an international currency and the City of London as an international financial centre offer no prizes commensurate with the strains it places on the economy – that it is a quixotic pursuit of grandeur.

Of the first 'delusion of grandeur', as he termed it, let me say that the record of Great Britain in giving aid and exporting capital to the emergent nations is nothing of which to be particularly proud. If fault is to be found on the score of inadequacy of capital investment in industry, it is not because too much of our resources have in recent years been sent overseas. On capital account – and it is a two-way account – the net outflow has represented a pathetically small proportion of the national income and in some years (1961, for example), we have been more invested against than investing.

But it is the second accusation that really riles. Sterling is not an international currency by reason of a conscious decision on policy but because it has grown into that role over a century and a half of international enterprise by British manufacturers, investors, merchants, insurers, shippers and bankers. To pull down the shutters on all this would damage the rest of the world as well as ourselves. It would deprive international trade of much of the financial services on which it now depends. It would mean much more than a loss of the direct income earned in these different ventures. A great deal of our exports are secured because the buyers are represented by subsidiaries and purchasing agents in the City of London, because they maintain their working balances in sterling, because they are, in effect, part of the world-wide sterling system. The livelihood of Clydeside shipbuilding workers, of textile operators in Bradford, of electrical engineers in Rugby, may depend on orders placed because of the financial and merchanting services provided by the City of London.

Balance of payments crises

But the reconciliation of the position of sterling with the wider interests of the British economy goes beyond this direct, specific assistance which the financial services offer to trade and industry. It is my firm conviction that the kind of economic expansion which will prove most endurable and be most soundly based is one that goes hand in hand with reasonable price stability and with equilibrium in the balance of payments. The growth that leads to balance of payments deficits and threatens the stability of the currency is *ipso facto* suspect, since it has weakened the competitive fibre of the economy. Economic history abounds with examples of countries whose economies have expanded so fast that they land in a morass of external insolvency. The latest of these object lessons is the Italian 'miracle', so often held up for our admiration and edification, which in the early weeks of 1964 had to be saved by a massive international rescue operation.

Growth will thrive best if it goes with stability of the currency and if it is subjected to the salubrious impact of competition within the domestic market and from other countries. That is why not only exchange restrictions and their protective cover must be minimised, but every effort made to reduce the tariff walls and quota barriers behind which inefficiency can shelter. The Kennedy round of tariff negotiations under GATT will give Britain an opportunity of serving this good cause. Our membership of EFTA is another window through which the bracing air of competition will blow through large parts of the economy. A day will surely come when the area of competition – and of opportunity – will be further extended by joining the two economic communities in Europe: the Common Market and the European Free Trade Association ('EFTA').

'The 57 varieties'

Satisfactory progress has been made since 1951 in dismantling the major part of the structure of sterling exchange control. What were once known as the '57 varieties' of sterling have been reduced to a mere four : non-resident sterling arising out of current transactions which is wholly convertible; resident sterling which can readily be used in payment for imports and, within generous limits, for travelling abroad; security sterling which represents the proceeds of sales of capital by non-residents; and, finally, the sterling which is used by residents wishing to invest outside the sterling area and which in acquiring the necessary foreign currencies has, in the not very distant past, had to pay premiums of up to 14 per cent.

Although good work has been done in simplifying the system of exchange control, it still contains some odd and damaging anomalies. Take, for example, the fact that a foreign investor buying sterling securities is told that when he sells them the proceeds will be in security sterling, known once upon a time as 'blocked' sterling. What an advertisement for a currency with pretensions to world status ! In fact the sterling in question is not blocked. It is available for reinvestment in other sterling securities by other non-residents. So far there has been a good demand for such sterling and there is a very free market in which it has been quoted at a minimal fraction below the rate for convertible non-resident sterling. But this is an unnecessary blot on the escutcheon of sterling close on twenty years after the end of the war. It is no defence of sterling: on the contrary, it must have deterred and turned away many millions of pounds of good foreign money which would otherwise have been invested in sterling securities.

Overseas investment discouraged

Equally damaging is the system under which British firms which wish to invest overseas by setting up subsidiaries or extending otherwise their own enterprise, must for the most part obtain the currencies they need in the investment dollar market and pay the appropriate premium which has recently been as high as 14 per cent. This is laying a heavy handicap on what are presumably regarded by the firms as profitable ventures that would bring benefit not only to them but to the balance of payments and are therefore in the national interest. The damage is the larger and resentment the stronger to the extent that some favoured firms may receive permission from the exchange control to obtain their currencies in the official market and, therefore, without having to pay any premium. This entails a form of discrimination which should be left to the decision of the market place and not exercised by a group of officials however above suspicion the motives behind their decisions may be.

Control of imports

There are other discrepancies in the system. The existing provisions for travel allowance, namely £200 per head per journey, gives the would be exporter of capital fair scope for his activities, especially as customs inspection of what currency a traveller is taking out of the country has lost most of its severity. This is not to condemn the freedom with which the British resident can now travel and spend his money abroad. But it contrasts oddly with the premium an enterprising British firm has to pay when it decides to make an investment in non-sterling countries – assuming, that is, that it is allowed to do it at all. The most dangerous aspect of the remnants of exchange control is not the restrictions on payments overseas, which the astute operator can usually circumnavigate, but that it provides a readymade mechanism for future control of imports. It is through exchange control that imports can most easily be restricted, since every import requires an authorisation to buy foreign currencies or to transfer sterling to the account of a non-resident. In recent years British import policy has been agreeably liberalised; but while exchange control exists there is an ever-present temptation to meet balance of payments difficulties by checking imports. This remedy appeals to the politician who can sublimate such a proposal into a measure that will protect British workers from 'unfair' foreign competition. And it is surprising how many eminent economists as well as politicians fall for the superficial but dangerous simplicity of this solution.

Less control over inflation

If the balance of payments runs into deficit it is *prima facie* evidence that prices at home are too high, that the domestic market is absorbing too much of what is being produced and that this buoyant domestic market is also pulling in competitively priced imports. In such circumstances to check the flow of imports cures nothing except the immediate symptoms. The deeper ills are made worse. Inflation can proceed a little further. The inefficient are protected. All the forces that led to the balance of payments difficulties gather strength. No better formula could be devised for perpetuating and accentuating the tendencies making for disequilibrium in balance of payments and undermining the stability of a currency. That way lies an ultimate and inevitable depreciation and devaluation of the currency.

This is an issue of burning topicality. The balance of payments has been under some strain : some of it justifiable and representing no more than increased stockpiling by a dynamically expanding British industry; but some of it beginning to reflect a slight overheating of the economy. In these circumstances, as one would expect, there is talk of selective import controls. The word 'selective' usually intrudes because it seems to give a virtuous gloss to what is a thoroughly iniquitous procedure. No 'selection' would save the process from the basic defect that it would aggravate rather than cure the root causes of imbalance.

Before such import controls could be applied, Britain would have to get special permission from the General Agreement on Tariffs and Trade ('GATT') and this in turn would require a kind of 'certificate of need' from the International Monetary Fund justifying Britain's action. That would set in motion a train of events which would call for something far more drastic and unpleasant than mere 'selective' control of imports.

Apart from all this, resort to import controls would in the present context of world tariff history be a strategic blunder of the first magnitude. The Kennedy Round of tariff negotiations under the aegis of the General Agreement on Tariffs and Trade has been started. Here lies the great hope of an appreciable demobilisation of world tariffs and of minimising the damage that might be done to world trade by the discriminatory character of the Common Market and also of the EFTA arrangements. Here is a momentous initiative in which the United States have hitherto received assurances of support from Great Britain. To stoop to import controls, however selective, would be to ring the death knell of the Kennedy Round, even before it had started.

JACK WISEMAN

I am the youngest son of a family of Lancashire cotton weavers, grew up in the depression and went to work at fifteen (no brass or scholarship). I was introduced to economics in evening classes in Burnley, and fired with enthusiasm by a fine teacher. In 1939 I was awarded a scholarship for evening study at the London School of Economics, but I was in the Territorial Army and it was 1946 before I got to London. Like Lionel Robbins after the first World War, I arrived a socialist and ripe to set the world right.

LSE was full of social fervour. I met an intellectual bombardment from all directions: from Laski to Hayek. The abiding influence on me was Lionel Robbins, but it was Laski who first gave me doubts about socialism. He was a fine man, but he told us he was interested in presenting a point of view rather than a balanced case, and we must get the other viewpoint from elsewhere. I did, and liked it. Having been poor, I have never been able to tolerate the patronising attitude of paternalists to my kin.

I was a Lecturer and Reader in economics at the LSE from 1949 until the end of 1963. In January 1964, after a year at the University of California as visiting Professor of Public Finance, I was appointed Professor of Applied Economics and Director of the Institute of Social and Economic Research at York. There I joined Professor Alan T. Peacock with whom I have had a long-standing association in joint publications on public finance and welfare services.

My hobbies are economics, arguing, eating and drinking, arguing, cricket and arguing.

6: GROWING WITHOUT NATIONALISATION

JACK WISEMAN *assesses the arguments for nationali-sation advanced in recent writings. In particular he analyses the new argument, based on an old argument, that the market does not take into account 'social costs' and concludes that there is little in it for practical public policy. He counters by proposals for subjecting the nationalised industries to competition with private sup-pliers where possible, or, where not, for denationalising them and returning them to the discipline of free markets.*

THERE have been frequent expressions of dissatisfaction with the internal performance of nationalised industries, but to a remarkable extent debate has concentrated in recent years upon the details of administrative and organisational change in the existing corporations, with little discussion of whether the scope of nationalisation might suitably be extended or existing corporations returned to the private sector. The enthusiasts of nationalisation and economic growth rarely recognise that the weaknesses of the nationalised industries may themselves have retarded the growth of the economy as a whole or that they must call into question the very principles of nationalisation if public corporations are to be judged by their past results.

The increasing weight of the nationalised industries on Britain's economic performance is clear. From 1938 to 1962 total annual investment in the U.K. grew from £656 million to £4608 million, or about seven times. But the investment of the public corporations during the same period has risen from £10 million to £927 million, or over ninety times. The proportion of all investment has grown from about one-sixtieth in 1938 to one-fifth in 1962. (This fraction does not include investment by local and national government which was £1013 million in 1962, or a further fifth.) The public corporations predominate in fuel and transport and also in communications of other kinds (telephones, broadcasting). They produce goods and services bought and used by the private sector of industry, whose own efficiency in part depends on them. If the nationalised industries are inefficient private industry will also be unavoidably inefficient.

The Case for nationalisation

There can be no simple way to demonstrate how nationalised industries have influenced growth in Britain because we cannot know precisely what would have happened had the enterprises been in private hands. But it is clear that the efficiency of the large public sector must influence the whole economy. It is therefore fruitful to ask why the economic efficiency of public corporations should be expected to be superior to that of the private enterprises that might replace them. The advocates of nationalisation use arguments of a broader social character as well as narrowly technical ones. The two groups of arguments merge with each other, and the incautious critic is liable to find dissent about one of them countered by argument concerning the other. We shall begin with the broader arguments on the political and social ends of society and move to the narrower and more technical issues.

The nationalisers do not agree about first principles. Here is Mr C. A. R. Crosland in the *Future of Socialism*:

... the ownership of the means of production has ceased to be the key factor which imparts to a society its essential character,

and

monopoly, even when it is public, has definite drawbacks.

Here, in the opposite corner the late Mr John Strachey in the *Political Quarterly* in 1953:

The British people must and will assume the ownership of the means of production which they operate, and in the conditions of large-scale modern industry this can only be achieved through collective ownership.

This kind of difference continues to plague British socialists intellectually and emotionally. But the case for public ownership is weak. First, their arguments of principle against private property *per se* are implausible and unconvincing. (It does not follow of course that any given pattern of property distribution or any existing structure of property law is incapable of improvement. I myself would favour heavy inheritance taxes.) Second, the destruction of private property must imply the concentration of political and economic power in the same hands. This must be expected to result, and has in the past resulted, in a severe (and for me intolerable) curtailment of individual freedom. Third, even if the arguments of principle against private property were accepted, they would lead to support for universal public ownership rather than for the existence of a few public enterprises in a predominantly market economy. But no one proposes universal nationalisation in current policy for Britain. Fourth, and arising out of the others, nationalisation is to be judged by its results, and the onus is upon those who wish to destroy private property to show why their proposals are to be expected to bring advantages massive enough to outweigh the dangers and objections.

Social costs

A second line of approach has come into prominence. It does not attack private property as an institution but argues rather that free markets fail to take account of 'social costs' whereas public corporations can do so. The public discussion of social costs is wreathed in obscurity. Two broad strands of argument can be discerned, the one vague or confused, the other technically interesting but inconclusive in its support for nationalisation.

The most naïve form asserts that markets function unsatisfactorily because the 'wrong people' get the goods. But if a rich old lady can buy eggs for her dog while a poor mother cannot get enough for her children, the reason is unlikely to be the imperfection of the market for eggs. The target of reformers should be the distribution of capital and/or income. To blame the market for the poverty of some who trade in it is to misunderstand what markets can be expected to do.

An apparently more sophisticated, but effectively more obscure, argument of this general kind is that private ownership of resources encourages 'social inequality'. Thus, Mr Shanks claims that there is a strong *prima facie* case for believing that the transfer of big industrial assets from private to public hands would promote greater 'equality'. Equality, and even more social equality, appears to be something we should encourage, in the same way that we are against sin. But as in the case of sin, there is need for more precise specification if the moral imperative is to be a guide for action rather than simple jabberwocky. Since Mr Shanks does not explain what he means by 'social equality', it is a little difficult to make any judgement on the plausibility of his *prima facie* case. If he means *economic* equality, then the *prima facie* case is certainly not made out. The belief that the distribution of income is uniquely determined by the pattern of ownership is both technically implausible (no consistent economic model is ever suggested to support it), and in our present context disingenuous in failing to recognise that 'public ownership' is ownership by people : it is vested in those who can get and hold political power. Equally, the strong *prima facie* case is unsatisfactory if it refers to earned incomes. Wage differentials are wider if anything in the Soviet Union than in Britain : the spread between the highest and lowest paid workers in the early 1950s was commonly as high as 15 to 1.

The narrower form of the social cost argument claims that the values established in competitive markets do not take account of costs falling on the community or benefits accruing to the community, whose interests may therefore be bypassed. The modern formulation originated with the late Professor A. C. Pigou. Pigou has recently been rediscovered and the claim advanced that Labour thinking on social policy derives from his writings, as Mr Peter Hall claims in *Labour's New Frontiers*.

> We have begun to grope our way towards a practical concept of economic planning which may prove, in a few years time, to be as revolutionary in its implications as was the Keynesian revolution in economics thirty years ago. It also originated many years ago with a Cambridge economist: Keynes' contemporary Pigou. It is the concept of social costs and benefits.

But the claim that any unique relation can be traced between, say, Pigou's classic *The Economics of Welfare* and a definitive social programme is preposterous, and can suggest only that those who make it are more familiar with say, geography, than with the pioneering works of Pigou or the voluminous literature to which they have given rise.

Let us consider the nature of divergencies of private and social benefits and costs in more detail. The classic illustrations are well-known. My factory emits smoke which dirties your clothes, but I do not pay to have them laundered. Or my railway train runs past your wheat field, and emits sparks which burn your crops. But what to do? Recent discussions of social cost problems in economic literature have clarified the relevance of the concept to issues of public policy. The most significant development is that it has been convincingly demonstrated by Professor R. H. Coase, Professor J. M. Buchanan and Mr Ralph Turvey that while so-called divergencies of social and private costs and benefits (essentially similar to the external economies and diseconomies of business enterprise) may affect the efficient use of community resources, they need not do so and frequently do not. For example, in the 'crop burning case' the 'efficient' solution (depending upon the circumstances) from the point of view of the use of community resources might be for example to fit spark-preventing devices, to leave the land by the railway uncultivated, or simply to accept the risks of crops being burned. But that ideal solution can be reached by market transactions, whatever the particular rights of the affected parties. If there are no obstacles in the way of creating the market institutions, the use of resources by the community would be the same whether or not the railway owners have to compensate the farmers for burned crops. And similarly with the smoke nuisance case, which Pigou made famous. Essentially, therefore, the social cost problem becomes one of deciding on forms of compensation, which is in effect a decision about the laws of property.

The argument has several corollaries. First, social cost problems are not confined to particular industries but are relevant to all activities that involve the specification of property rights – in effect, the whole of economic activity. Second, the character and existence of social costs is less obvious than is commonly assumed. They may involve subjective assessments, and there is no agreed method of identifying and valuing them or of deciding which 'costs' are the proper subject of public policy. If I hang my weekly wash in my front garden, my neighbour may find the display offensive and argue that I have imposed a social cost upon him, but it does not follow that the *community* should take cognisance of it. Or consider the effect of cinemas upon members of the Salvation Army, to whom their presence was at one time an offence (a cost). By what criteria are we to decide upon the appropriate course of public action or inaction? Third, the existence of adequate market institutions is crucial : many of the examples of social cost problems turn out on examination to be cases in which demand cannot produce a market response. Consider for example Mr J. R. Sargent's discussion of social costs of road transport in *Lessons of Public Enterprise* :

> . . . The social costs of traffic congestion are what they are because the motorist is not generally made to bear the cost of his parking space, and because the traffic congregates in morning and evening peaks. To reduce these costs charges for parking must not only become the general rule but must be made to vary according to the time of day . . .

The factual description is accurate. But the problem of public policy arises out of the absence of a satisfactorily competitive market in road use or in parking places. Agreed, there are technical difficulties in creating such a market, but it would be more efficient to try to solve them than to conclude (as Mr Sargent does) that there should be a public monopoly of parking space. A monopoly must inhibit the creation of the necessary market conditions rather than encourage them.

Public ownership does not help

This brings me to the final point. Of itself, the substitution of public for private ownership does nothing to make policies to deal with problems of social cost easier to formulate or implement. If the government is not to abdicate its responsibility for policy-making, the public enterprises will have to be subjected to general rules specifying the social costs to be taken into account, and how. Exhortations, for example, to cover costs while promoting the (unspecified) 'public interest', are fruitless. They must lead public corporations either to give no more attention to 'costs' they are not required to pay than private enterprise would, or to the use of the 'public interest' injunction to avoid public accountability or to assume social responsibilities for which they are politically and structurally unfitted.

What happens if public corporations are allowed to determine 'social costs'? Suppose the Coal Board decides against closing a high-cost pit because miners would become redundant and the Board cannot move them elsewhere (or is unwilling to bear the cost). Such a policy must raise the cost of coal, so that the 'social cost' is borne by coal users. But the Coal Board cannot know the full implications of its decision : the government itself is concerned about distribution of industry and labour over the country as a whole, and there is no more reason to allow the Coal Board to take such a decision than to allow or expect a private producer to do so. If we must have a nationalised coal industry (I argue below that we would be better without it), it should be required to follow normal economic criteria so far as they can be applied. A proposed closure might be notified to the government (in the same way that one would expect private enterprise to give advance notice of a major redundancy), but the decision on the necessary 'social' adjustments would be for the government alone. Further, if it was desired to keep the pit open, logic would suggest that a specific subsidy from general taxation should be provided for the purpose.

Similar arguments apply to many other common proposals, such as that for the subsidisation of railways to reduce urban congestion. Thus, Messrs Ernest Davies, Austen Albu and Michael Shanks in *Lessons of Public Enterprise* support the view that 'responsibility for defining the public interest and for seeing that the nationalised industries conform to it is the Minister's' (as opposed to the boards of management). But if this is so, the Minister's (i.e. Parliament's) responsibilities in social cost/benefit problems embrace the whole of the community's economic activity and provide no reason for the nationalisation of parts of it.

In practical politics, no serious attempts have ever been made to deal specifically with such social costs as public corporations might be generally agreed to create. We do not compensate those who live near gasworks, or in the houses bordering Mr Sargent's congested roads. Indeed, it is not unfair to say that in its purer forms the social cost/benefit argument has never been reflected in public policies towards nationalised enterprises : on the contrary, the crude assertion that the industries confer social benefits has been used to impede the development of market procedures that might improve their economic efficiency and accountability.

In short, the social cost/benefit arguments do not produce support for nationalisation, but argue rather for the need for constant attention by government to definitions of property rights and to the development of market institutions. These are not easy tasks, but they can hardly be lightened by replacing private markets by statutory monopolies.

Nationalisation to control private monopoly?

We now turn to other (economic) arguments in favour of public ownership : first, the need to control or prevent private monopoly.

There are many examples of the willingness of statutory monopolies to raise revenues or to defend their position, protected as it is by law, by measures that would be condemned in private industry. A recent illustration is provided by the violent reaction (including proposals for preventive legislation) to the 'pirate' radio stations which dare to offer pop music in competition with the BBC. On the other hand prevention of private monopolistic practices by law is feasible given determined government. But by a strange alchemy the competition whose absence is said by some to make nationalisation essential becomes unnecessary and even 'harmful' once a public corporation has been created. On the other hand, other supporters of nationalisation share a belief in the virtues of competition :

> 'It may be regrettable', said Mr Hugh Gaitskell in *Socialism and Nationalisation,* 'but it seems to be a fact that people's enthusiasm about almost any group to which they belong is enhanced by competition.'

I would disagree only that it may be regrettable. But this kind of view does not lead to support for denationalisation, only to suggestions for more competition within and between public corporations. For both philosophical and practical reasons such views have had little influence, and cannot be expected to have much in the future. Genuine competition requires that enterprises should be able to go bankrupt. What is the difference between this and denationalisation? Anything less can be only a sham.

Secondly, there is the argument that in some industries nationalisation is the best means of increasing economic efficiency. The notion that a competitive market for some products is 'inefficient' or 'impossible' has been very common, but it is unlikely that there are many industries in which technical factors alone require for efficiency a minimum scale of production so large that competition between efficient units is impossible. The minimum capital investment needed to build a modern strip mill is absolutely large, but the output is a tiny proportion of the world demand for steel. Private capital after all built the railways, yet who can doubt that if such a task were envisaged nowadays there would be a chorus of despairing voices saying that it was not a task that private industry was competent to perform? More usually these apparently 'technical' difficulties turn out to have their real roots elsewhere – for example, in monopoly conditions in bordering markets or in the influence of legislation upon the competitive process. The most satisfactory solution for such problems is to take steps to remove the *obstacles* to enterprise and competition, rather than to superimpose a public monopoly upon them.

Disadvantages of nationalisation

The nationalised industries are statutory monopolies vulnerable to political interference and to the pressure of vested interests, whose resistance to competition and to change is as effective as a set of tariff walls. In the words of the White Paper *The Financial and Economic Obligations of the Nationalised Industries*, 'economic objectives are blurred by political expediency'. For this reason and others already explained, the public corporations suffer and must be expected to continue to suffer, from disadvantages of size, unavoidable over-centralisation of management and control, and inability to pursue efficiency by the devolution of authority (e.g. to give local managers effective power to vary pricing policies in response to variations in local market conditions). Among other things the corporations have to solve problems of pricing policy which are inherent in the form of organisation, and particularly in the lack of competition. If the corporations are not to be left to decide what is the 'public interest' when fixing prices (we have argued the case against this), then Parliament must. But what competence have ministers in such a matter? We should recognise that this problem like many others is largely artificial, created by the existence of the public corporations and most efficiently resolved by their abolition.

An important aspect of these difficulties has recently been exemplified in the attempts to subject the public corporations to more realistic financial discipline. While laudable as an effort to improve earlier confusions, the proposals fail to establish satisfactory criteria for borrowing, investment policy or rates of return. They are not explicit about the social costs and benefits which are held to be relevant, and effectively accept Ministerial (i.e. political) control of pricing policy. These problems cannot be solved by administrative reform, or even by the removal of the statutory monopoly unless this implies a willingness to let corporations that cannot pay their way disappear.

We come finally to stabilisation policy. The influence of Keynes was to encourage the belief that a large public sector might be used as a weapon for promoting economic stability, for instance by increasing nationalised industry investment at times when the level of unemployment showed signs of rising. Actually Keynes' own views were less simple as the following forthright quotation from the *End of Laisser Faire* shows :

> there is for instance no so-called important political question so really unimportant, so irrelevant to the reorganisation of the economic life of Great Britain, as the nationalisation of the railways.

Postwar history has also refuted this view. The rapid rate of growth of investment by nationalised industries has hardly contributed to stability. This is not surprising : it is not easy to see how large-scale investment of the kind these public corporations require can be geared to the needs of short-term stability. The very existence of these large organisations makes the marginal adjustment of investment more difficult than it needs be and interferes with the efficient functioning of the market for capital.

Taken together, these objections to nationalisation seem to

me overwhelming. They suggest that public organisations
not only create problems in themselves, but frequently have
serious repercussions on the economic and social organisation of the community. It is a mistake to regard the issues as
unimportant or unworthy of serious discussion, as in the
1963 *Encounter* symposium, or to treat nationalisation as an
irrelevance, a sort of coelacanth as Mr P. J. D. Wiles des-
cribes it in *The Unservile State*, or to concentrate on administrative and organisational reform like the contributors to
Lessons of Public Enterprise. The issue of nationalisation is
fundamental; the solution is the eventual denationalisation
of all activities capable of private operation and the sub-
jection of the rest to all possible competition.

Reorganisation of the nationalised industries

Since the weaknesses of the nationalised industries derive
basically from their large size, their statutory monopoly and
their susceptibility to misuse for social and political purposes,
the cure lies in removing all three. At the least, they should
be broken into smaller and competitive units, subjected to
outside competition, and required to act as commercial
undertakings. If possible they should be returned to private
ownership. How?

As a first step, I would propose the appointment of a
Select Committee of the House of Commons aided by a
permanent secretariat to act not as an instrument for direct
control but as a reviewing body for pricing and investment
policies. More important, it would decide upon the need, if
any, for given nationalised industries to remain in public
control.

We might divide the nationalised industries into two
groups:

Group 1	*Group 2*
Coal	GPO
Rail Transport	BBC
Gas and Electricity	Bank of England
	Cable and Wireless
	Civil Aviation

Group 2 is the more heterogeneous, the unifying element being that enterprises are all affected by generally accepted social or political factors which influence the most economically satisfactory form of organisation. This is not to say that commercial considerations are not relevant to their operation. Indeed, it is clear that in the GPO and civil aviation, for instance, they are of first importance. Nor does public participation in these services of itself require public monopoly. The need for public access to means of communication, for example, is perfectly compatible with competitive services. The public interest is not less well served because the BBC is in competition with ITV; indeed, more competition, for example by metered services, would improve the situation further. Wherever public enterprise is held to be necessary for this kind of reason, it should be a first principle of public policy to encourage competition in the most equal terms possible with private producers. Furthermore, pricing policies should as far as possible be organised so that payment is related to quantity consumed and is not on a flat rate basis (as with TV licences). The public subsidy to this form of activity should reflect ideally only its value to government.

Denationalising railways and coal

In Group 1 it is possible to make more far-reaching proposals for reorganisation. Commercial considerations are here of dominating importance for policy. It should be remembered that the four industries did not come into public ownership as the result of decisions of principle of the kind examined earlier but rather from a combination of intense competition (as in gas and coal) that encouraged the industries themselves to accept controls and of measures of public policy that inhibited competition (such as the Coal Mines Acts and the Road Traffic Acts of the 1930s). These influences contributed far more to the pattern of post-1945 nationalisation measures than doctrinaire insistence on the superiority of nationalisation as a form of economic organisation.

Once created, nationalised industries of this kind can exist for longer than the market would allow them, for absence of the dynamic of competition retards change and inhibits adaptability. The first requirement is therefore that we should get rid of this irreversibility : the prime purpose of the proposed Select Committee would be to keep the possibilities of denationalisation regularly under review.

Let us consider some particular instances. In transport it is clear that the railways enjoy no general monopoly power because of competition from road transport (and airlines). The first requirement is to set about creating the preconditions for 'fair' (efficient) competition between road and rail. This is a difficult task, but the very difficulty is a good reason for us to cease to ignore it : there is clearly much that can be done and some interesting suggestions are contained in John Hibbs' *Hobart Paper, Transport for Passengers*. Dr Beeching's streamlining operations, while welcome as a recognition of a need, must be unsatisfactory in detail pending the creation of such a genuinely competitive background (which would include *inter alia* the elimination of 'common carrier' obligations and of economically unjustified cross-subsidisations). Thereafter, if rail transport still fails to pay its own way, why should the public corporation be allowed to continue? For that matter, if the railways did not prove to have significant monopoly power, why should they remain in public hands even if they can make a profit? It should be the function of the Select Committee to consider such questions, and if appropriate to recommend procedures for orderly denationalisation. There might be local areas in which some monopoly power continued to exist, but these are unlikely to be significant, and would be easily controlled by measures far short of nationalisation. Similarly, if the government itself has a strategic or other interest in particular lines, the appropriate procedure is to furnish specific subsidies where these are needed.

Even more obviously than the railways, the coal industry could and should be returned to a competitive system. The basis of competition was destroyed not by technical factors but by the property laws and the quota legislation of the thirties. It is time to think about how to recreate a private and competitive market.

Leave gas and electricity nationalised?

Gas and electricity pose more difficult problems since technical factors make the creation of a satisfactory basis for competition difficult. The difficulty of generating a competitive market does not arise out of the size of the production units but rather out of the indivisibility of the distribution network. In fact in recent years imports of cheap oil have posed problems for the public corporations which have gone some way towards restoring healthy competition and more forward-looking attitudes. (They have also produced successful pressure for heavier taxes on fuel oil.) This new breath of fresh air might be reinforced by action on the part of the public authorities : the grid for instance might be operated independently with individual suppliers selling power to it. But there is perhaps more room for debate here than in coal and railways : the costs of creating a market might themselves be high, and it would have to be considered whether unsubsidised public corporations in this field could be left alone once the size of the nationalised sector had been reduced in other directions. Charges for gas and electricity should of course be kept under review by our Parliamentary Select Committee, to prevent misuse of monopoly power.

In recent years, Dr Beeching (in tackling problems of cost) and Lord Robens (in tackling problems of marketing) have shown that the internal organisation of public corporations can be improved in ways that conduce to efficiency. But they are being asked to cure cancers with corn plasters: both the structure of the public corporation and its relations with Parliament and with the rest of the economy place the fundamental problems beyond the reach of internal reform. Even more, they are not to be dealt with by the kind of proposals for administrative reform now proposed by the nationalisers.

The cure for bureaucratic management and political control is not more bureaucratic management or more political control. The only way to ensure that service to the public is put before administrative convenience, spurious social purpose or political party manoeuvring is to press first for competition and second for denationalisation. The solution to the problems of public corporations is to abolish as many of them as possible and to subject the rest to as much outside competition as possible.

GWYN JAMES

My birth, in Swansea, coincided with, but in no way inspired, the General Strike of 1926. Rumour has it that despite a considerable effort on my part as a young child, I narrowly missed an open scholarship to an approved school. Instead, the local grammar school accepted me and duly trained me for a University education at Aberystwyth, where a benevolent examiner awarded me a First in Economics. Then, on to King's, Cambridge, where I staggered my tutor by gaining another First in Agricultural Science, and an amazed University awarded me the T. H. Middleton Prize.

Since then I have confined my apparent talents to research and teaching in agricultural economics, first at Cambridge, then at Aberystwyth and now at Bangor University. There is no truth in the rumour that I have applied for membership of the local NFU. I have published a number of articles and books on agricultural policy and management. My latest book, *Farming for Consumers*, written jointly with Graham Hallett, was published by the Institute of Economic Affairs in July 1963.

My economic philosophy revolves around the sovereignty of the individual. I abhor compulsion and rebel against all forms of authoritarianism. I regard progress as the product of individual initiative.

7: BACK FROM THE LAND

GWYN JAMES *casts a critical eye on British policy on agriculture and argues it has discouraged rather than encouraged efficiency and expansion. He opposes the system of marketing boards for intensifying monopoly and weakening competition. He concludes that there are too many farmers and that the only way to enable a smaller number to produce better or cheaper products on larger farms is to pension some off.*

AGRICULTURE is part of the British economy whose policies require a 'face-lift'. It resembles a new model, Rolls Royce, Silver Cloud saloon, fitted with a 1900 Ford 8 engine. The exterior looks modern and impressive – it is one of the most highly mechanised industries in the world; the farmers themselves give an outward show of prosperity, symbolised in the Jaguar of the farmer and the fur coat of his wife; its production levels rise annually – but in many ways this is a façade which hides serious weaknesses.

Miss British Agriculture of 1964 is heavily made-up. Wearing her false wig of guaranteed prices, her wrinkles of uneconomic holdings and inefficient farmers camouflaged behind a thick coating of assured markets, she seems certain to win the Miss World Agriculture Beauty Contest. But as with many real-life Beauty Queens, when the make-up has been scraped off and the hair loses its artificial waving the glamour also disappears.

The case for subsidising farmers

In fairness to the National Farmers' Union it must be said that, as seen by the farmer, an apparently infallible case can be made out for the current method of guaranteed prices and assured markets for many products. It can be claimed, for instance, that they have given the farming community a sense of economic security that has encouraged farmers to plan long-term investments and adopt technical innovations more readily. Moreover, the resultant prosperity has been supplemented by related investment to improve conditions in the countryside, through better roads, piped-water supplies, the near-completion of the electricity net-work, bringing radio and television to farm households, and simplifying many laborious farm tasks. The housewife has also benefited through lower food prices; and although the real cost has had to be borne by the taxpayer, this method serves social justice, since taxation is (supposedly) related to the ability of the individual to pay while food prices are the same for rich and poor. It appears that assured markets have provided more orderly marketing arrangements by rationalising the channels of distribution, eliminating unnecessary cross-transport costs and reducing marketing costs.

These are achievements that no-one would seriously question. Farmers and their workers should benefit from improvements in living conditions in the same way and to the same extent as other members of the community. Television sets, washing machines, refrigerators, motor cars and the other tangible benefits of higher living standards should not be the prerogative of the town-dweller. Differences in income between farming and other occupations are not sacrosanct, and I welcome any narrowing of the gap. But I do not agree that these achievements are the result of increased efficiency, that government policy has raised the efficiency of the agricultural industry as a whole, or that the economic climate created by current policy will encourage further increases in the future.

The efficiency of British farming has grown since the war. For instance, since 1945 the net output of our national farmers has increased by near 20 per cent, even though the agricultural labour force has fallen by about 20 per cent. The productivity of agricultural labour has thus risen by about 40 per cent – or roughly 4 per cent a year – an achievement of which many manufacturing industries would be proud. Nevertheless, I maintain first, that this increase in efficiency has been achieved *in spite of*, rather than because of, our agricultural policies since 1947; second, that if these policies had been directed along different lines, the increase in efficiency would have been even more impressive. Post-war agricultural policy has retarded rather than encouraged efficient production.

Reasons for increased efficiency

One of the most important reasons for this improvement has been the increase in mechanisation, particularly since 1947. It is doubtful whether any industry has undergone such a rapid development in the use of mechanical equipment as has British farming. Without the extensive adoption of mechanical aids, the large increase in food production since the war would not have been possible. Another contributory factor has been the application of work study to agriculture, by which many laborious tasks have been reduced to simple, routine operations. This has often been the natural result of increased mechanisation, for the use of large machines often demands the rationalisation of farm design. But equally, labour shortages have compelled farmers to economise in its use, often by simplifying farm work at little additional cost.

Other causes of increased efficiency have been the use of scientific and technical aids, the development of a National Agricultural Advisory Service, the electrification of farms and the application of new scientific knowledge to the practice of farming – new crop varieties, improved pasture management and livestock husbandry, artificial insemination, and so on.

Nonetheless, I suggest that parts of our national agricultural policy have made the level of efficiency of the national farm *lower than it could be*. In other words, while I wholeheartedly support the Government's objective of creating and maintaining an efficient agricultural industry, I do not believe this can best be done by guaranteed prices and assured markets. I am critical of the means, not of the end.

Guaranteed prices harm the farmer

Let us look first at guaranteed prices. In times of national food shortage, guaranteed prices are an effective and possibly indispensable instrument for achieving maximum output. Are they equally effective now that the emphasis has shifted from maximum to *efficient* food production? There are three criticisms of guaranteed prices. First, an artificially created price imposed on a freely determined market price weakens and often destroys the ability of the marketing system to convey changes in consumer requirements to producers through changes in the price. Price changes should indicate to farmers how they should adjust production plans in the light of changing economic conditions. If prices are rising this indicates that more is being demanded by consumers than is available on the market and that farmers might do well to produce more. Price acts in effect like a set of traffic lights with amber representing a normal and stable market condition where demand is equal to supply, green rising prices with demand exceeding supply, and red falling prices with demand below supply. But the imposition of an artificially created support or guaranteed price blurs the significance and function of market price; it may change the red to amber or the amber to green so that farmers unwittingly react in a way contrary to that required by consumers. As a result, consumers are presented with either more commodities than they require, or a lower quality standard than they are prepared to pay for. And either distortion ultimately harms the producer.

Second, it is unlikely that under a system of guaranteed prices and deficiency payments the market price, that is the price which consumers actually pay in the shops, is that which consumers are prepared to pay. Subsidised production distorts demand as well as supply.

Third, although the present policy of the Government is towards competitive production, guaranteed prices encourage an even larger volume of output; they incite farmers to 'over-produce'.

Aim to the under-nourished

Over-production is synonymous with inefficiency in the use of resources in the sense that the products have no market value if they cannot be sold. To most people it is unrealistic (and to some ethically wrong) to talk of food surpluses when there are so many people in the world, particularly in the Asiatic countries, living on a bare subsistence diet. The simple solution, it is suggested, is merely to dispose of these surpluses in countries where food requirements outstrip the supply. There are, however, two serious obstacles to such a simple solution. First, if the transfer of food surpluses from one part of the world to another is to be effected by a growth in the volume of aid to the undeveloped countries, the task would appear to be beyond our capabilities. The contribution of institutions such as Freedom from Hunger, OxFam, War on Want towards feeding the world's hungry is minute in relation to the demand. And even if aid on the scale required can be given, is this in the best ultimate interests of the underdeveloped countries? Aid is urgent, but it can be only a short-term relief measure. What these countries need most in the long run is not charity but the ability to enter world markets and buy food. The best form of help is, as Sir Sydney Caine has argued, that which helps them to help themselves.[1] Long-term measures designed to overcome the problem of food surpluses through aid to underdeveloped countries will, through discouraging enterprise, run into serious difficulties over time. The Labour Party is pledged to a policy of maximum food production from British farms on the assumption that the food surpluses can be disposed of in the underdeveloped countries. Such a programme would weaken rather than strengthen the economic position of British farmers.

[1] For a fuller discussion of these issues see Sir Sidney Caine, *Prices for Primary Producers*, Hobart Paper 24. Institute of Economic Affairs, 1963.

Assured markets by marketing boards

What of assured markets? Guaranteed prices themselves provide assured markets in the sense that producers are prepared to sell irrespective of market price knowing that the difference between the market price and the guaranteed price will be made-up by the government by a deficiency payment. The more usual form of assured markets is that provided by compulsory marketing boards. A producer-controlled marketing board acts for all producers; it represents the interests of the majority – efficient and inefficient, well and poorly situated, big and small, producing good and poor products. But progress in agriculture, as in most other economic activities, spring from the initiative of a few enterprising and untypical individuals. A compulsory marketing board blights the initiative of the pioneering farmers, by making them conform to the existing order of things and removing the incentive to progress. Secure in the knowledge of an assured market at a guaranteed price, producers are less inclined to think of progress and innovation.

The chicken and the egg

There is a danger of confusing the efficiency of the individual farm with that of the national farm. Consider egg production. As production costs increase, the individual farmer is persuaded by his local advisory officer to increase his output by keeping more hens. This reduces his costs per unit of output by spreading his fixed costs over a larger output. He is therefore more efficient. But do we want more eggs in this country? From the standpoint of the national interest, might not production be more efficient if some of the resources used were transferred to other enterprises, either within, or even outside, the agricultural industry?

Can we blame the local advisory officer for persuading the farmer to increase production of a product, for which there may be no demand? He is motivated by the guaranteed market available for eggs at the guaranteed price; moreover, his first loyalty is to his client, and hang the national consequences. In many ways, the position of the advisory officer is similar to that of the local medical doctor, who is called to treat a sick patient in the full knowledge that the country is over-populated. It is a sobering thought that doctors discount completely the national interest when treating their patients. Long may they continue to do so.

Production is not an end in itself; it is (or should be) a means to an end – the satisfaction of consumer requirements. Market demand represents that part of total output which consumers are prepared to buy at prevailing prices. Consequently, one can only speak of an assured market in terms of consumer demand. No one can talk of assured markets in terms of total output, part of which may remain unsold. Yet this is precisely what a marketing board sets out to do, for it is compelled to accept all the output of its members. The producer of an agricultural product controlled by a trading board is sure in the knowledge that whatever he produces he can sell. His horizon is the farm gate; factors and events outside are of little concern to him. Consequently, production becomes an end in itself : farmers continue to produce what *they* find convenient rather than what the consumer desires.

These two pillars of national agricultural policy – guaranteed prices and assured markets – create an occupational vacuum, within which British farmers are hermetically sealed and insulated against external events. National agricultural policy should have as its major objective the well-being of the nation. But measures designed to protect or safeguard the interests of the *individual* producer can conflict with the interest of his country as a whole. Post-war agricultural policy in Great Britain can therefore be indicted on the charge that it has been preoccupied with serving the interests of individual farmers, and has overlooked national priorities.

It is relatively easy to be wise and critical after the event; it is also unfair, unless one is prepared to make alternative suggestions. I should like to make four.

Four-poster for farmers

The first refers to guaranteed prices. If on political grounds the Government continues to regard subsidies as the most effective method of protecting the British farmer (with which I do not agree) I make a plea that they should be designed to encourage rather than retard efficiency. This can be done if the size of the guarantee payment is related to the quality of the product, as a means of encouraging producers to meet market requirements. If, for instance, the market requires light weight lambs, the market guarantee can be used to penalize the farmer who produces a heavy lamb. This change could lead to a fall in the size of the subsidy bill, if the present guarantee level were given to the 'quality' producers and a substantially smaller guarantee (or none) were given to the others. Financial support is now running at nearly £1 million a day and the Government is right to have indicated that steps must be taken to limit it.

Second, there should be more encouragement of forward contracting. The growth of contracting is connected with the development of supermarkets and large-scale processors who require large and regular supplies of a uniform and high quality. The supermarkets want to make contracts with farmers to supply stated quantities of named types of produce. By linking production more closely with consumption, forward contracting reduces the risk of the two getting out of step, as can happen when farmers produce for an anonymous market. Contracting can be allied to cooperative marketing, especially where the individual producer is small. The development and success of cooperative contracting should reduce, and ultimately remove, the reputed need of farmers for marketing boards. This is not to suggest that non-trading boards should be abolished (there is a strong case for abolishing the compulsory trading boards) but that membership should not be obligatory on the farming community. Hats off to the Verdon-Smith Committee on Meat Marketing which, in its recent report, rejected the plea of the National

Farmers' Unions for a Meat Marketing Board on the ground that it would in no way improve the efficiency of meat marketing. History suggests that the Marketing Boards do not best serve the interests of either producers or consumers.

Third, producers need more information on marketing trends and prospects. The farmer needs to know what, when, and how much to produce. He must know more about consumer tastes and requirements and of likely changes in consumer habits; this is market research. Moreover, he needs to know the volume of supplies entering the home market and likely changes in them; this is market intelligence. Some progress is being made : the new Chair in Agricultural Marketing at Newcastle University and the announcement of a five-year research project into meat marketing and production (in that order) are signs of serious efforts to undertake studies in marketing. Private firms have also been established to specialise in this field.

These efforts should be widened and extended, and I would strongly advocate the establishment of individual Commodity Commissions to co-ordinate these marketing functions. I agree with the recommendation of the Verdon Smith Committee that a Fatstock and Meat Authority should be established with a wide range of functions relating to the production, marketing and distribution of fatstock and carcase meat. But the problems of the beef, lamb and pig industries are so diverse and specialised that I would favour individual Associations for each livestock product, rather than an all-embracing Authority as recommended.

Finally, the problem of disseminating the information obtained by market research and intelligence agencies between farmers is as important as the need for the information. Farmers have a free National Agricultural Advisory Service, and I suggest that in future it should focus more of its attention on to the market than on the farm, and that its work should be assisted by specialist Agricultural Marketing Officers.

Import controls are no solution

In May, 1963, the Conservative Government announced a system of import control through minimum import prices combined with the extension of the 'standard quantities' concept to fatstock and cereals (which together account for over 80 per cent of the present price guarantee bill). Such a scheme suffers from two major weaknesses. First, it prevents commodities being purchased in the cheapest market. It ignores the fact that the person most likely to benefit from cheap imports is the consumer, who in future has to pay more for meat and cereals. It reduces the housewife's freedom to buy in the cheapest market. And it does not provide any incentive to increase the competitive position of our agriculture. The motive appears political – to put a break on the increasing subsidy bill.

I do not believe that British farmers want or need to be protected from competition, provided they are given the economic environment within which they can operate to the best of their ability. The inefficient producers, whether their trouble is bad management or uneconomic holdings, must be induced to leave their farms. Incentive to change should be the major aim of British agricultural policy during the next decade. My fourth suggestion is therefore a fundamental improvement in the structural efficiency of British farming, an aspect of agricultural policy that has been completely overlooked during the past fifteen years.

The need for such improvements is clear. 51 per cent of the holdings in Great Britain (over 5 acres) are under 50 acres; 72 per cent are under 100 acres; only 5 per cent are over 300 acres. What can be done to increase the average size? The number of holdings has decreased by about 9 per cent over the past ten years. Some have been acquired for afforestation; others have been bought by local authorities for urban development; some have disappeared through the creation of reservoirs to meet the water needs of growing industrial areas; and some have been amalgamated with other farms to make more viable units – but we do not know how many under each head.

Encouraging amalgamations

Sweden offers an interesting example of a state-sponsored policy aimed at creating economically viable holdings. The Swedish Land Acquisition Act of 1945 has two aims : to prevent non-farmers from acquiring farm (and forest) land and unsuitable amalgamations. Private persons have to apply for permission to acquire farm land by purchase, exchange or gift (though not by inheritance). If permission is refused by the County Agricultural Board (acting on behalf of the Minister of Agriculture), the contract to purchase becomes automatically invalid, but the Board has a legal obligation to buy the land at the price previously agreed if the new owner still wishes to sell. Land thus acquired by the Board is normally transferred to farmers in need of additional land as soon as possible. But some is leased to local farmers to create a land reserve to facilitate amalgamation at a more opportune time. This scheme in no way resembles land nationalisation,

The Swedish policy of farm amalgamation is strengthened by financial assistance by the government to enable farmers to buy land to improve the viability of their holdings. The government guarantees loans from private credit banks, which may cover the whole of the purchase price and have to be repaid over a maximum period of 30 years. In addition, Government grants are made for approved schemes, such as land drainage and ditching, farm road, and farm building improvements. The attractiveness of this policy is that there is no compulsory purchase. The County Agricultural Boards can buy farms only if the owners offer them for sale. But the speed of reform is limited by the availability of farms on the market. If private owners are not prepared to sell, the amalgamation of holdings is retarded.

Pensions for farmers

A solution could be found by offering farmers a financial inducement to sell beyond the market value of their farms. Such a measure, allied to Swedish experience, could result in a major reform of British agriculture. I would urge the Government to introduce legislation, akin to the Land Acquisition Act, which would empower the Minister of Agriculture to buy land for amalgamation. The Act should be an enabling rather than a directing measure, so as not to violate the freedom of the individual. The willingness and readiness of farmers to offer their land for sale would be considerably strengthened if, in addition to the selling price of their farm, they were offered an unconditional annual pension for life. A sum related to the average earnings of farm workers would be realistic; I would suggest an annual pension of £500 a year.

The cost of such a scheme can be estimated. Suppose the number of farms in Great Britain under 50 acres were halved from 163,000 to 80,000, the average age of the farmer accepting the pension was 45 years, and the pension is paid in full for 30 years. The total cost would be £1,200 million, or £40 million a year. This represents about one-eighth of the cost of Exchequer support to the agricultural industry. The net cost to the country would probably be much less, for the resulting increase in efficiency would mean a saving in subsidies. The real attractiveness of such a policy is that it would be geared towards solving the problem of non-viable holdings, whereas the present policy merely perpetuates it.

Such new policies would create the economic climate within which the flower of agricultural efficiency would blossom. The goal of agricultural policy should no longer be the protection of producers but the well-being of the industry and the country. I do not deprecate the achievements of British farmers or minimise the contribution of agriculture to the national economy. But I want to see an efficient, virile, competitive, prosperous industry, worthy of its place as Britain's biggest industry. I want to celebrate the rebirth of British farming, not to mourn its untimely demise.

JOHN A. LINCOLN

I was born on the longest day out of union hours, but no-one concerned with the event including myself was paid time and a half. In 1919 I served for a year on the staff of the Organising Committee of the International Labour Conference (Washington). During the 1920s I spent six years at the Ministry of Labour and the India Office. I then enjoyed the freer air of journalism for several years.

Two years as political adviser and public relations consultant to the National Conference of Friendly Societies and the National Deposit Friendly Society led me later to initiate the Voluntary Social Service enquiry, for which I was one of the assessors with Lady Wootton and others to Lord Beveridge and served as secretary to the enquiry. In 1955 I acted for the Amalgamated Society of Engineers and Firemen during the railway strike. I fear my publications, *The Strange Case of the Friendly Societies*, 1946, 'The Problems of the Friendly Societies' in *Evidence for Voluntary Action*, 1948, *Brought to Book* (Epigrams 1949), 'Human Rights in Industry' in *Agenda for a Free Society*, 1961, and the present contribution may earn me a violent end from a trade unionist who does not recognise a friend. But I hope to keep both my friends, who have been good *to* me, and my enemies, who have been good *for* me.

8: UNIONS AND THE LAW

JOHN A. LINCOLN *looks at the legal powers of the trade unions in conditions of full employment. The trade unions are widely blamed for obstructing economic advance by opposing improvements in machinery, methods and the use of man-power. Many critics preach at them to mend their ways. This essay argues that the trouble is more fundamental and the cure more radical: that the unions will command public support only if they are voluntary, and that the law governing their powers and privileges needs to be reformed.*

POPULAR discussion of the trade unions concentrates on problems of organisation and structure, or on their responsibility for the success (or failure) of the government's fanciful incomes policy. Fortunately for Great Britain the decision of the Law Lords in the case of *Rookes v. Barnard* has brought to the headlines a problem of more importance for our political and economic future; namely the relationship of trade unions to the law.

In my *Journey to Coercion* I have traced the development of trade union law in some detail. In the mercantilist era wages and conditions of employment were subject to state control. The Combination Acts of 1799 forbade the combination of workers for industrial action. A period of comparative immunity for their activities followed the 1824 Combination Act until the passage of the Conspiracy and Protection of Property Act (1875) and the Trade Union Act (1871). These acts confirmed union responsibilities and rights before the criminal law. But the Trade Disputes Act of 1906 did the reverse. It established their legal immunity before the common law, and it is this immunity that is now, after

several warnings in legal actions, under challenge from the
Rookes v. Barnard judgment.

Since 1950 a surprisingly high number of trade union cases
have come before the Courts. Seven were concerned with
the wrongful expulsion of union members; *Lee v. Showmen's
Guild* (1952) and *Bonsor v. Musician's Union* (1954) were
the most important. *Spring v. National Amalgamated
Stevedores and Dockers Union* (1956) challenged the legality
of the Bridlington Agreement. Other cases involved unlawful dismissal, imposition of discriminatory levy and two
cases of conspiracy, *Huntley v. Thornton* (1957) and *Rookes
v. Barnard*.

The situation disturbed responsible trade union leaders
and there were warnings of a possible major legal clash
ahead. Mr George Woodcock[1] commented sharply and
bravely :

> At one time the courts looked upon trade unions as among the
> most genuine of voluntary societies of working men for mutual
> aid ... Since 1950 there have been several cases in which indi-
> vidual trade union members have obtained the protection of the
> courts and, in some cases, damages against the union itself. It
> may be that the courts have noticed a spread of the practice of
> insisting that all the workmen in a factory or doing a particular
> class of work shall be a member of the union and have there-
> fore decided that a time has come when the workman's right to
> be in a union and his rights inside the union need to be safe-
> guarded by an impartial and authoritative body.

A new and disturbing element is that all the cases concerned union disputes with individual members, not between
unions and employers. Once again unions were involved in
common law wrongs and *Bonsor v. Musicians' Union* and
Huntley v. Thornton respectively established their liability
for damages for breach of contract and for conspiracy.
These were clear signs that the unions' use of collective
power against the individual (inevitable in enforcing membership) would jeopardise their whole legal position. The
warnings of Lord Denning and of union leaders like George

[1] BBC Broadcast, 'A Problem of Power,' *Listener*, 23 July, 1959.

Woodcock, Charles Geddes and others were ignored.

A marked hostility to union methods of membership compulsion was shown by the public, not least because they were harmed by inter-union disputes. The unions' acceptance of government policy on restraint of trade and legislation dealing with monopolies and restrictive practices attracted growing comment concerning their exclusion from the scope of this legislation. But union methods continued unchanged and their divergence from public policy, government policy and the law became more and more obvious. Finally the inevitable clash with the law occurred in *Rookes v. Barnard*, and the unions faced a 'HALT' sign on their road to coercion.

What Rookes v. Barnard means

Mr D. E. Rookes, a draughtsman, was dismissed in 1956 by the BOAC after it had been threatened with a strike by the Association of Engineering and Shipbuilding Draughtsmen (AESD) unless he was withdrawn from the design office. Rookes refused to rejoin the union; he was removed from the design office and his employment ended by proper notice according to his contract. The union had an agreement with BOAC which barred strikes; moreover they did not give proper notice.

In the High Court Mr Rookes was awarded £7500 damages. This judgment was set aside by the Court of Appeal. The House of Lords re-affirmed the original judgment that he was entitled to damages but ordered a new trial to re-determine the amount.

Mr Rookes claimed damages from Messrs Barnard, Fistal and Silverthorne for the loss of his employment which he alleged was due to their wrong acts. Barnard and Fistal, officials of AESD were employed by BOAC; Silverthorne, the district organiser of the union, was not.

Mr Rookes' case was that the wrongful acts were the threat against BOAC to unlawfully secure a strike in breach of their contract of employment and that they had committed the 'tort' (civil wrong) of intimidation, that as a

result BOAC had dismissed him, that he had suffered
damage and was entitled to damages. The defence countered
firstly by denying that the tort of intimidation existed and,
further, that granted that it did exist, that it was limited to
criminal acts and did not cover a threat to break contracts.
Section I and 3 of the *Trade Disputes Act* 1906 were relied
upon by the defence to provide their immunity from any
actionable claim.

Allowing Mr Rookes appeal the Law Lords held :

(1) that the tort of intimidation was an established fact
and included threats of breach of contract and that the
defendants had committed the tort of intimidation.

(2) that Section 1 of the *Trade Disputes Act* 1906 provided no protection to the defendants as the act of intimidation could have been committed by a single person and
was actionable if done without agreement or combination.
Further, Lord Reid held that Section 1 did not mean a
comparison with the *precise* act in question but required
comparison with the nearest *equivalent* action.

(3) that Section 3 of the Act means that if interference is,
or has been, a tort then there is no liability, in a trade
dispute, 'on the ground only' of interference. The complete
Section does not protect the inducement of breach of contract or interference with trade, business or employment
where they are brought about by intimidation and other
illegal means. Section 3 did not protect the defendants
because their interference with Rookes' employment was
brought about by unlawful intimidation.

The defendants' cross-appeal on damages was allowed
and a re-trial ordered to determine the amount.

It is important to remember that the issue was liability
for damage caused by unlawful acts against an *individual*.
This was no dispute between employers and a trade union
involving a claim for damages. However, consideration of
the case could not be separated from a *general* review of the
protection afforded to trade unions by Sections 1 and 3 of
the 1906 Act. Irrespective of any desire the Law Lords may,
or may not, have had to confine their judgment to a par-

ticular issue – their judgment was bound to affect the *general* limits of trade union indemnity.

Results of Rookes v. Barnard

The judgment clearly affects trade union methods and their means of securing compulsory membership and the 'closed shop'. Many trade union leaders would privately admit to relief at the legal check on irresponsible militant activity by a minority of union members and unofficial leaders. Unfortunately the judgment has left in doubt union liability for strike activities in a dispute between union and *employers* arising from negotiations on hours, wages and working conditions.

The tort of intimidation, threatening a strike in breach of contract, immediately reveals a discrepancy between the right to strike which is perfectly legal (i.e. a collective termination of contract by the required notice) and the right to strike as understood and practised by the union where

the object of the strike notice was not to terminate the contract – the object was to break the contract by withholding labour but keeping the contract alive for as long as the employer would tolerate the breach without exercising the right of recission.

Thus a strike notice that was not a proper notice of termination of the contract of employment, could be held in breach of contract and if accompanied by any threat constituted the tort of intimidation thus depriving the union of the protection of Sections 1 and 3 of the 1906 Act.

The trade unions can rightly demand that the present uncertainty of the law should be removed; whether they are right, or wise, to demand the reversal of the *Rookes v. Barnard* judgment in order to restore their imagined 1906 position is open to serious question. Obviously an inquiry into trade union law is necessary; trade union hostility to it is disturbing for it promises a repetition of the repeal of the 1927 Act if a Labour Government is returned to power. It would be disastrous if under the parrot cry of 'back to 1906' the House of Lords judgment were reversed. Trade union moments of inertia are measured in quarter days but a backward journey into time, virtually 1871, is carrying this activity too far!

The danger of an inquiry into trade union law concentrating on the problem of keeping the unions outside the law is very real and has many precedents. Any inquiry which concentrated on bringing industry, employers and unions alike, within the law would be more likely to make a lasting contribution to the solution of the current problems of both the law and the trade unions.

Proposals for trade union law reform

> Trade union law, like commercial law, has rested for the last hundred years on the assumption that the persons concerned are *free contracting parties* ... In substance, apart from the indemnities of the Trade Disputes Act, 1906, the law relating to trade unions has not seriously been modified since 1871. How long it will continue in its present artificial state is uncertain.[1]

Lord Justice Sir Henry Slesser in this passage reveals the basis of trade union law and of trade unionism – *the assumption that the persons concerned are free contracting parties*. That this assumption can no longer be made threatens the law and the unions alike. If the unions abandon or compromise their voluntary status they cannot maintain their position at law as workers' associations. Whether they enjoy the freedom we reserve for voluntary associations or suffer the strict regulation we impose on public utilities depends on their own decision. To attempt compulsory unionism under the immunity of voluntary association would irretrievably damage the common law and extinguish trade unions as workers' mutual aid associations.

The *Rookes v. Barnard* judgment holds, rightly, that it is unlawful to secure membership by unlawful means – intimidation. *Any demand by the trade unions for the reversal of this finding is de facto a positive claim by them for compulsory rights. The unions cannot shirk or disguise*

[1] Rt Hon. Sir Henry Slesser, P.C., Q.C., 'The Legal Status of Trade Unions', *Agenda for a Free Society*, Hutchinson for Institute of Economic Affairs, 1961.

this decision. Abraham Lincoln declared :
> 'a nation cannot live half slave and half free.'

The trade union movement cannot exist half voluntary and half compulsory. Already their threat to the rights of others has threatened the security of their own.

Trade union law, acting on its basic asumption that it is dealing with *free contracting parties*, has to meet the problems of 1871 and of 1906 plus the problem posed by union methods of 1964. It has, therefore, to protect the collective power of voluntary associations of workers seeking equality of bargaining power with their employers' association, and to secure the common law rights of the individual.

Any lasting solution requires (1) that the law secures the unions' right to employ their collective power for negotiation, agreement or dispute with other collective associations on the *privileged occasions* of a *trade* dispute, and (2) that the unions accept a statutory disbarment of the use of their collective power directly or indirectly against *individuals*.

The first requirement could be met by an amendment of the Contract of Employment Act, 1964, to provide that every contract must contain a clause permitting the *suspension* of the contract after seven days' notice. This would restore the 1906 Act protection to the unions because withholding labour after due notice would not be a breach of contract.

The second requirement, for individual security, can be secured by amending the definition of a trade dispute in Section 5 of the 1906 Act to exclude a union dispute with or involving an individual. (A similar exclusion could be considered for disputes arising from restrictive practises or inter-union disputes). A strike against the employment of an individual should be made illegal.

Section 4 of the Trade Disputes Act, 1906, should be amended to cover only the *privileged occasions* as in Sections 1 and 3. The unions' total immunity, constituting them a *privileged group*, should be repealed.

The infringement of individual common law rights by union contracts with the member (the Rule Book) could be checked by empowering the Chief Registrar of Friendly Societies to check, revise or rescind Rules and to ensure that the Rules provide member safeguards, disciplinary procedures with fines and penalties related to the offence, an independent appeals tribunal control and inspection of voting and elections – termination of the contract by the member and limit the size of branch to the facilities available.

The union mutual aid and sickness benefit funds should be separated from the general fund and come under the Friendly Societies Act and to constitute a separate membership.

The review of the law concerning the *withdrawal* of labour should also examine the law on the *dismissal* of labour. The right of an employer to dismiss with due notice any worker, in any circumstances, without any given reason, is almost unique to this country and should be limited especially as workers' reactions against dismissals account for most unofficial strikes.

The basic human rights in industry – the right to work, to contract, to associate, and to negotiate – should be made statutory rights, thus presenting the trade unions with a new trade union charter embodying the workers' rights for which they fought.[1]

From status to contract

Sir Henry Maine in his famous aphorism declared 'the movement of progressive societies has hitherto been a movement from status to contract'. That movement continues to bring those concerned within the law. Industry, employers and unions alike, cannot hope to keep their feudal status with its jousts and tournaments.

Meantime, can we deprive ourselves of the common law protection of our rights and freedoms because the common law hinders the trade unions not in their restraint of trade activities but in their pursuit of the 'closed shop', and at the same time pass legislation against restraints of trade –

[1] See the author's 'Human Rights in Industry', in *Agenda for a Free Society*, Hutchinson for Institute of Economic Affairs, 1961.

monopolies' restrictive practices and resale price maintenance?

Have we arrived at some Orwellian 'Legal Farm' where
'law' means that 'all are legal but some are more legal than
others' and where the trade unions declare the courts and
the law illegal because they are in restraint of trade unions?

After all, laws are most needed when the urge to break
them is strongest. So, paradoxically, are trade unions.

Trade unions after Rookes v. Barnard

To trade union apathy *Rookes v. Barnard* points a cure –
namely, a free and participating membership. Compulsory
trade unionism is proving as damaging to the unions in the
1960s as was syndicalism in the 1920s.

The legal check on the coercive methods of securing compulsory unionism affords the unions an opportunity to halt
its progress. Communication and participation are the essen-
tials for union recovery. The collective agreement that covers
so little because it has to cover so much – the active minority
which dreads any sign of returning membership life – and
the leaders with no members to lead – these are a few of the
problems the unions must face. Only with a voluntary membership can the unions face and solve them.

The unions must differentiate sharply between union
membership as a *condition* of employment and membership
as a *qualification* for employment and avoid compulsory
unionism like the plague. Trade unions are not privileged as
far as the laws of history are concerned and with them, as
with us, if we cannot digest history it will repeat itself.

George Loveless, leaving the Dorchester Court in 1834
to face the 'hulk' and transportation threw a paper with this
message to free men down the centuries –

> God is our guide! No swords we draw,
> We kindle not war's battle fires,
> By reason, union, justice, law,
> We claim the birthright of our sires;
> We raise the watchword 'Liberty':
> We will, we will, we will be free!

DENIS THOMAS

I was educated at a grammar school, in the Burma jungle with the Chindits, and at Oxford where I earned the distinction of becoming the only editor of *Cherwell* ever to get a black eye playing rugger. Editorial posts on magazines led me eventually into the Coronation Streets of England and Wales as an industrial journalist – an experience I cannot recommend to any Stagnant Society gospeller who is anxious to hold on to his prejudices. I have also been a television and book columnist for national newspapers, but I prefer nowadays to make TV programmes instead of criticising them, and to write books instead of reviewing them. My personal stake in a regalvanised Britain includes a youthful wife, and three schoolboy sons.

9: FREE AS AIR

DENIS THOMAS *looks at broadcasting and the other 'mass media'. He finds that broadcasting was stagnant until the coming of competition in television. He argues that TV and newspapers can best remain independent of state control if they are run by private firms in competition with one another, and that trade union restrictions threaten the free development of communication. He concludes that, in spite of its drawbacks, competition is better than monopoly, public or private, for giving the people the entertainment, amusement, information or education they want and eventually for raising the standard of what the public demands.*

'WE hear the news at nine o'clock,' writes Mr Arthur Koestler in his editorial introduction to *Suicide of a Nation*, 'but where are the eagles and the trumpets?' We'll come to them in a moment. But first, what's this about *hearing* the nine o'clock news? These days we do nothing of the kind – we watch it, often at the very moment it is happening, on television. What's more, within fifteen minutes or so we have a choice of bulletins. Gluttons for news most evenings of the week can even see both. And it would be no compliment either to the BBC or to Independent Television to suppose there's nothing to choose between them. There is, and both sides know it. The only argument is where the difference lies.

But this is not the true burden of Mr Koestler's rhetorical question. As a literary eagle himself, and no mean trumpeter on his day, he echoes the familiar complaint that we – that is to say, the rest of us – are short of a moral purpose, an incentive, a collective sense of mission that will somehow save us from our complacent and over-indulgent selves. In his introductory essay 'The Lion and the Ostrich', he cites 'some of the causative factors of our economic, political, and cultural maladjustment' which contributors to *Encounter*'s symposium propound in their articles. These include 'fixation on the glories and the miseries of the past' and 'rule by mediocracy', otherwise identifiable as 'the cult of amateurishness' and contempt for expertise. As one who makes his living in what other people call the mass media, I sometimes wonder if the Stagnant Society brigade and I are living in the same country.

Past and future

It is certainly possible to exaggerate the 'glories and miseries of the past', and to find false comfort in the lessons and examples of history. But these are only basic qualifications of nationhood, as spelled out by Ernest Renan a century ago :

> To have common glories in the past, a common will in the present; to have done great things together; to wish to do greater: these are the essential conditions which make up a people.

Doesn't that fit us? A bit later there is even a line about 'an inheritance of glories and regrets'. When he came to quote this passage in *The Revolt of the Masses*, Ortega y Gasset screwed the message home with a couple of turns of his own :

> If the nation consisted only in past and present, no one would be concerned with defending it against attack. Those who maintain the contrary are either hypocrites or lunatics. But what happens is that the national past projects its attractions — real or imaginary — into the future.

Not to have a past which can be projected in this way is to feel deprived, as I suppose new nations like Zanzibar might after a tame and orderly progression from colonialism to statehood; needing those glories and miseries, they deliberately bring them about by violence. But what about that

other qualification, 'a common will in the present'? This is
the point at which Mr Koestler strains his eyes and ears in
vain for the eagles and the trumpets.

Individuality in the press

The obvious place to turn to is the day-to-day record of
our lives and behaviour, the press. Since ours is a free society,
and the press is not under state supervision, no common or
collective voice comes through loud and clear – not the
leader writers' and certainly not the advertisers'. The general impression is as formless as protoplasm. The press contains all the elements of our lives but only momentarily
holds in focus life itself. Individual newspapers can and do
strike individual attitudes (unlike radio and TV organisations, they are not forbidden by law or charter to 'slant' the
news) – from the *Daily Worker* to *The Times*. You can hear
trumpet blasts in both, though not often in the same key :
the *Worker* is a propagandist sheet drumming gospel truths
into the already converted, while *The Times* every once in
a while rumbles its bellyful like a stage thunder machine
without overtly trying to bring down governments or start
a revolution. Seekers after truth might distrust both papers
for the same reason – that they are committed to preconceived notions of society and behaviour. Between these ex-
tremes the other papers cover the whole range of contemporary manners, though in some cases the very term 'newspaper'
has become as strained as a well-filled bikini.

The popular papers are still the ones which cause the
least disturbance to people's thought-processes. As *The
Times* once put it,

> 'readers are won in their millions more readily by what is trivial
> than by what is serious. We are still in all too early stage of
> universal education', it added – this was seven years ago – 'for
> first things to be put first, where its reading is concerned, by a
> proportion of the population sufficiently large to support all
> existing newspapers.'

Since then, newspapers have continued to die at regular
intervals and Mr Cecil King has forecast that in the end we

shall be left with only the *Mirror*, the *Express* and the *Telegraph* among the national dailies. The prospect is one which should alarm the Stagnant Society-ites no less than the rest of us, for already the agglomeration of newspapers into a few huge groups threatens to standardise presentation and stamp out the last few sparks of irreverent individuality which flicker in the popular dailies. Even the political balance of opinion could be altered for the worse (in France, a model of technocratic government and economic 'growth', the press is under commercial pressure to be polite to President de Gaulle; in Ghana, which has an unexceptionable 'common will in the present', the press is a mockery). The most recent casualty among British newspapers has been one of the most politically committed, the *Daily Herald*. For years it laboured to endear itself to a mass readership while plugging the orthodox TUC–Socialist line, and only when it was faced with the last desperate bid for circulation did it bring its appearance and its tone of voice more into line with that of its main competitors, the *Express* and the *Mail*. When that failed, as every journalist in Fleet Street knew it must, there was nothing for it but to pack up. (In fact it decided to start all over again with a different name and a new, carefully market-researched image.)

Newspapers will continue to flourish or die for much the same reasons as people. Prosperous ones, like the *Express* and the *Sunday Times*, generate confidence and energy. Ailing ones are querulous and strained. Some, like the *News Chronicle*, die of sheer anaemia. Transfusions of new capital can raise the red-corpuscle count, but in the end only the paper's own intrinsic life-force will save it.

The life-force, on the other hand, can be drained away by restrictive practices. These operate more severely against small newspapers than against big ones, who can generally afford to meet the extra costs which arise from over-manning of new, supposedly economical machines, and the payment of wages to non-existent 'ghost' workers. Cases are known of compositors who have to be paid for setting which has already been done outside, and of packers insisting on a supper break before starting work so that they can charge overtime while actually on the job. In some sections of television, equipment and ideas which would introduce new techniques in programme making are resisted by the technicians' unions for similar self-protective reasons. Meanwhile, both industries cry out for adventurous management and new creative techniques.

The fiercely realistic view of a newspaper's fortunes is that if enough people don't buy it, it deserves to go under. The altruistic view is that the more newspapers we have, of whatever quality, the better it will be for us and our democracy in the end. What is both priggish and dangerous is to watch with satisfaction the death of newspapers which may in their time have been 'yellow' or semi-pornographic, on the grounds that they only got what was coming to them. Every newspaper is a voice, and every time one is stilled – even one that jars on educated ears – our society takes another step towards conformity.

Control of the 'communicators'

For newspapers, like television and radio, are part of our popular culture. As such they come under the suspicious scrutiny of sociologists who see in them dangerous or cynical abuses of literacy. Mr Raymond Williams, in a Penguin Special, has argued in favour of a new system in which all the means of communication would be publicly owned, but vested in trusts which would hire out their facilities to independent professional companies 'run by ordinary democratic means, with all the members having an equal say.' In the case of newspapers, 'functionless financial groups' would be cut out, and local trusts set up to 'guarantee the independence of editors'.

One can but shake one's head in admiring disbelief. This is the academic *reductio ad absurdum* of the argument that 'communication' must be separated from production and trade, which is to say from the profit motive. Newspapers flourish or fail because people choose whether or not to buy them. Television companies gain popularity or lose money because people choose either to watch their programmes or switch them off. The true communicators are not 'a few irresponsible men who treat our cultural means as simple commodities,' as Mr Williams thinks. They are, of course, the men and women who produce and write the newspapers and the television programmes. They are not unduly corrupted because they are paid for it. On the contrary, achieving success in a skilled job under the combined stimulus of ambition and competition gives them no less a pride in their work than, say, university dons have. 'Functionless financial groups' may in some instances pay the salary cheques; but these same bogey-men are answerable to shareholders or boards of governors. Who would stand trust for the trustees? I feel sure it was not a press run by committees that Milton was hoping for when, in the *Areopagitica*, he spoke out against regulating 'all recreations and pastimes, all that is delightful to man.'

The mass communicators follow more often than they lead. It is their business to sense what their public wants to know, or what it enjoys, or would enjoy if it were given the chance. Newspapers, it may be, have only a marginal vote-getting effect on General Elections. Yet it is perfectly possible for a paper which 'sells' success, brightness, optimism – as the *Express* does – to bring its readers to a state of mind in which political change is seen as a threat to the rosy vision of the *Express*-type good life here on earth. It is equally possible for a paper which bangs away at class attitudes – as the *Mirror* does – to persuade a lot of people that a council school is a better training-ground for a potential Prime Minister of this country than the playing fields of Eton.

More scepticism and television

But there is something new in British public opinion : an awakened sense of scepticism. With better education and more worldliness – higher wages, the break-up of socially inbred communities, foreign travel – has come a quickened critical faculty which newspapers and television have done much to foster. Also, over the past ten years pressure of competition has forced the predominantly Tory press to sharpen its attitudes to government policies : in a circulation war, the editorial guns have to keep firing. It would be extraordinary if any government could disregard such a dangerous fallout from their own side.

The papers' collective power is still immense, but its direction is shifting. This is due partly to a tendency away from hard political attitudes towards more purely social ones, and partly to the new competitor, television. Night after night, the television bulletins anticipate tomorrow's front pages with pictures and story, interviews and follow-ups. Professionally there may not be much to choose between the newspaper journalist and the television journalist (the latter, anyway, is still quite likely to have a Fleet Street background) but in terms of sheer technology the advantages are all with television. In neither world is there a vestige of amateurism left. Getting the news, and getting it out to the nation, is a single-minded professional operation, conducted with cool precision. Contempt for proficiency and expertise? *Mediocrats*? Not here, Mr K.

A new sense of public service

Competitive television has been with us long enough now for earlier, pre-ITV impressions to have faded. But every one of its present advantages can be seen to have stemmed directly from the breaking of the BBC monopoly in 1955. In the days of Lord Reith, Mr John Ardagh recalled in a recent isue of *New Society*, 'the BBC was sure of its moral and cultural mission to the wasteland of Philistia. Radio announcers wore dinner jackets to read the news; programmes reflected "British mentality at its best"; top executives were calm in their faith that they were there to give people what the BBC thought was good for them.' Today the BBC's popularity stands far higher than in the days of Reith. *Out* is the old sense of patrician righteousness. *In* is a new sense of public service which doesn't– or didn't – funk scandal or sensation of the kind identified with TW3.

Whatever has happened? The breakthrough came with the death of paternalism as the guiding force in British broadcasting. It is amazing, thinking back, how long it kept its hold. During the thirty years in which the 20th century revolution came to the boil, the great British public were treated as so many million Larry the Lambs, quite likeable but slightly delinquent, who could not be trusted to know what was in their own best interest. To charges that he was giving the public only what *he thought* they wanted, Reith replied that 'few know what they want and few what they need.' In defence of the indefensible – monopoly of broadcasting by the state – Reith told the Beveridge Committee that it was 'the brute force of monopoly' that had made possible the BBC's 'policy of moral responsibility'. But all pretensions were exploded when at last ITV came on the air. From being a cosy bourgeois recreation, BBC-accented and liberally sprinkled with middle-class recognition signals, television suddenly burst its bonds. With the salesmen and the sweatered comperes and the journalists with cruel spectacles came the energetic vulgarity which set it free. Television has never been the same since, and it will never be the same again.

And yet, as if in response to instinctive British sympathy for the underdog, the BBC has now been given back much of the advantage it enjoyed before its monopoly was broken nine years ago. Independent Television will have its second channel too, but not before the BBC has had the first chance to seize for itself another slice of the nightly audience. In addition, experimental licences to operators of coin-in-the-slot TV can be expected to shave off a measurable slice of 'minority' viewers, though these may well affect the BBC's figures before they begin to show on ITV's. The race for the ratings is on – for none of the new generation of BBC producers pretends that audience ratings don't matter. Meanwhile the ITA has had its functions more sharply defined in the new Television Act: to act as 'a public service for disseminating information, education and entertainment' – the same rubric, word for word, as appears in the BBC's charter; to ensure that the programmes 'maintain a high general standard in all respects'; and to secure 'a wide showing for programmes of merit.'

Breaking monopoly by competition

This is one of the watered-down effects of the Pilkington Report, which was so sparing in its tributes to the achievements of Independent Television that to get a pat on the back from it, according to one recipient, felt like wearing a Victoria Cross in a Ban-the-Bomb parade. The Pilkington Committee might have shamed ITV out of its less lovable excesses if they had managed to keep in check their basic antagonism to the whole concept of independent television. As it was they missed the central point : that the best way to break a commercial near-monopoly (the network system) is to enable other commercial groups to set up in competition. The case against the BBC having their advantage restored can be stated in principle : a public service dependent on the state is not as free as a public service dependent on competitive private enterprise. The point was made by David Sawers in a Hobart Paper published shortly after Pilkington :

> British experience in the last fifteen years must by now be seen to confirm the teaching of political philosophers since Hobbes, that the state is not a disembodied force concerned only with the welfare of society. A public corporation is made up of individuals, who have points of view. However hard they may try to present a balanced picture, on the subjects where they feel strongly their feelings are bound to appear. And if these bodies depend on the Government for their finance they cannot escape covert desires to avoid offence.

Commercial power is also suspect; but at least it can be held in check by competition.

It would be a bad look-out for broadcasting in Britain if the eventual pattern were to emerge as a carve-up with each side, BBC and the independent producers, settling for a tacitly agreed share of the audience. What must be resisted is any polarisation towards 'pop' television on some channels and 'serious' television on the others. Something like this is happening outside television, in the Sunday paper market, where in recent years the casualties have been among the middle-weight papers. Steadily the survivors have eased over to the flanks : on one side the 'quality' papers, and on the other the mass-circulation sheets whose cash registers ring as merrily as bedsprings. No section of the communications industry more depressingly supports the Two Nations concept than Britain's Sunday press.

Some of the blame for this must lie with the advertising agencies, whose ruthless slide-rule assessments of value for money militates against papers with static or fluctuating circulations. But in a hard world there is no passing the buck. When people with a free choice stop buying a product in sufficient numbers to ensure its survival, out it goes.

As it happens, the last casualty of the kind among the Sunday papers was the *Dispatch*. During its last days I turned up the first issue, published (as the *Weekly Dispatch*) on September 27th 1801, to see how far it might have moved from its original intentions. Across the hundred and sixty years came the voice of its first editor, in a tribute to

> that laudable spirit of competition which has raised the Literary as well as the Commercial character of Great Britain to unrivalled eminence.

The paper, he said, would 'convey the most authentic, interesting and useful Information up to the last moment of its being Put to Press.' It would be 'Independent, unconnected with Factions or Parties'. And it would be 'not inattentive to occurrences of a subordinate kind'.

All these are sound, and for their time imaginative, principles. They look ahead to Northcliffe's famous injunction to the staff of the *Daily Mail* a century later : 'Be bright, but dignified.' Brightness and dignity are not irreconcilable, as some newspapers, and some television programmes, demonstrate every day; and while the worst may get worse, the best gets steadily better. In the next half-century, if we can prevent the consumer-protectionists from setting up

committees to mind our own business, more and more
control over mass communications will be by discriminating
free choice. The state has gone as far as we should ever allow
it in monopolising the free air. And when the state ceaseth
(as Nietzsche put it, anticipating – even capping – Mr
Koestler),

> look my brethren – do you not see the rainbows and the bridges
> of the beyond?

PART THREE

WELFARE FOR AFFLUENCE

Generally speaking there is no-one who knows what is for your interest so well as yourself – no one who is disposed with so much ardour and constancy to pursue it.

Jeremy Bentham (1795)

It is an abuse of the principle of equality to demand that no individual be permitted to be better off than the rest, when his being so makes none of the others worse off than they otherwise would be.

John Stuart Mill (1848)

The spirit of self-help is the root of all genuine growth in the individual, and exhibited in the lives of many, it constitutes the true source of national vigour and strength ... Whatever is done *for* men and classes to a certain extent takes away the stimulus and necessity of doing for themselves; and where men are subjected to over-guidance and over government, the inevitable tendency is to render them comparatively helpless.

Samuel Smiles (1859)

We may look forward to the time when the labouring population may be safely entrusted with the education of their children; ... the assistance and superintendence ... of the Government for that purpose ... (is) ... only a means of preparing the labouring classes for a better, but remote state of things ... in the latter part of the twentieth century ... when that assistance and superintendence shall no longer be necessary.

Nassau Senior (1861)

COLIN CLARK

I was a Labour politician in the 1930s, Economic Adviser to the Queensland Government from 1938 to 1952, since then Director of the Agricultural Economics Research Institute in Oxford University.

I am accustomed to finding myself in intellectually isolated positions – I supported Keynes before he became fashionable. I have opposed the protection of manufactures in Australia and of agriculture in Britain and have been questioning since 1939 the supposed high rate of economic growth in Soviet Russia. I argued in 1945 that 25 per cent of the net national income was the economically safe limit for taxation and advocated dismantling the Welfare State and handing back to the average family a large part of the 30 per cent of their income which they now pay in taxation, believing that they could then make better provision for their own welfare. I consider that economic growth takes place mainly as a consequence of improvements in human resources and cannot be artificially accelerated by excessive investment; find it quite erroneous to describe half or two-thirds of the world's population as undernourished, though their poverty in other goods deserves our active sympathy; believe that population growth usually provides an economically beneficial stimulus.

10: TAXATION FOR EXPANSION

COLIN CLARK *argues that we tax ourselves too heavily, nearly 40 per cent of the net national income, and that high taxation holds back production by weakening incentives and stimulating inflation. He says that taxation ought to be brought down to about 25 per cent of the net national income and that this can best be done by reducing the structure of state welfare. He outlines the principles of taxation and how to apply them in such a new system.*

MANY writers in our day argue or imply that the remedies for our misfortunes are to be found in further actions by the central government. The idea that some of them might be put right by restoring some powers to individuals and families to act for themselves, and by decentralising the powers of government, is rarely considered.

Keynes, whose aphorism 'In the long run we are all dead' is so often quoted to support crash programmes and crass policies he would have abhorred, was no supporter of unlimited state action. And we do well therefore to remind ourselves of his too-little-known assessment in the *General Theory* of the advantages of individualism, emphasising the gains from the decentralisation of social power and economic action :

> They are partly advantages of efficiency – the advantages of decentralisation and of the play of self-interest. The advantage to efficiency of the decentralisation of decisions and of individual responsibility is even greater, perhaps, than the nineteenth century supposed; and the reaction against the appeal to self-interest may have gone too far. But, above all, Individualism if it can be purged of its defects and its abuses, is the best safe-

guard of personal liberty in the sense that it greatly widens the
field for the exercise of personal choice. It is also the best safeguard of the variety of life, which emerges precisely from this
extended field of personal choice, and the loss of which is the
greatest of all losses of the homogeneous or totalitarian state.
For this variety preserves the traditions which embody the most
secure and successful choices of former generations; it colours
the present with the diversification of its fancy; and, being the
handmaid of experiment as well as of tradition and of fancy,
it is the most powerful instrument to better the future.[1]

Those who turn to the state as the solve-all for social problems should bear in mind this assessment of the advantages
of a liberal economy; for the dominance since the war of
pseudo-Keynesian economics is not a little responsible for
the unprecedentedly high rates of taxation.

That the authors of the article in *Encounter* (July, 1963)
for example completely ignore the problems of public finance
– of excessive government expenditure and the inefficient
system of taxation by which it is financed – is, one fears,
more than an editorial slip. It appears that the fundamental
problem of the proper role of the state, of which the organisation and extent of public finance are important aspects, is
beyond their vision. But this is the problem we shall discuss.

Principles and forms of taxation

Many people still regard public finance as the predominantly practical problem of raising taxes somehow and getting
the budget to balance. An easy-going approach to this type
can have, and has had, extremely serious consequences in the
long run. Let us therefore state a few general principles that
should govern the administration and collection of taxes.

Tax collection is the monopoly of government and with it
go heavy responsibilities. Politicians must carry, in a manner
fully visible to all, responsibility for their decisions. And in
a democracy this implies that electors should feel some general responsibility for the decisions made on their behalf.
Such behaviour is hardly characteristic of the practice of

[1] *The General Theory of Employment, Interest and Money*, 1936.

contemporary politics, whereby all parties seek to buy the support of the electors with expensive bribes which have to be paid for by someone, meanwhile working their hardest to convey to each elector the impression that it will not be he personally who has to pay. Financial journalists and economists join the conspiracy to keep public opinion in the dark about the extent to which the average family is taxed for its share of the 'welfare state'. Carefully though the facts are concealed from them, people are discovering them all the same. Is it too much to hope that a time will soon come when a politician will introduce a new measure by saying : 'This is going to cost us another 2 per cent of our incomes, and you will all have to pay it, except the very poorest; but I still think that it is worth it, and I hope that you will agree with me, and continue to vote for me'?

The designer of a system of taxation has to take into account social justice, economic efficiency, and administrative practicability : and it is regrettable to find how often these requirements conflict with one another. Social justice does *not* mean taxing those classes of the community of whom you disapprove in order to pay money to those of whom you approve; rather the opposite – it means ensuring that no social group should receive money from public funds beyond that for which they can show a really just claim; and that no social or economic group is taxed beyond the share it ought to contribute to public needs. At the same time we must remember that no government can, or should attempt to, provide perfect justice; domestic quarrels for instance are outside the province of governments.

The state should also levy taxes in a manner compatible with economic efficiency and growth so as to discourage as little as possible, and indeed to encourage where possible, the potentially fruitful aspirations of individuals and companies. The obligation of economic efficiency may frequently conflict with that of social justice – a government which was only concerned with economic efficiency, for example, might impose heavy taxes on the necessaries of life, which could not be avoided, and so make the poor work harder. It is quite compatible with social justice however for the state to require that individuals and families in general should make social welfare provision for themselves but give generous assistance to those who are not able to do so.

The economic criteria of public finance require in the first place that productive resources (labour, capital and land) should be free from unemployment or under-employment through a general inadequacy of demand (which was the economic problem of the thirties); but also that they should be given incentives to produce as much as they can. Serious offences against this principle are to be seen in the purchase tax, levied at high rates on specifically designated commodities. Producers may in this way be induced to make costly alterations in the design of their products to avoid high rates of tax.

Equality is not the aim

How can these broad principles be applied to specific proposals? We may first note the idea that taxation should aim to bring incomes as near equality as possible. This notion lost much of its primitive appeal for the early Fabians when it was realised that the major part of the world lay outside Britain and was on average much poorer. The objective is clearly incompatible with our economic criterion since in such a nation enterprise and hard work would go unrewarded, and stagnation would follow. It is also important to realise that equality of incomes would not long survive equality of opportunity, since individual abilities and energies differ. We may finally dispose of equalitarianism by noting that it conflicts with our criterion of social justice, since it could be properly realised only where all means of production were owned by the state, with the consequent loss of all meaningful freedoms.

Taxation should be moderately progressive

We now turn from this extreme doctrine to the more moderate one of progression in taxation. It says that while the state is not entitled deliberately to redistribute income, it should design its tax system so that the burden falls relatively more severely on the rich than on the poor. The opposite state of affairs is known as 'regressive taxation', whereby the poor pay in taxation a larger proportion of their incomes than the rich. It would be regarded by no-one as just (though present British and United States taxation is in fact regressive over considerable ranges of income).

Some American economists and political philosophers believe that social justice demands strictly 'proportional' taxation, the case for which was originally stated by Adam Smith in *The Wealth of Nations*

> The subjects of every state ought to contribute towards the support of the government, as nearly as possible, in proportion to their respective abilities; that is in proportion to the revenue that they respectively enjoy under the protection of the state.

An equi-proportional tax on incomes, accompanied by a small equi-proportional tax on capital, might be found just and practicable : but my own conclusion is that income taxation should be progressive, so long as the progression is moderate. A moderately progressive tax system would not significantly conflict with our criterion of economic efficiency.

There has been so much talk about tax progression that we tend to believe we are living, in common with other western nations, under a highly progressive tax system. This is far from true. Recent calculations of the Central Statistical Office have shown that when all taxation, including direct and indirect taxes and rates, have been taken into account the burden is almost uniform over the larger part of the income range, with most families taxed to the extent of 30 per cent of their incomes (tax rates become progressive, when all taxes have been taken into account, only at a high income level) – and only the poorest families get back what they pay. In direct taxation the rapidly growing social insurance contributions fall heavily on low incomes; and indirect taxation is increasing and becoming more regressive, not least because the taxes on beer, tobacco and gambling are levied on the principal recreations of the people with lower incomes.

Sir John and Lady Hicks and W. B. Rostas, in *Taxation of War Wealth*, written in 1939–40, reached the common-sense conclusion that, even in war-time, it is wise to let any taxpayer, however rich, keep at any rate £1 out of £3 of any additional earnings, on grounds of economic efficiency and social justice alike. I would suggest maximum tax rates of 50 per cent of increments of earnings in peace-time, and these maximum rates should be scaled down in smooth progression so as to avoid inequalities between adjacent income groups.

It is desirable to exempt people with very low incomes from taxation, though ideally our principle of encouraging electoral responsibility would apply to all incomes however small. Tax exemption should be virtually complete below a limit of £500 income for an average family (more or less for varying family responsibilities).

How much should the state take?

But how much is it desirable that the state should take in taxation? This is perhaps the crucial question.

In 1960 the percentage of net national income at factor cost[1] claimed by local and national government was 35·4 and in 1962 it was 38·9. Under the stimulus of competitive electioneering from the politicians, the Sizzling Sixties show every sign of really swingeing rates of tax from all social classes. Table 1 shows how these taxes were spent.

Is it desirable that taxes should be at this level? In 1945 I published a paper in the *Economic Journal*, entitled 'Public Finance and Change in the Value of Money', which concluded that where taxation (or taxation plus government

[1] This is the total of all wages, salaries, rent, dividends and interest received by individuals, including income in kind, the income of entrepreneurs and undistributed profits of companies and corporations before deductions of taxes. For our present purpose it is a better measure than Gross National Product which includes depreciation and indirect taxes and excludes subsidies, and which is therefore itself effected by changes in government policy in the budget.

TABLE 1

Percentage of National Income spent by Local and National Governments.

	1952	1957	1962
Defence	13·0	8·3	7·5
Debt Interest and Finance	5·9	4·7	5·3
Roads and lighting	0·9	0·9	1·3
Police and justice	0·8	0·7	0·9
Overseas services	0·6	0·5	0·6
Other services necessarily falling on public authorities	2·6	2·0	2·3
	23·8	17·1	17·9
National insurance, pensions and assistance	6·5	5·9	7·2
Education and child care	4·2	4·4	5·3
National Health Service	3·9	3·5	3·8
Agriculture and industry[1]	4·1	3·0	3·4
Housing	3·5	2·1	1·9
	22·2	18·9	21·6
All expenditure[2]	46·0	36·0	39·5

[1] This total includes certain necessary regulatory services but largely consists of direct or indirect subsidies (to agriculture, railways, etc.) which on the whole do not really enrich even the recipients, but serve to postpone necessary economic readjustments. On the whole, these can be described as the price which the country has to pay in order to enable politicians to defer unpopular decisions.

[2] Totals are higher than those for taxation because some expenditure from loans is included.

Source: *National Income and Expenditure*, Tables 1 and 44.

deficit), exceeded 25 per cent of the net national income at factor cost forces were set in motion which resulted within the space of two or three years in a general rise in costs and prices. Keynes, who was then editor, wrote to me :

> In Great Britain after the war I should guess that your figure of 25 per cent as the maximum tolerable proportion of taxation may be exceedingly near to the truth. I should not be at all surprised if we did not find a further confirmation in our post-war experience of your empirical law.

A recent re-examination of my earlier results has confirmed the findings as Keynes predicted. Since the war nearly
all countries have levied taxation at a rate much above 25
per cent on national income. They have also experienced
rates of price increases much higher than ever before. Moreover countries with higher rates of taxation show higher
rates of increases as Table 2 shows. (We should bear in
mind that, in the world as it has been since 1945, even countries with low rates of taxation cannot help 'importing' a
certain amount of cost increase through their trade with
other countries.)

TABLE 2

Taxation as a proportion of National Income and Average Rates of
Increase of Costs

(per cent per year)

Taxation	1953 to 1963	Increase in Costs
under 25%	Japan Portugal S. Africa Switzerland	1·0
28–34%	Australia Belgium Canada Denmark New Zealand Sweden (1953-7) USA	2·7
34–40%	Finland Italy Netherlands Norway (1953-7) Sweden (1957-63) United Kingdom	3·3
over 40%	Austria France Germany Norway (1957-63)	3·7

Taxation raises costs partly by discouraging productive effort and, more significantly perhaps, by causing industrialists to become careless about costs. (If half of any increase is 'on the Treasury' they will take much less care to avoid it, whether in the wages bill or the expense account.) Furthermore those who pay not far short of half their incomes to the government may understandably look to it for the solution of a good many problems, and this encourages a weary and unproductive paternalism in politics.

Let us be quite clear about the undesirability of price increases. The pursuit of economic policies that lead to persistent price increases is unjust, for it plunders the savings of people who do not have enough money or knowledge to buy ordinary shares or real property, which may be able to keep pace with inflation, and who have to hold their savings in insurance policies or savings banks, which do not. Furthermore it discourages savings and leads to a devil-may-care attitude to the future, provision for which comes to be regarded as a lamentable and eccentric folly.

There is strong evidence to suggest that if people realised just how much of their earnings they are giving to the government they would be angry and horrified. Can one imagine the results of a social survey which asked people of all classes, 'How much of your income do you wish to give to government?', returning the answer 'Just under half'! The idea is preposterous, almost as preposterous as that which suggests that one can collect nearly 40 per cent of the national income through a progressive taxation system. Any such attempt must bear extremely heavily on people with lower incomes if only because if it does not do so the wealthier, more knowledgeable, and enterprising elements will quit the country. We should therefore seriously aim at conducting the business of government on a budget of not more than 25 per cent of the national income, at all times except war, or similar emergency.

Reducing taxation

How then can the present excessive tax-levels be reduced?
In 1963 the Institute of Economic Affairs' survey *Choice in Welfare* found that over 50 per cent of male married heads of households would prefer that the state should take less in taxes for the provision of welfare services. The solution to our problem seems clear. If the expenditure could be curtailed in favour of private provision, perhaps through insurance, then we should have gone a long way to reduce public expenditure by the required 15 per cent of national income.

There is of course one absolutely essential condition for the working of such a system of private insurance, namely the end of the general rise in prices which has now been going on for 25 years. If it continues personal insurances are bound to become inadequate. We must therefore make a most important addition to the principles of taxation outlined in the foregoing section. *We must ensure that governments never pursue policies which lead to a general persistent rise in prices*; in particular they should confine their activities to such as can be financed by a budget not exceeding 25 per cent of net national income at factor cost.

The new tax system

A system of taxation compatible with this change in state welfare policy must reflect the required principles. The responsibility of politicians for their decisions must be clear and the tax system should encourage a general sense of responsibility and interest amongst electors; taxes must not conflict with social justice and should be levied so as to encourage productivity and foster growth. A moderately progressive income (and capital) tax is compatible with these canons of taxation and should therefore be the principal source of government revenue. But the government should never in time of peace attempt to collect more than 25 per cent of net national income in taxes, nor should it pursue policies which lead to general and persistent price increases, for this would jeopardise the systems of private insurances that must replace the welfare state. Furthermore public expenditure and taxation should be transferred, wherever possible, from national to local authorities in the interests of accountability and efficiency.

There seems to be no reason in economics or justice why 'real' capital gains should not be treated for tax purposes in the same way as income. But if this is to be so there is little reason why capital should be further taxed on the death of the tax payer; the estate duty should therefore be abolished (incidentally releasing for more productive pursuits the platoons of lawyers and accountants employed to evade estate duty). Taxation on the realisation of capital assets should be combined with a full rebate on savings such as there now is on life assurance and mortgage interest saving.

A new land tax should in part replace the local rates which discourage development because they are levied on buildings and other improvements to land. Furthermore much of this revenue represents in effect a tax upon housing, which is very regressive upon the lower income families and on those bringing up young children. The ratio of land values to national product is now much less than it was in the 1870's, when the Henry Georgeites were advocating a (single) tax on land, and both for this reason and because the proportion of expenditure in the hands of governments is higher now than then too much should not be expected of a land tax. But it remains one of the most economically efficient forms of taxation, because it does not injure anyone's incentive to produce (land cannot be produced) : and indeed may often encourage people to make better use of their land in order to pay their tax. (The sites of buildings of historic or architectural interest, or land of outstanding national beauty, or available for public recreation, if *permanently dedicated* to these objects, should however be exempt.)

Should companies be taxed as such or should the tax laws regard them as only a 'vehicle' for the taxable incomes of their shareholders? Most countries treat companies much more severely than we do – the United States, until recently, has taken a straight half of their profits in taxation, which is clearly excessive. The case for taxing companies as such is however that those who have received the special privileges arising from limited liability should also be prepared to pay for it through taxation of company profits, the more so perhaps since the interest of society at large demands that as many men as possible should remain as individual traders responsible for their own debts. Though now modified by the profits tax the British system still gives too strong an incentive to trade as a company rather than as an individual. Furthermore, despite the contrary report of the Richardson Committee, the French system of taxing the value added (i.e. deducting from taxable sales the amount spent by the industrialist on purchasing material or equipment) and the taxing of payrolls is economically superior to a lower rate of sales tax levied on all transactions valued gross, or to the British system of heavy taxation of profits, for they give incentives to economise on labour, expense accounts, and other costs which the British system does not.

Spreading indirect taxation

A limited amount of taxation on commodities (e.g. tobacco, drink, gambling) which the state believes we should consume in smaller quantities is proper, but it should not be carried so far that it distorts production and consumption. Other indirect taxes so far as they are necessary should be levied over the whole range of goods on the market.

The following figures indicate roughly the possible orders of magnitude which the various components of the state budget might have under such a tax system : they are percentages of net national income at factor cost.

The principal source of revenue would be the personal, and now progressive, income tax, which despite the exemption and the limit of 50 per cent on even the highest levels of income, would produce $11\frac{1}{2}$ per cent as opposed to the 10·3 per cent of the current income tax. The tax on capital would produce $1\frac{1}{2}$ per cent, and those on company *profits* (at a rate of 10 per cent) 2 per cent. The land tax might raise 3 per cent, and those on drink, tobacco and gambling (assuming a decline in cigarette smoking) 2 per cent. The general tax on value added should produce $2\frac{1}{2}$ per cent. The total taxation would in this way reach $22\frac{1}{2}$ per cent of national income. This total would be sufficient for government purposes including assistance to education, old-age assurance and so on.

And so we can achieve our target of limiting taxation to 25 per cent of national income, encouraging efficiency and maintaining social justice. And there is little doubt in my mind that this response to the wishes of the electorate would in a little time be rewarded by the resurgence of productivity and new advances in living standards.

ARTHUR SELDON

I was born in the First World War and graduated by national insurance and state education to the London School of Economics. There I read voraciously Lenin, Laski, Strachey, Dalton but was more influenced by Robbins, Plant and Hayek. The war and postwar siege economy, several years as editor of a trade journal, ten years as an economist in industry and five years working in fruitful partnership with Ralph Harris at the Institute of Economic Affairs have reinforced the view I had acquired from a teacher that the nineteenth century was the great age of emancipation and that the classical economists were basically right.

The limitations of even the best-intentioned politicians have strengthened a general prejudice against entrusting them with power and in favour of letting people learn by making mistakes in free markets.

At the 1924 General Election I joined in cheering the Labour cars and booing the Conservative and Liberal cars. In my lifetime the Tories have enlarged state authority by fits of absent-mindedness, and my political sympathies have been Liberal, but I prefer to think of myself as a conservative radical: conservative about preserving the principles of a good society but radical about reforming the institutions required to preserve them in a world of change.

I live near Sevenoaks with my wife, three sons, two dogs and one cat, with cows and sheep for neighbours.

11: WELFARE BY CHOICE

ARTHUR SELDON *reviews the state welfare services, which take a fifth of total national income, and argues that they cannot provide services efficiently or match the varying needs or preferences of individuals. He shows how thinking on the social services is changing in response to social and economic developments. And he concludes with suggestions for refashioning the social services by transferring them increasingly from state control to private choice.*

CAN our economy grow faster? Are our moral standards weakening? These are the dominant issues of our day. They fill our newspapers, television screens, paperbacks, political manifestos, church sermons. What bearing have they on our social welfare policy, and what bearing has it on them?

Recent thinking on the social services sees them as an umbrella to shelter everyone against the storms of unemployment, sickness, old age. If there was ever any doubt about the influence of private ideas on public policy the development of the social services can leave none. The major intellectual philosophies that have shaped them (and influenced politicians) are represented by three very different kinds of thinkers: Keynes, Beveridge, Titmuss. Keynes, the most fertile economist of our time, was thought by many of his followers to have destroyed the classical theory of individual spontaneity and to have replaced it by a new concept of government foresight and wisdom that would maintain full employment at all costs, in all circumstances and in all parts of the country. The warnings he uttered in his last years against forgetting the value of a social system in which initiative was dispersed were ignored by economists who welcomed the increasing domain of the state on principle.

Beveridge dreamed of a world for the 1950s that would solve the problems of the 1930s. He too had regrets : he deplored the inflation that politicians could not resist, and the weakening of voluntary action that the state action he recommended made inevitable; but no-one listened.

Professor R. M. Titmuss evolved the 'badge of citizenship' for everyone to mark the sharing of communal services : its origin was the sense of solidarity formed by wartime evacuation emergencies, improvised schooling, makeshift medical services, the public provision of pensions for grandparents, rent tribunals for parents, orange-juice for grandchildren. All this was to form the blue-print for a post-war society in which fellowship would abolish conflict and state benefaction replace commercial self-seeking.

Early after the war Professor (Lord) Robbins, who had a large hand in running the war economy, warned against the totalitarian effects of 'the mystic joys of tribal unity' urged by paternalists. But post-war governments proceeded to inaugurate the millenium. They gave us bureaucratic education with little room for the individual preferences of parents; a health service that put free dentures before new hospitals and weakened the trust between doctor and patient; housing policy that miraculously combined over-housing with over-crowding; pensions that have made a mockery of insurance. All together they have aggrandised the state, shrunken the individual, enmeshed welfare with national finances and party politics, denied administrative and political talent to indispensable public services, and intensified dependence on the state.

Welfare and wealth

National income is £25,000 million. Individuals are made, by taxes, rates and the poll tax called social insurance, to yield some £5000 million for centralised compulsory state welfare : a fifth of the national wealth. State education costs over £1000 million, public authority housing £500 million, the National Health Service nearly £1000 million, the state pensions another £1000 million.

They may raise national output by improving education, health and living conditions; but the case for them as 'investment in humanity' has been over-stated since to a large extent they use manpower and capital for consumption. We simply do not know how efficiently they are run. We do not even know enough of their costs to be able to judge their methods or the people who run them. When the Ministry of Health was asked recently for the cost of the National Health Service or parts of it for men, women and children per head, it replied that it simply had not worked out the figures. For a service spending nearly £1000 million such ignorance is hardly likely to strengthen confidence in its managers. Many of the costs are administrative overheads which cannot easily be 'imputed' to individual patients, beds or hospitals; but this in itself is a fundamental criticism of state services – they have to be so big that they cannot see what is going on.

The state services are the sole, or dominant, buyer in Britain of the services of doctors, nurses, teachers and of the products of numerous firms. It is hardly likely, except by accident, to pay salaries or prices that precisely represent the maximum value they could contribute to the economy in other uses. The consumer of state welfare services has almost no say in how much of them he is freely prepared to pay for, except at General Elections in which his judgement on state welfare is mixed up with his judgement on numerous other aspects of government and politicians. The decisions are taken supposedly for his good by administrators and officials on the job, and we cannot tell whether too little or too much of the nation's resources are going into them, and therefore whether too little or too much is going into other uses in which they might do more public good.

Probably too little of our national resources have been going into welfare, precisely because we are being compelled to buy it from the state; if we could buy to suit individual tastes we might buy more. In the USA, where health services are mostly private, total expenditure has been rising faster than in Britain. In countries, such as Germany and Italy, where state pensions have developed most, private services have grown least. Continuing state welfare on a large scale has meant less welfare in total than people would otherwise have chosen.

Through the welfare services the state and its local organs influence the whole economy. About a million people work directly for the state in education and many more in health services alone; there are numerous civil servants in White-hall and local government officials in every town; indirectly many more millions 'work for the state' by selling it services or products. They are largely at the mercy of the state as a buyer. There is a small private sector of public and prepara-tory schools – perhaps 5 per cent of total education, a much larger sector in housing – perhaps 50 per cent, a tiny sector in health services – one per cent or less, and a sizeable sector in pensions – perhaps 30 or 40 per cent. If doctors or nurses are dissatisfied with the terms offered by the state they can emigrate, as Dr John Seale has shown in the *British Medical Journal* many have done to North America and other coun-tries; and if British firms are dissatisfied with the state's terms they may be able to export. But the state remains the dominant buyer; and the salaries or prices it pays are not decided solely by their worth to the community but by political influences, ranging from well-intentioned but in-accurate political judgements of future needs (doctors, teach-ers, scientists, laboratories, colleges) to narrow party interests.

We do not know whether private education, health ser-vices, housing or pensions would be more efficient than the state because there is no free choice. The family that prefers the private service must pay for the state service it does not use. There is a counter-weight in the tax rebate on life assurance policies for education and pensions and on the interest on mortgages or other loans for housing, but not for health services. Choice is confused and the consumer is frustrated.

What does the state fear? If its services were better than

private services people would prefer them; if not, there is no reason for refusing the people something better. There are two good reasons for supposing that private services would often be more efficient. First, they would have the spur of competition from other private services and from the state. Second, if a choice were offered and some people preferred private services, it would be possible eventually to reduce taxation, and the resulting relief in the pressure on incentives would raise individual effort and output.

The old fallacies

How can free choice be introduced into welfare? The first requirement is to discard the old thinking that has stood in the way since the end of the war. We are witnessing five major retreats by social scientists who argued that the way ahead lay with the state.

The case for 'public control' of the welfare services has long been urged on the general ground that only the public official would be concerned for the public interest and accountable to public control. Private commercial suppliers of welfare or other services were concerned only to make a profit; the consumer was at their mercy; and there was no way of controlling them. Public officials would put the public first; they would give the best possible service; they would be answerable to Parliament which would see to it that 'the public interest' was served.

These hopes are being dashed because they rest on wishful thinking about human nature and ignorance of the working of large institutions. To make a man a public official is not to make him a public benefactor. If large-scale welfare organisations in education or health are to work efficiently, or at all, they cannot be subjected to daily questioning by politicians concerned for party advantage. The national services multiply on an elephantine scale the growing disadvantages of over-centralisation, rigidities and remote control of large-scale management. And the consumer feels no sense of control over (or personal ownership of) state education, the National Health Service, council housing or state pensions. He does not even know how much he pays for them. He tends to regard them like tap water, not worth a thought.

Another obstacle has been the bogey of 'commercialism'. Commercialism has its defects : they are clear enough in poor schools, nursing homes and housing; but these defects could be removed by more vigorous competition or state standards and inspection. The only alternative to commercial control is political control, the defects of which are more difficult to remove. It is not easily disciplined by Parliament, the cockpit of conflicting ideologies and interests in which (except in war-time) 'the public interest' emerges barely recognisable. The pleas by doctors, teachers, actuaries and others that education, health, housing or pensions be 'taken out of politics' suggests little trust in control by politicians.

It is perhaps the confusion about the meaning and measurement of poverty that has done most damage to social policy since the end of the war. Professor Titmuss, Professor Peter Townsend, Dr Brian Abel-Smith and others have erected a concept of poverty that produces strange conclusions. Some have spoken with fine moral fervour of 'the submerged tenth' (five million people) or even 'the submerged fifth' (ten million) and have created the impression that the problem of poverty is no less than it was before the war. This notion can be made to seem plausible, and even supported by statistics, if it is defined as poverty relatively to the standard of living in the community as a whole. A community that is becoming more prosperous can then have a growing problem of 'poverty', even though living standards are rising in all income groups. In that sense every community, capitalist and communist, American and Russian, Polish and Polynesian has its submerged fifth or tenth, or fiftieth. A poor country can have a less troublesome problem of poverty than a rich country. Poverty becomes perpetual. The richer we become the more the poor are with us. Whatever it means, and however it is measured, the 'poverty' of the minority is then made the argument for state services for *everyone*. This *non sequitur* has had a long run.

The confusion on poverty has in reality been a discussion of equality. And the tragic irony is that the concern for equality has been indulged at the expense of humanity. Social benefits, it has been argued, must be free, equal, compulsory and permanent. No-one may have more than anyone else. So for years two or three million retirement pensioners living only or mainly on their pensions could not have higher benefits because all five or six million pensioners had to have more. Benefits, grants, allowances to the sick, the unemployed, the widowed with little other income could not be raised because *all* the sick, *all* the unemployed and *all* the widowed would have to be given more. Have we built a humane society?

The morality of state welfare

The case for equal benefits has indeed been inhuman and immoral. It has sacrificed the needy to the creed of equality. The advocates of equality cannot pose both as uncompromising advocates of the creed and compassionate champions of the poor.

State welfare encourages the notion that 'the state' should provide, not the family or individuals; it has thus impoverished us by inciting us to beggar and demean one another. Doctors are mis-used for trifling ailments. Council houses are occupied by tenants who demand garages. Children who can support their parents throw them on the state – in hospitals that become hostels. Students who demand higher grants to avoid dependence on their parents see nothing wrong in depending on other students' parents. Politicians who tell pensioners that a means test implies dependence on their children see no wrong in keeping them dependent on other pensioners' children. We have all become accustomed to taking money – allowances, grants, 'insurance' benefits, pensions – we do not need (and have probably not paid for). But a society in which we are allowed or encouraged to get as much as we can from one another does not foster self-respect, morality or integrity.

State welfare has created 'topsy-turvey' scales of values. It is considered proper to spend money on the pleasurable – clothes, drinking, smoking, amusements, holidays – but not on the essential. A man who spends on education is accused of buying privilege, but he is 'with it' if he spends lavishly on record-players, cars, a fortnight in Spain. Since private spending on welfare is socially ostracised and consumption socially approved, is it any wonder that so much advertising and productive resources are diverted from welfare to consumption?

Not least, 'free' state welfare has invaded the province of the individual spirit. It deprives us of individual decision, impairs the will to assert individuality, degrades us to the level of supplicants who must ask for what we get though we increasingly pay for it.

In contrast to Professor Titmuss's 'badge of citizenship' we might conceive of a personal 'declaration of independence' by the man who does not accept social benefits he does not need. How many do not draw pension benefits, family allowances or other grants? The 'declaration of independence' would do more than the 'badge of citizenship' for personal choice, freedom and dignity. And it would be a faster way to reduce taxation than any Chancellor has yet found.

The conflict between equality and humanity could not be denied much longer. Fifteen years after the war Professor Titmuss generously confessed error in *The Irresponsible Society*:

> Many of us must ... now admit that we put too much faith in the 1940s in the concept of universality as applied to social security. Mistakenly, it was linked with economic egalitarianism. Those who have benefited most are those who have needed it least.

It took another three years for the lesson to be learned. In October of 1963 some Young Fabians told their elders that 'it would be utterly naïve' to suppose the basic pension could be raised enough to take most pensioners off National Assistance:

There is no other solution [than some] kind of means test.

Two months later, after years of castigation of the means test, the Labour Party took up a device some of us have been urging for several years, an income code as an automatic indicator of entitlement to assistance. Soon after the Conservatives – as usual – followed suit. The intellectual case for rigid equality had collapsed.

The economic, social and humanitarian case for giving social benefits according to need had invariably been met by the objection that it was 'politically impossible'. The assumption – by politicians of all parties – was that there was a near-universal desire for growing universal social benefits. Yet no post-war government has done anything – even through its own research unit, the Social Survey of the Central Office of Information – to see whether it was right. Political parties, which talk knowingly about 'what the people want', have not used much of their funds to find out. Yet private research suggests that governments and politicians are wrong. In 1960 Research Services found for *Socialist Commentary* that 40 per cent of a representative sample of 724 people aged 18 and over preferred not to pay more taxes for more social benefits. In April–May, 1963, a survey by Mass-Observation for the Institute of Economic Affairs found that 20 per cent of a sample 2005 male married heads of households of working age favoured concentrating state education on people in need and a further 27 per cent favoured individual contracting out (total 47 per cent); for the National Health Service the figures were 24 and 33 per cent (total 57 per cent); for state pensions 22 and 34 per cent (total 56 per cent). Where is the universal demand for universal state welfare? Who have misled the politicians?

The latest capitulation has been signalled by Dr Brian Abel-Smith in a piece of courageous writing, *Freedom in the Welfare State*, that marks a climacteric in the intellectual debate on welfare. Hitherto we have been led to believe that once public control was established all would be well. Dr Abel-Smith now concedes the case of what he calls 'the liberal economist' that without consumer choice all is far from well in the state services, that only *the power to withdraw custom* will ensure that the services are run for the good of the consumer.

> 'When shortages of staff generate rudeness from public servants, the customer is seldom in a position to take his custom elsewhere.'
> 'We have to get rid of the autocratic frame of mind of some civil servants, local government officers and councillors – even Labour councillors.'
> '. . . people should be allowed to make their own choices . . .'

And he sees the next step clearly : that if the individual is to exercise choice he must be helped by cash and not in kind by state services supplied by state officials in state buildings.

What is this but the case for choice in free markets that 'liberal economists' take in with their first reading of Adam Smith? 'Customer', 'custom' – this is the language of the philistine commercial market. The failure to understand the function of markets has created the horror of commerce and the incapacity to use competition and the profit motive to serve the consumer in welfare as much as it has done in consumption goods or capital investment. Dr Abel-Smith still does not see that free markets provide the only institutional environment in which choice can be exerted *effectively* because they offer *alternatives*. Monopolies respond sluggishly to complainants whose custom they cannot lose. The only way to make state education, health and other services better is to make it possible for parents and patients to take their custom elsewhere.

The principles of state action

What has gone wrong in the welfare services? We have spent years building an enormous structure of state provision by piling the 'administratively practicable' on to the 'politically possible'. We are so obsessed with patching up the past that we are frustrating the future. We are told by politicians and administrators that we must be 'practical';

we must devise policies that are 'politically possible'. But we are preparing for the 1970s and 1980s; education is teaching a demand for individuality; at 4 per cent a year incomes will double by 1982. We should not be persuaded into short-term 'practical' steps that are often short-sighted and lead us farther away from our long-term goal. It is time we asked where we are going. What are we really aiming at? What principles do we want to apply? What should the state do and what should individuals insist on being left to do for themselves?

Adam Smith in 1776 in *The Wealth of Nations* said :

> The sovereign has . . . the duty of erecting and maintaining certain public works and certain public institutions which it never can be for the interest of any individual or small group of individuals, to erect and maintain: because the profit could never repay the expense . . . though it may frequently do much more than repay it to a great society.

Some 80 years later Abraham Lincoln said the state should

> do for the people what needs to be done, but which they cannot, by individual effort, do at all, or do as well for themselves.

In 1932 J. M. Keynes restated the classical principle in strangely similar language :

> The important thing for government to do is not to do things which individuals are doing already, and to do them a little better or a little worse: but to do those things which at present are not done at all.

What individuals are doing for themselves is the outcome of what they have been accustomed or brought up to do. For 60 years or more the mass of the people have not chosen schools; for 50 years they have contributed compulsorily to the national health services; and for 40 years to the state pension. Millions have never known the art of choice. The state should leave to individuals not only what they *are* doing but also *what they could be allowed, educated or encouraged to do.*

The creation of choice

Six steps to choice in welfare are now socially, economically and politically possible.

First, people with low incomes should receive generous cash money grants or vouchers to enable them to assert themselves in the market place by exerting a choice between state and private welfare services. Poverty has never provided a reason for state provision of a service in kind. If some people have incomes too low to enable them to buy the education, the health services, the housing, the pensions considered desirable, the solution is not 'free' state services but cash to enable them to indicate their choices between competing suppliers. Assistance with money has two advantages; the consumer would learn, by choosing, to choose better : the faculty of choice is stifled if it is never used; and the supplier would have an incentive to improve : the headmaster of a private school in competition with others has more to gain – or less to lose – by constant improvement than the headmaster of a state school protected by zoning.

If people are judged incapable of making sensible choices they can be given vouchers that can be used to pay only for education, health services (through fees or insurance), housing or pensions.

There would remain some people who might have to be given help in kind. But they would account for a small fraction of the enormous structure of state services we have created for people who increasingly do more for themselves.

Second, in an age of increasing equality of income it is wasteful to redistribute income through the state by massive taxes and massive grants or free services; the better way is to redistribute it through the family. There could be a new advance to family endowment by encouraging sisters, brothers, grandchildren, nephews, nieces and others to support less-well-off relatives by extending the system of dependents' allowances. The allowance is now a maxium of £75, so that if two sons support an ailing father one deducts, say, £40 and the other £35 from taxable income. The allowance should be increased to £150 or even more; and each person should be able to give an allowance to a needy sister or other relative if he is able. The family would be helped because the giver would pay less tax at his higher rate and the receiver would pay at his lower rate.

We might even redistribute income privately by allowing people to help others outside the family.

Third, the state services would be confined to people in need by excluding others as their incomes rise, or by allowing individuals to contract out by tax rebates on the costs of private services, by vouchers or excusing taxes.

Contracting out in groups has been shown to be practicable in pensions. Individual contracting out might be more inconvenient. But systems are made for people, not people for systems. There is no difference *in principle* between contracting out from pensions, education or health services. The reason why it is not allowed in education or health services is what the pragmatist would call 'practical politics' : that nearly 11 million people with votes are accumulating private occupational pensions while only $1\frac{1}{2}$ million are insuring for private health services and only half a million families or so have children at private schools.

Fourth, until rising incomes gradually teach the value of spending money on good teachers and doctors and of saving money to accumulate income in retirement, it may be desirable for the law to require minimum expenditure on them. Parents are required to educate children to stated standards, at school or at home. In health minimum insurance could be required, as with third party motor insurance. In pensions it may be necessary only to give larger tax rebates on contributions to or premiums on life assurance policies which yield a pension. If they fail to generate enough voluntary saving to avoid dependence on the community in retirement, it may be desirable to require a stated proportion of income to be saved, defining it in terms of amount saved or retirement income accumulated.

Fifth, in time – perhaps 20 years – the expansion of private welfare would make it possible to denationalise much of compulsory state welfare. People under 45 today have not lived through general or prolonged unemployment, and they have mostly earned good pay. By 1985 no new pensioner would have known poverty. Schools could be sold in stages to private individuals, partnerships, companies or trusts. Doctors' private lists would increasingly replace NHS lists : their income would come from patients' fees rather than from the NHS. Hospitals would make more rooms, facilities and staff available for private patients. The National Insurance Fund, a pitiable £1,000 million compared with the capital of £25,000 million required to pay national insurance benefits, could be returned to national insurance contributors in cash or as a transfer value to life assurance on other private pension schemes. A Permanent Commission on the Social Services would advise which state services should be run down and which expanded.

Sixth, not least, the government would need to construct a competitive framework for private enterprise. Private welfare is run in large part by dedicated professionals rather than by commercial entrepreneurs. Education is run by scholars, clergymen, Boards of Governors who have forgotten or never known commerce or competition; health services and medical insurance by doctors, dentists, accountants, actuaries, secretaries; life office pension schemes in large part by actuary-managers. The professional and the 'mutual non-profit-making' attitude have inhibited the expansion of private services. There has been little new enterprise, capital or entrepreneurship in the life assurance market, and it may be desirable to overhaul the legal framework to facilitate it. If the three medical insurance organisations, the British United Provident Association, the Hospital Service Plan and the Western Provident Association, are to expand faster – fast enough to deprive politicians of the excuse for expanding state medicine – they will have to recognise that they are in a competitive market, that they must use modern marketing methods, that they may have to build private hospitals if the politicians and administrators obstruct the increasing demand for choice in medicine, and that they will probably

have to enter the capital market and pay current rates of
interest for money to enable them to build. Private schools
will have to concentrate on attracting more pupils by proving
their excellence and reducing their costs rather than be
diverted into appeasing the advocates of state control by proposals for 'integrating' private and state education. The best
defence – politically as well as economically – of the private
sector is to multiply its customers by showing it is better than
the state.

The counter-revolution

Until recently academic thinking on the welfare services
in Britain was cornered by economists, sociologists and political theorists who could see nothing but increasing direction
by the state. Their purpose was basically equality, and they
found little difficulty in devising institutions untrammelled
by the requirements of liberty.

The post-war reaction has come from social scientists who
considered they should study institutions for a society based
on the preservation and development of personal freedoms.
Their spiritual ancestors were the classical economists who
for a century had been dismissed with derision. In the last
ten years the classical teaching has been re-interpreted to
suit the post-war world. In its application to the welfare
services the movement was sparked off in 1953 by Mr Colin
Clark's *Welfare and Taxation*, a private enterprise analysis
of the taxes paid and the social benefits received by households. His finding, that even working men were paying
nearly as much as they received, was greeted with scepticism
and worse. But he was amply vindicated nearly ten years
later when official statistics collected by the Central Statistical Office largely confirmed his findings.

The accompanying table shows the amounts paid in 1962
in tax, rates and social insurance contributions by a family
with two children.

Income of a family with two children in 1962
before and after paying tax and adding social benefits

Original income	Value of benefits received	Amount paid in taxes, rates, social insurance	Increase or decrease in FINAL income	
			increase	*decrease*
£	£	£	£	£
559 to under 676	219	176	43	
676–816	192	213		21
816–988	181	249		68
988–1,196	218	298		80
1,196–1,448	201	330		129
1,448–1,752	206	347		231
1,752 and over	210	490		280

Only the family in the lowest income group with £559 to
£676 a year received more than it paid; the families earning
above £676, roughly £13 a week, paid more than they received. (The average manual earnings of a man in industry
were £15 10s. in 1962, £16 10s. in 1964.) A family with two
children and income in 1962 from £676 to £816 a year
received £192 and paid £213. In short, the net effect of
these to-ings and fro-ings of taxation from the family to the
state and social benefits back from the family to the state
was to leave the family very much where it was. The jour-
neyings were hardly necessary. Another example : a family
with three children and an income from £988 to £1,196
received £326 and paid £313; Shakespeare might have
called it 'much ado about nothing'. Even where the family
is left much better (or worse) off, it seems hardly sensible to
raise huge sums in taxes and pay vast proportions of them –
60 or 70 per cent – back in kind or cash.

The whole machinery of the welfare state is thus becoming to a large extent a vast engine for carrying coals to Newcastle. Moreover, in the process it burns up between £100
million and £200 million worth of labour and capital, part
of which could be better used in providing welfare. Since
1953 further writings by Mr Clark, Mr Walter Hagenbach,
Professor John and Mrs Sylvia Jewkes, Professor Michael
Fogarty, Dr A. R. Prest, Dr D. S. Lees, Professor A. T.

Peacock, Professor Jack Wiseman, A. R. Ilersic and others have made the case for indiscriminate expansion of state welfare look very weak.

National economic expansion can best be helped by putting welfare by stages into the market where the consumer will rule instead of the politician, and where he will be able to command all the resources that can respond to his demands rather than only those that can be organised by officials. Conversely, the welfare services will develop best the more efficient the economy. The market creates more wealth than state direction because it mobilises the resources and talents of every individual, who can use knowledge that is beyond the capacity of officials or planners to organize or even envisage. It makes planners, entrepreneurs, managers, and economisers of us all. It benefits society, widens choice, raises living standards because it emancipates the individual by replacing the badge of citizenship with a declaration of independence.

E. G. WEST

I was born in 1922 in Goldthorpe and went to a co-educational grammar school after failing the then 'eleven plus' at the first attempt. My parents attribute this setback to the antics of local education officials who made me change my school to suit their 'zoning'. We moved to Exeter in 1936 where I attended a grammar school for boys, but by the time I had settled down in it my father thought I should get a nice quiet job somewhere. After working for a while in local government offices, I entered Exeter University in 1945 with a government grant. I emerged with a degree in economics and a teacher's diploma. Nervous as a student, I was terrified as a teacher. However, I survived my first post in a secondary school in the Black Country and moved to a technical college in Guildford to teach economics. In 1956 I went to teach at the Oxford College of Technology where a few staunch colleagues helped me launch a strenuous full-time London University degree course in 1958. Apart from this history, experience as a taxpayer has given me a vested interest in educational reform.

In 1962 I left Oxford and local authority education to become Lecturer at the University of Newcastle upon Tyne. Following articles on monopoly legislation, the history of economic thought, the economics of education and the problem of local unemployment, I am writing a book on the economics of education for the Institute of Economic Affairs.

12: PARENTS' CHOICE IN EDUCATION

E. G. WEST *attacks the fashionable notion that education needs increasing state financing and state control. He gives reasons for thinking the opposite: that it would be more progressive, more efficient, and more healthy if it were taken as far as possible from the state and the influence of parents were increased in a system of competing private education.*

THOSE who exert themselves most in pointing to supposed economic failures in our society usually get themselves particularly excited when they get round to education. For here they know that they are always assured of a willing and expectant audience. All men are equally wise about the need for a good education; to assert that we need more of it is to be a good chap in any company. It is only when the more independent persist with the question of *how* education should grow that the irritations begin. Thus Mr John Vaizey in *Encounter*, July 1963, answered his own question of why a trebling of expenditure between 1938 and 1963 had still not begun to transform British society by pointing to the crucial need for more places in higher education, in other words more public expenditure on it. No doubt when this gap is filled such critics will point to deficiencies in other parts of the system. Meanwhile, increased public expenditure on education can always be relied upon to produce at least the discovery of the need for still more public expenditure.

The real failure of our system stems from the very success of these critics in persuading us that the only way to assuage our guilt feelings on education is constantly to resort to the public purse until the proportion of our national income devoted to it places us high in some international league table. The Ministry of Education is triumphant that education's share of the national income is now about 4.9 per cent compared with 3.1 per cent in 1951. But when should we relax? When it is 5 per cent? 10 per cent? 25 per cent? Within the private sector any announcement that total costs have increased meets with the immediate suspicion that inefficiency has probably crept in. It is time we considered this possibility too in state education. For nobody has yet proved that it is impossible to get more education from constant or even declining expenditure. If we rely upon dispersed decision-making in the private sector to keep a downward pressure on costs and an upward pressure on quality, there seems to be no good reason why we should not also attempt to incorporate it where possible in the public sector. That there are, for instance, far more parents than state education administrators suggests the need for a serious investigation into the possibility of reducing the strong predominance of the paid official.

Do officials know better than parents?

It is natural that officials think they always know best. It would be unnatural if education officials ever claimed that the system of instruction they administered was so successful as to turn out people who could judge at least as well as they could. Thus at present it is irritating to them, for instance, that too many of us want schools that are 'streamed' instead of 'unstreamed', or exercise discipline instead of 'free discipline', or are traditional instead of comprehensive. They still insist on over-ruling us even when we remind them that they themselves are divided on all these alternatives. But their biggest irritation occurs when the odd citizen questions the wisdom of that 'great' 1944 Education Act for having turned out to be the most ingenious piece of parental manipulation of all time. It was this Act which empowered the state to protect children from an education unsuitable to their 'age, ability and aptitude', a secret formula known apparently only to Directors of Education. Meanwhile, no doubt, education officials are impatiently waiting the genius in political theory who can explain convincingly why parental judgement is supposed to be so inadequate to choose the 'right' schoolmaster *directly* and yet adequate enough to choose the 'right' government representative to secure the schoolmaster *indirectly*.

Most citizens undoubtedly accept in principle that the state has specially protective duties towards children since they are among the most defenceless of its members. Most would also accept the corollary that in some cases the state has to protect children against negligent parents. But fuzziness begins when the average person tries to conceive of proper machinery for state control. To some theorists the 'state', especially in the educational context, is an abstract father figure beyond all reproach. Even for some to whom 'the state' does manage to manifest itself in real flesh and blood officials and representatives, there is probably still some lingering intuition that these mortals are somehow 'different'. How else can we possibly begin to understand the evolution of the curiously cumbrous apparatus through which the state now attempts to fulfil its educational obligations? But apparent schizophrenia among voters is nothing compared with that of the state. For see how differently it responds to similar duties in different contexts. Protection of a child against starvation and malnutrition is presumably just as important as protection against ignorance. It is difficult to envisage, however, that any government in its anxiety to see that children have minimum standards of food and clothing would pass laws for compulsory and universal eating or increase taxes and rates in order to provide children's food 'free' at local authority kitchens or shops. It is still more difficult to imagine that most people would unquestioningly accept this system, especially if it had developed to the stage where for 'administrative reasons' parents were allocated shops which happened to be nearest to their homes; or that any complaint or desire to change their pre-selected shops should be dealt with by special and semi-judicial enquiry after a formal appointment with the local 'Child Food Officer' or by pressure upon their representatives on the local 'Child Food Committee' or upon their local MP. Yet such measures are typical of English state education as it has evolved by historical accident or administrative expediency.

Parents in revolt

In some quarters, at least, there is a new awareness of all this incongruity. Recently established parent organisations, for instance, are now voicing their discontent. If, with the abolition of resale price maintenance, parents can be given more freedom to buy from the more efficient supplier in retailing, why not in education? Such cumulative murmurings, it seems, have even reached the hustings:

> 'We aim to enlarge the area of individual choice, whether it be the housewife deciding what to buy, the industrialist deciding what to manufacture, *or the parent deciding what sort of education he wants for his children* . . .' (italics supplied)
> Sir Alec Douglas-Home, at Swansea, January 20th, 1964.

It is difficult to know as yet what to make of this pronouncement since it was followed up in the very next week by the announcement of the intention to raise the school-leaving age to 16 – a measure which substantially reduces the choice of many parents who agree with the complaints of their 15-year-olds that they are wasting their time at school. Nevertheless, discussion will continue. On what can the growing criticism be expected to focus its first attention?

Parts of the 1944 Education Act are obviously ripe for reform. Consider for instance Section 76, which was an apparent attempt to see that justice was done, or seen to be done, to the parent:

> . . . as far as is compatible with the provision of efficient instruction and training and the avoidance of unreasonable public expenditure, pupils are to be educated in accordance with the wishes of their parents.

It will be noticed that this provision precludes the parent from making the final[1] judgement about what instruction is 'efficient'. It is not surprising that this section has now become a dead letter. Theoretically the parents' influence could make itself most effective over the choice of school, just as the parents' choice of shop for the child's clothing is effective in encouraging the supply of the most efficient product. In practice the parent has only 'Hobson's choice' as a rule. If, for instance, he does not approve of the primary school allotted to his child because it is of the 'free discipline' variety, and prefers the one with the 'old-fashioned stricter methods' a little further away, there is nothing to stop him voicing his preference. It will not get him far. The parent will usually be met with formidable bureaucratic reasons why his choice cannot be exercised. If the authority cannot prove that the parents' wishes would involve 'unreasonable public expenditure' (Section 76), they can always resort to the old formula that the chosen education does not suit the 'age, ability and aptitude' of the child.

Zoning prevents choice of school

The process which, whatever its purpose, holds back parents from a school which has become noticeably successful and keeps their children in inferior schools is known in official circles as 'zoning'. Educationists approve of 'zoning' on the ground that under free choice it is only the middle-class parents who are quick off the mark to transfer their children to the improving schools. If this is allowed, the 'experts' argue, it will 'tip the social balance' so that there remain predominantly middle-class (good) schools and working-class (bad) schools.

Up to now ordinary folk have been too readily silenced by such slick speculation. But now that people's commercial imagination is being stimulated by the new freedoms in shopping they may soon be able to do a little theorising for themselves. They will see perhaps that competition does not necessarily result in the good getting better and the bad getting worse. On the contrary, the standards of suppliers usually rise, keeping reasonably in step with one another. With really free choice, an initial trickle of children transferring to efficient schools would threaten, in the eyes of the inefficient school directors and staff, to become a tidal wave of mass emigration and so draw public attention to their inefficiency. Automatically the inefficient would be prodded into removing the source of their weakness and to catch up with the efficient. The ability of parents to 'vote with their children's feet' is ultimately the only sure way of getting parental wishes really respected, and it would certainly be more powerful than all the parents' associations put together.

So far, however, the recently established campaign groups of parents seem to be resigned to a policy of pressing for improvements of the state service *within* the present framework, an attitude which involves the assumption that the state should continue to play the predominant part. It will be surprising if these tactics meet with much more success than, say, the representations of Consumer Councils to the nationalised industries. Improvements in the coal industry, for instance, are far more likely to have come from the stimulus of a major competitor such as oil rather than from the meagre representations of consumers on official committees. By contrast, the most solemn inadequacy in state education is the absence of any such powerful competitor. Private schools cannot properly fulfil this role under the present system, since their competitive potential has been crippled by state opponents with the advantage of always being able to dip into public revenues to cover their costs. Incidentally the lack of market discipline on these costs may hide waste, inefficiency or worse. Public revenue replenishments, of course, flow in from compulsory taxes, the yields from which quietly and automatically increase as national income grows.

The only way out of this dilemma is to facilitate the return to a much wider system of fee-paid schools which would use mainly fee revenues to bid for teachers, equipment, buildings. I say a *return* to such a system since most parents *were* paying fees for the privately sponsored education of their children a century ago (a fact rarely taught in social history today). To anticipate the protests against such suggestions it is necessary to review old arguments which attempted to justify the original provision of state schools and see whether they are true today.

State monopoly in education

First, it was claimed that a state school was often needed to offset the tendency of monopoly in one region by a private school. This anti-monopoly argument now stands on its head. The substitution of state monopolies for private ones makes the situation worse, for statutory monopolies more easily entrench themselves. With a private monopoly at least there is a chance that one day it will be challenged by a newcomer. This chance is much less likely under the state system because a monopoly state school can ward off any challenger by using the advantages of public revenues to outbid it. If, for instance, the salaries of state school teachers are paid out of compulsory taxes, then, in the words of Adam Smith in *The Wealth of Nations*, such salaries :

> put the private teachers who would pretend to come into competition with them, in the same state with a merchant who attempts to trade without a bounty in competition with those who trade with a considerable one.

The second argument was that parents cannot make wise choices if left to their own devices because they do not know all the relevant facts. (This paternalistic view is often held by people who send their own children to private schools: are they in favour of a state 'soup kitchen' education only for other people?) Such an argument assumes that the state's choice of the best kind of education is based on unanimous professional advice. But teachers and educationists do not speak with one voice; their advice had swung from one extreme to another in the past. Above all the argument that parents cannot be trusted to avoid bad private schools is *irrelevant*, because all private schools are vetted by the Minister. Indeed, over 60 per cent of private pupils are in

schools recognised by him as efficient. The remainder have
to be registered by the Ministry, which implies that they are
not inefficient.

Third, would the alternative of a free market result in the
rich getting the best, when uniformity of access to schools is
needed for better social cohesion? Put this way, of course,
the argument cannot be held at the same time as the second
one because it makes contradictory assumptions about the
capacity of parents in judging which is best. But it resolves
itself into an objection to *all* the superior educational influences that children have by living in richer homes or in
homes in which parents put education relatively high in
their scale of values. Ultimately this is an attack on richness
are such and should be made openly in proposals for
more progressive taxation. If we decide that we cannot do
without money incentives, then inequality of income has to
be accepted, and no educational purpose is served by trying
to disguise it from children or by protesting, as, for instance,
Elizabeth Young did in *Encounter* that 'the public schools
have a higher pupil-teacher ratio because they are able to
pay their teachers more . . .'.

If we really want equality of opportunity, how is it nobody
ever argues that we should be spending, for instance, about
twenty times more on physically and mentally handicapped
children, or three or four times more on some West Indian
or Pakistani children, than we do on the poorest ones in our
state schools? More important, the state system, far from
achieving social mixing, makes things worse, since working-
class people tend to live in working-class districts so ensuring
that the local primary school takes predominantly working-
class children. Rationing of school places geographically is
the obvious and easiest criterion which presents itself to
official administrators. Arguments in terms of Mr R. H. S.
Crossman's 'educational apartheid' or Mr Vaizey's 'caste
divisions' should be preceded by attempts to solve the apparently inherent contradictions in the state system which is
supposed to put these wrongs right. (Another fact of life is
of course that most people, including many opposed to

private education in principle but who now send their own children to private schools, do not really wish to abolish independent schools anyway.)

Who can pay fees?

Finally, are some parents too poor to pay school fees, or even if they could afford it would not value it sufficiently if left to themselves? This was the way that the classical economist, Nassau Senior, argued for temporary state intervention in the nineteenth century. Even at that time, nevertheless, when education was not compulsory, the Royal Commission on Education of 1861, of which Senior was a member, reported that ninety-five per cent of parents throughout the country were buying *some* education for their children. Their fees were subsidised by endowments and grants from the state, but there seems to have been a lively desire to pay more where specially good tuition was offered. Moreover, Senior openly argued that the poor were themselves most important contributors to the state subsidies since taxation was in those days very regressive, falling heavily on commodities in daily consumption. Although theoretically we cannot today identify which tax pays for which state service, it is useful to keep informing ourselves about the sources of government funds. The £885 million quietly collected on tobacco alone in 1962 was more than the current expenditure of £789 million on education. Taxes on spending, many of which are acknowledged to be regressive, amounted in 1961 to £2759 million or more than two-fifths of all taxation. The net is wide : it includes taxes on petrol, oil, motor vehicles, beer and tobacco, besides stamp duties, import duties and purchase tax. It is hardly surprising that many people are too poor to afford private education.

But let us suppose for a moment that these indirect taxes were drastically reduced. Should we suppose that after nearly a century of state education the ordinary person would go out and squander the balance? And supposing the state decided to contract slowly out of education, as it would be forced to do if its indirect tax revenues were cut, so that it could no longer supply 'free' education : why should we not presume that ordinary people would devote much of their balance to the purchase of education for their children? They vote for their own money to be spent on education *in public*, judging by its prominence in election manifestos, why do we assume so readily that they would not spend it directly *in private*? One thing could be certain, the voice of the parent would receive far more respect once he was restored to a more central position in matters of the purse. And the resulting improvements in efficiency would be shared even by those who would voluntarily spend least of all on their children.

Vouchers for education

Attempts to strengthen the private sector have so far not been very successful. It is unfortunate, for instance, that proposals for state bursaries to enable children of poor parents to stand a chance of entering the public schools (on the lines of the Fleming Report) have never amounted to much. Whilst the government has lacked enthusiasm on this kind of suggestion, the local authorities have been more interested in the development of their own schools. A more modest plan which may stand a sporting political chance in view of the alarm over the impending large shortage of primary school teachers would be to explore the possibility of enabling *some* parents to do a deal with the government at the very commencement of their children's education. Supposing the central and local government has to be ready to spend £60 per annum for the schooling of a child entering school at 5 years old. If this money were simply handed to the parent in the form of a voucher[1] so that it was earmarked for education, the government would be relieved of one more headache. There are several technical ways of doing this – an extra coupon in the family allowance book, for instance.

[1] The proposal for education vouchers is worked out by Professors A. T. Peacock and Jack Wiseman in *Education for Democrats*, Hobart Paper 25, Institute of Economic Affairs, 1964.

It will, of course, be objected that this measure would give money to rich parents who would have sent their child to an independent school anyway and that, therefore, the government would be involved in a net increase in its payments from a fixed revenue. But this objection refers to inequality of income generally, so it can be treated in the context of taxation as a whole. A second criticism might be that although the immediate pressure on the most congested state schools would be eased, the increase in spending in the private sector would either simply increase the size of the queues already waiting to get into the private schools, or, if places were found, there would be more teachers in private schools and less in the state system. But there is evidence to show that not all local authorities are prepared to staff the schools up to the limit of the available supply of teachers. This is especially so at a time of heavy pressure to keep the rates down after the shock of revaluation. Again, independent schools, not being confined to rigid restrictions such as age limits or regional quota systems, can draw upon a wider range of people to staff them. In 1963 the State recruited 30,000 new teachers and fatalistically 'lost' 25,000. No doubt the independent schools could find more imaginative ways of cashing in on this pool of expensively trained but shockingly wasted talent if they were confronted with many newly liberated parent customers flourishing their vouchers at their doors. Further, if parents were given £60 vouchers spendable on schooling, many of them would begin to add to it marginal amounts so boosting the net effective demand for education. The added expenditure would result in a net increase in the recruitment of school teachers through the attraction of higher salaries. If these suggestions are too revolutionary for political acceptance at the moment, at least there would be some virtue in a pilot experiment in a county or borough. It would reveal the extent of the demand for a wider choice of school and the other possibilities about staffing mentioned above.

The family versus the expert

It has been unnecessary to become involved in the deeper philosophical question whether a parent should have the right to *absolute* control over his child. In a free society no one individual, whether parent or state official, should have absolute power over another. The function of supervising a child is such a delicate personal matter that it is probably best to visualise it undogmatically in the form of a balance of influence between one individual, the parent, who by nature is closer to the child and therefore has the best opportunity for gaining a comprehensive knowledge of its needs, and other individuals, perhaps appointed by the state, who can at least check that the child is not being neglected. But generally, if the family is regarded as a desirable institution, the onus should be upon those who wish to interfere with it. That parents will make mistakes is not a sufficient argument for placing them under the present degree of constraint. It has to be shown not only that they will fail to learn from their mistakes but also that the mistakes made by state representatives will not be bigger still. But whatever happens we must not allow the 'expert' to be the only judge of mistakes. For the moment we do, we hand over gratuitous support to those, such as Mr Vaizey, who tells us in his *Economics of Education* that reliance on the family as the basic unit of society 'is not one that would readily stand up to sociological analysis', and that education can be regarded as 'an intervention to save the individual from the family'. Since when did we start drifting into a 1984 world in which sociologists not only received their salaries from us via compulsory taxation but made our value judgements for us as well?

More choice would increase expenditure on education

The present method of state intervention in education is not divinely inspired. The attitude is all too common that private schools are 'the ones that got away' and that a method should be devised to 'integrate' them somehow into the public service. Why should we not equally consider the opposite possibility : whether states schools should be 'integrated' into the *private* system, especially where it can be shown to be superior? The state would still be accepting its major responsibility to supervise the quality and quantity of education. There is never any need for a government to provide the schooling of children if the parents would do it anyway. Local experiments are continually needed to see what parents would do with fuller responsibility and given *quid pro quo* tax reductions, or at least money vouchers. If the experiments showed that parents could still not exercise sufficient responsibility, then something would be very much wrong with the state schools that produced them. If, on the other hand, the parents accepted their new powers with good sense, then a wider choice of schools would result. The consequent availability of alternatives to state schools would give the parent more power *vis a vis* local administrators and greater competition and flexibility would result. There is little risk of a parent making a positively bad choice of school since the whole of the private school sector is now underpinned by Ministry inspection and registration.

> Parents have one great superiority over the Government or the administrators. Their faults are mainly the corrigible faults of ignorance, not of apathy and prejudice. . . . They have the wish to arrive at a true conclusion, the data are before them, they must be the judges in the last resort, why should we shrink from making them judges at once?

Such were the words of Sir Robert Lowe on the eve of the revolutionary Education Act of 1870. Some may not care for his opinion, but no one could dispute the framework of alternatives in which it was expressed.

Robbins and higher education

But so accustomed have we become to the idea of the government spending our own money for us on the education of our own children that many do not seem to notice how the state juggernaut is now lurching its way into *higher* education too. The debate about the Robbins Report did not centre on the question whether the proposed substantial increase of expenditure from £200 million to £750 million by 1980 should be handled mainly by the government or by individuals and families. The participants in this debate argued rather about who was to be the overlord; should we have one or two ministers? Yet the Robbins Report justified this vast increase of public expenditure on the grounds that:

'To spend more on higher education would almost certainly be the average family's individual response.' (Report, page 208.)

In other words, if the state *reduced* taxation and played a smaller part in higher education, families would buy higher education themselves. And this does not mean only rich families, for remember the vast amount of regressive indirect taxation required – at the 1964 budget it was taxes on beer and tobacco to which the Chancellor resorted in order to find the money for new public expenditure programmes. If people would spend the money on education anyway, why the need for the state to spend it for them via its cumbersome bureaucratic machinery?

If more freedom were restored to the family by tax reduction, the question whether there should be one or two ministers would settle itself more easily. For in that case there would be *thousands* of ministers of education, as many in fact as there are heads of households. If we are to accept with such fatalism the tendency of our tax system to monopolise the sources of educational finance, then the government will inevitably intervene in education more and more. The reverse policy, that of reducing taxation, is the only way in which we can secure that the control of education is shared by all and not confined to academics and government administrators.

Many writers on education and many educationists tell us that increased choice in education is only possible if we have *more* education. The argument here is the converse, that *we can have more education in the end only if we have increased choice.* Parents must not be put off with the argument that choice is impossible because of shortages. For choices in education are in fact made every day when new appointments are being negotiated, new curricula introduced new schools built. These choices need not be the monopoly of officials if the parent's wishes are taken into fuller account by allowing him the freedom not only to vote periodically at the ballot box but also to choose directly from the day-to-day supply. Grown-up people in an affluent society should demand nothing less, especially if they wish their children to enjoy still greater affluence in the future.

ALAN BARKER

I was born in 1923 and educated at Rossall School. After war service in the Royal Artillery in North-West Europe (wounded 1944) I took up a history scholarship to Jesus College, Cambridge, and received my BA in 1946. From 1947 to 1953 I was an assistant master at Eton, taught at Queens' College, Cambridge, as Director of Studies in history till 1955, spent a year at Yale as a Commonwealth Fellow, before returning to the playing fields of Eton, that won the war at Waterloo.

I live in Cambridge, where I have been Headmaster of The Leys School since 1958 and a County Councillor since 1959. As a public school headmaster I am one of Mr Anthony Sampson's 'awesome and formidable men . . . wielding immense power, maintaining exact if sometimes irrelevant standards . . . figures of massive integrity and moral uprightness'. My way of life, 'combines monasticism with worldly ambition'. I am 'insulated against the outside world, living in the midst of the country surrounded by inferiors both masters and boys.'

My hobbies are bridge, golf and American History. I've written a book on the American Civil War and two text books on English History. At present I am a member of the Committee of the Headmasters' Conference.

13: INDEPENDENCE AND THE PUBLIC SCHOOLS

ALAN BARKER examines the criticisms of public schools and replies that in spite of their drawbacks they should be valued and more people encouraged to use them as centres of independence in education where family decisions count for more than state influence.

'WHAT we need is a single system of Schools, which would include all our children, not just most, with their teachers paid what they need in salary and amenities to assure them dignity and independence.' So Elizabeth Young concluded her attack on the public schools in *Encounter* (July 1963). It revealed the ambivalence shown by most critics of the public school system : a recognition of the advantages of smaller classes, good facilities and a certain leisure for the educational process combined with the charges which make the public schools the scapegoats for all the ills to which our society is heir. This latter theme has been present in other *Encounter* writings as when one writer relates homosexuality to our lagging national productivity; once more 'that remarkable anachronism the English public school' is held responsible. So much heat is generated by this anachronism that a dispassionate analysis is impossible. Little point would be served by examining the charges one by one; our opponents are not open to conviction. They hold with fanaticism the faith that the world and human nature can be reformed by administrative order.

Analysis and prejudice

There is a considerable literature about public schools apart from the fiction and memoirs written by discontented alumni who recognise that scandal is more profitable than truth. Many people criticise their upbringing on reflection in later life, but a Simon Raven or a David Benedictus speak only for the discontented few to whom all authority is suspect and all established institutions are perverse and obsolete. For those wishing to understand something of the public schools today, the starting point must be the Fleming Report. It contains the best short study of the origin of public schools. Besides this two books with the same title : *The Public Schools and the Future*, the first written by Donald Hughes in 1944 and the second by John Dancy in 1963, give the best informed, most balanced and imaginative assessment of what these schools offer and can offer to our society.

Of course, as two public school Headmasters, both Hughes and Dancy have a recognised point of view and make no effort to disguise it. This is in striking contrast to the recent supplement *The Public Schools* produced by the recently founded Advisory Centre for Education in Cambridge. This Centre claims to be an independent research institution and in its supplement sought 'to inject a little objective information into the mass of opinion and speculation surrounding any discussion of the public schools.' Unfortunately its objectivity was questionable, its information superficial and its so-called 'research' both elementary and statistically unsound. Whatever its declared pretensions of objectivity ACE is quite clearly a pressure group. Beneath its appearance of detachment the prejudices and opinions of its managers are plain from the tone and approach of most of the articles in its magazine *Where*? Their dislike of all forms of independence in education is evident. I have no doubt that the intention of ACE's Director, Mr Brian Jackson, is to assist in the abolition of independent schools and to direct change within the maintained system on preconceived lines. He is fully entitled to work for these aims but not, I should have thought, through ACE which claims to be unprejudiced. It is alarming that a body of this kind is too often accepted at its face value by the general public. It should be recognised for what it is: a pressure group of *pronounced prejudices* and opinions, not a research body of independent and objective character. The supplement on public schools revealed the truth of this quite plainly.

The attack on independence

Much more important, however, than the specific charges against public schools is the general attack on independence in education implied by Mrs Young and Mr John Vaizey. In the whole independent sector of education the public schools are merely the best known but not the largest part. For parents this independent sector permits a definite freedom of choice. The range of choice is wide : from local day schools to country boarding schools; from individual music lessons to dancing, secretarial and correspondence schools. The range of fees is equally wide from less than £60 to over £500 a year for schools, to a few guineas for a course of music or secretarial lessons. Obviously only a very limited number of parents can exercise a choice at the top end of the fee scale, but the solution is to extend the ability of parents to choose, rather than to prohibit it altogether as many critics would wish. I shall examine this problem later.

The range of choice in the independent sector is wide also in the variety of schools available. There are boarding schools and day schools and some which are both : large, small, Anglican, Methodist, Catholic, Quaker and undenominational; progressive, traditional, co-educational, and single sex schools. Some cater for particular aptitudes and interests in their pupils.

This range and variety can be provided only by independence. 'A single system of schools' demanded by Mrs Young under the combined control of the Department of Education and local authorities cannot provide it. Anyone who has sat on a Local Education Committee (as I have) knows of the limitations which a dependent system involves, however enlightened the administration. Top-heavy governing bodies with too many councillors on them, financial control from the centre which allows the headmaster no discretionary fund, a quota system which rations the supply of teachers, a building programme which forces every school into a queue – these are merely typical examples of the kind of limitation imposed. It is sometimes surprising that the maintained system produces such excellent results in the face of these difficulties. They may not continue to do so when the present generation of teachers appointed in the 1930s reach retirement, as they will in the next decade.

Dangers of political control

The hope that the taxpayer or ratepayer (or both) will be prepared to find the financial resources to improve salaries and amenities in schools thus assuring to the teacher 'dignity and independence' is a vain one. Independence of what and dignity in what sense? No one can believe that *increased* finance from public authorities will lead to *less* dependence of the maintained schools on local and central control. And dignity is related to independence. What is remarkable in the maintained schools is the way in which teachers have retained their dignity, although the threatened strikes of two years ago suggested the inherent difficulty. No single system of schools provided and financed by the state can, in fact, ensure dignity and independence for the teacher. It is asking too much of human nature that the piper who pays should not call the tune. The taxpayer and the ratepayer will not accept exceptional expenditure for one type of child or school unless it is for the disabled or abnormal. This refusal more than anything else supports the demand to get rid of the tripartite *system* of grammar, technical and secondary modern schools, and replace it by comprehensive schools. There are, indeed, educational and social reasons for this demand but the financial reasons are seldom loudly voiced.

The trouble about so many of the current arguments on educational administration is that they start from theory rather than practice. It is here that the history of the public schools provides a telling example. Essentially they were created in the 19th Century by private enterprise to meet the demands of an industrial age. The vast majority of public schools were founded or re-modelled in that century. Eton alone, perhaps, was the exception, then as in many ways she is today. These schools grew out of a demand for secondary education and in time they have modified themselves to meet it while imposing standards of their own. These standards have been re-interpreted periodically but throughout their history the three essential features of the so called 'public schools' have been their independence, their boarding character and their religious foundation. They have met a demand which, whatever may be said about 'snob' reasons, is based on family choice.

Family responsibility

When the state in 1902 began to concern itself with secondary education it was not family choice but the ability of the child which counted, and even in 1944, when secondary education was made compulsory for all, the choice was restricted by the principles of *tripartite* selection. Moreover from 1944 the state abandoned the principle of fee paying in its schools, thus creating a gulf between private and state schools which has widened with bitterness and envy in the past 20 years. So wide is this gulf that the payment of fees by a family is now held to be anti-social! Mrs Young argues that 'one need not take very seriously the argument that a comprehensive fee-less system is an intolerable infringement of an Englishman's freedom to spend his money as he likes'. I – and I have no doubt many others – do take this argument seriously, since there are very strong reasons for the belief that a parent has not only a right but a *responsibility* for the upbringing of his family. The state should insist on minimum standards and provide facilities for the children of parents who cannot or will not take the responsibility themselves, but not deny the right and the responsibility to parents who can, which in our day means not a small minority but a growing majority.

There are, indeed, two values at stake here : first the principle of personal liberty in a free society and, second, the responsibility of parents for the standards of the family. In

1944 these values were assumed and not argued about. Some people expected the public schools (the top of the iceberg of the independent sector) to disappear; others hoped that the recommendations of the Fleming Report would, by bringing state bursars into the public schools merge the differences between the two systems. Neither of these developments has occurred. Instead the maintained system has run into the rocks of selection, finance and the population bulge. Education has become political in a way it never was and it is now regarded as a major instrument of social justice and social change. In such a climate, the prosperity and differences of the public schools are an intolerable insult. Liberty and the responsibility of parents have become of secondary rather than of fundamental importance. Yet the family is more fundamental than the school, however much social planners may dislike or find it inconvenient.

Obviously it is necessary for the state to ensure the adequate education of its citizens, but in a democratic society this should be done as far as possible through the family. The rights of every citizen should include : *first*, education for his children up to the standard which the country decides it can afford for all; *second*, as wide a choice of schools as the country can afford to make available; and *third*, the freedom to spend his own money, if he wishes, on what he may consider to be additional advantages for his children. The first and second rights recognise the stubborn and irreducible fact that there are many claims on national resources and that education is only one of them. The third right not only preserves individual freedom but also diverts into the educational sphere money which might otherwise be spent in such luxury pursuits as gambling, drinking or smoking. It has always seemed to me absurd that our present maintained system prohibits the payment of fees. Not only are school meals subsidised and text books provided free, but a local community of parents cannot contribute directly to provide the salary of an extra teacher. All they can do instead is to provide peripheral amenities such as a swimming bath or fittings in a school shop.

A public school on the other hand enlists the direct interest of parents through fees. (And much the same is true of every private school). A school is enabled to build, to engage sufficient staff and to supply amenities, according to the fees it can command in competition with other schools. Its headmaster has a discretion and freedom which he can use to advantage, or abuse at his peril. His independence is considerable but it is similar to that of a prime minister. If either uses it irresponsibly he will be called to account, but at least it permits him to ignore temporary swings of opinion or subservience to the latest fashion. He may indeed have to contend with tradition and with the old guard, but this serves to remind him that the past has its claims as well as the present and the future. A public school serves more than one generation and by so doing can represent values which may appear obsolete and redundant to a single generation. The boys may be conscripts but the parents are volunteers, and this fact is of supreme importance. It is not that those who support public schools believe, as Mrs Young puts it, 'in the changelessness, past and future of the kind of society we live in.' It is rather that they believe in some unchanging values. This is expressing an ideal at its highest, but it is timely to do so when faced by appeals to social justice and equality.

The family and liberty

The gulf which has opened up since 1944 can be healed only by some fundamental rethinking of our educational principles. To obliterate the independent sector of education is an act of destruction, not of healing. Doing so would not only be complicated, slow and painful; it would also deprive the total pattern of education of principles which should give life to the whole. Since the public schools developed in response to a demand made through freedom of choice, the relevant question is whether this freedom can be applied in practice to the maintained system. Since independence is a major feature of public schools, the pertinent question is whether independence rather than dependence can be encouraged within the maintained system. If we believe in the

family as the basic unit of society and in liberty as a higher
ideal than equality, then the answers to these questions must
be, yes.

First, then, there should be a relaxation of control within
the maintained system. This could be done by the provision
every five years of 85 per cent of the money required to run
a school. The governors or managers would be given more
authority and independence by being required to find the
remaining 15 per cent through fees, and the percentage
could rise as national wealth and personal incomes increase.
Anything more they could raise would be used to improve
the amenities and facilities of the school for both child and
teacher. In this tangible way the interest and concern of the
local community would be engaged. Each school would develop on its own lines within its locality and could impose
its own standards of entry and attainment under the general
control of the Inspectorate. The functions of the local education authority would be to keep under review the educational needs of the area, to collect and disburse the five-
yearly grant and to provide specialist and advisory services
for the guidance of governors, parents and teachers. Responsibility, however, for running the schools would rest on the
governors. There would be much more freedom of choice for
parents – although this within limits – and the frustrations,
both of parents and child, would therefore become less than
under the present system. If parents know that their interest
and financial contributions are permitted directly to improve
the school attended by their children, then the maintained
system will develop at a rate impossible today when teacher
quotas, central control and rationed finance gear development to an average which allows little local variation, initiative or flexibility. Competition is as relevant to the maintenance of an educational system as it is to industry, commerce or business. Has it ever been suggested that universities, old or new, were prevented from expanding their facilities from private financial sources? If not the universities,
why the schools? Any wide difference in the economic resources of different regions could easily be regulated by the

scale of the state grants.

Second, the existing independent schools classed as efficient by the Ministry should receive directly a tuition grant equivalent to 85 per cent of the minimum cost of running similar maintained schools. Such a grant would appreciably reduce their fees and make entry to the schools available to a wider range of parent. This range is anyway increasing steadily with the rise in incomes and with encouragement will continue to do so even more. The fees of the boarding public schools, which cover board as well as teaching, would, however, remain high. The state could well take between a quarter and a half of places in these schools, making them available to parents by bursaries gauged to parental means. This assistance by itself would not be enough since if a boarding education (for some part of a child's life) is to be within parental choice there must be a wide extension of boarding facilities throughout the educational system. It is only in the past 20 years that 'boarding' has become a nasty word because the vast majority of boarding places has been in the independent sector. Yet the 1944 Act looked forward 'to the provision by local education authorities of their own boarding schools'. Administrative Memorandum 225 of 1947 envisaged a demand from parents 'which may be expected to develop as the facilities become more widely known', and anticipated that the day would come when 'increasing regard will be had to the potentialities of the child as an individual and to the benefits to him and to the nation, which might accrue from a period of boarding education.'

How different are the realities from the hopes! State boarding facilities have not developed because of financial stringency, and parents can hardly demand something of which they have no experience. With the understandable failure of most local education authorities to provide boarding schools, the effect of the past twenty years has been to maintain the boarding school as the preserve of the 'well-to-do' parent or of the less well-to-do who is prepared to save by insurance or other ways to meet the cost of steadily rising fees. The public school and the boarding principle are thus today under attack as divisive factors in our society. This is deplorable above all because the relative exclusiveness of public schools means that they cannot be judged objectively. They are accused of every vice, of being out of touch and unadventurous and of providing a ladder for the social climber. At times it almost appears as if their disappearance would solve all Britain's problems – a panacea I believe as disingenuous and false as President Sukarno's hope of solving Indonesia's problems by nationalisation and nationalism.

The advantages of independence

The public schools should be considered both for what they have been and for what they are. The Fleming Report of 1944, which was unanimous, while 'agreeing that things cannot be left as they are with the independent public schools confined almost exclusively to the children of those able to pay full fees' also recognised the undoubted worth of these schools. Apart from the religious affiliation of many schools, as a body they represent the principles of independence and boarding. Any educational system without these two principles is deficient. The public schools are not necessarily *better* than other schools, and it does not help their cause or the cause of truth when people say that they are. But they are *different* from other schools in important respects. Within them what is educationally desirable can take precedence over what is administratively convenient; they can go against the tide or run in advance of it; they possess the confidence that comes from knowing that in the long run they would not exist unless they satisfied their customers. Of course like all human institutions they are fallible and fall short of the best. But they are free institutions in a free society where independence does not mean irresponsibility. Freedom can be desired and used for responsible ends. Education is a personal thing, and room must be left for the unconventional and the experimental. A free society must seek to increase rather than circumscribe the liberty of all its schools and universities. As John Stuart Mill put it 'A general State Education is a mere contrivance for moulding people to be exactly like one another : and the mould in which it casts them is that which pleases the predominant power in the Government, whether this be a monarch, a priesthood, an aristocracy, or the majority of the existing generation.'

Mrs Young's 'single system of schools' would be moulded according to the mood of the moment, which would reflect the dominant political philosophy – or superstition. It would obliterate the independence which at present exists, in the hope that social class would disappear. As the study of any society would show, this is a vain hope.

The fundamental point is that every society is different from another, and the political and educational structure is the product of a particular society's history. Change must be made within the context of that history and tradition. Here in education the public schools point the way to the future. The gulf between the maintained and independent systems can be bridged, given goodwill and commonsense. For the gulf to remain is undesirable. Even more undesirable would be the destruction of the independence on which the public school was founded and on which a free society must depend. To ignore this principle neglects the lessons of the past and surrenders the defence of the future. Let us take a deep breath and count ten : perhaps then the word 'public school' may excite less passion and generate more light. Let us also recognise that these schools are national assets not scapegoats. It would be folly when rising incomes are enlarging the area of choice, to turn our backs on the very institutions which have set the pace for much of our educational advance.

A. R. ILERSIC

I was born in 1920 and graduated at the London School of Economics in 1940. After the war I taught economics at the University of Exeter from 1947 to 1953, since when I have lectured in social statistics at Bedford College in the University of London.

Local government affects our lives from the cradle to the grave but my own interest in it has been rather less constant. In between lecturing, writing several books (*The Government Finance and Fiscal Policy in Post-war Britain*, 1955, *The Taxation of Capital Gains*, 1962, *Relief for Ratepayers*, Hobart Paper 20, 1963) and sundry articles, I have become increasingly aware of the simple fact that British local government and the officers who run it are much better than the electorate in some areas deserves. Hostile reaction against the rating system and the pervasive but naïve belief in the virtues of central planning could bring about changes in the form and structure of local government which would be in the interests neither of local democracy nor of the individual citizen. In a revival of 'parish pump politics' lies the best means of redressing the imbalance between 'them' in Whitehall and 'us'. The sooner the public recognise this truth, the more likely we are to get a local government system suited to the needs of the times.

14: PAYING FOR REGIONAL GOVERNMENT

A. R. ILERSIC *examines the whole field of local government, which accounts for nearly one-fifth of total public expenditure and nearly one-tenth of total national income. He argues that if local government is to be efficient the active interest of the citizen must be maintained, and that this requires small units, but that for some purposes local authorities should be grouped into regions. In any event he argues that if taxpayers are not prepared to pay more in rates the solution is not to centralise the control of services such as education, since they would require higher taxes, but to levy direct charges in the form of fees.*

PUBLIC attitudes to local government affairs are best summed up in the phrase 'parish-pump politics'. There are some 7500 parish councils. There are also some 1500 local authorities in England and Wales, comprising 62 county councils and 85 county boroughs, 28 metropolitan London boroughs, to say nothing of 318 non-county boroughs, 564 urban districts and 474 rural district councils. Between them they employ some 780,000 persons, or 3 per cent of the entire labour force. Their annual current expenditure in Britain is nearly £2500 million, about 10 per cent of the national income; a further £800 million is spent on capital works. How much attention does all this economic activity get from those who have been busy telling us that the economy is stagnant, rotting or beyond hope? Precious little.

Yet local authorities are the bodies responsible for most of our children's education, for housing one quarter of our population, for keeping our streets clean and our cities healthy, for administering roads and police, for planning our towns and countryside. Their activities impinge upon the daily lives of every citizen and his family. Are they run efficiently or not? They cannot be ignored in considering the nation's future and its capacity for economic expansion.

The local curate's egg

Local government today is like the curate's egg : good in parts only. It remains the most democratic form of administration in a society in which power is being increasingly centralised. In local government John Citizen can talk to his political masters – or servants – man to man. If his cesspool overflows on to the road he can ring his councillor and hope to get action quickly. Yet there is much that is wrong. The government has recently announced two committees of enquiry, the first to examine the role of local government, the other to investigate the characteristics of the people prepared to give up their time to become councillors. The Local Government Commission is still reviewing local authority boundaries, the Allen Committee is investigating the incidence of the local rate upon householders, and yet another is promised to enquire into the the future of local authority finances.

Where is all this leading? What sort of local government do we want in Britain? Only one thing is clear : it cannot continue as it is. Much of the present structure is the product of the 19th century; parts even older. Neither can we raze the existing structure to the ground and build anew. What can be done is to meet the needs of the second half of the 20th century. We must keep the best features and cut out the bad. What policy would achieve these ends?

Three main problems

Whatever the policy advocated, it must answer three major questions. *First*, what do we want local authorities to do? Should they keep major services such as education and the police, or should they lose them to Whitehall? *Second,* what structure of local authorities is best suited to the most efficient yet democratic provision of the services? Should we have a few all-purpose single-tier authorities, or something like the present patchwork of large and small, ancient and modern authorities with a division of function? Or do we need a reorganisation of such bodies into larger regional units with a two tier-structure such as in the counties? *Third,* how is the new structure of local government to finance itself? At present, criticism of the rating system is so sharp that many critics are prepared to place the entire cost on to Whitehall and dispense with the rate. However much we may criticise the present local government system as an anachronism, its finances as regressive and inadequate, and the standard of its services as too variable, and even if it is proposed that the whole edifice be swept way we still have to put something in its place.

What many critics fail to realise is that all aspects of local government are interdependent. The larger the authorities and the more varied the services they provide, the more money they must have. The more funds Whitehall provides, the more say it will demand in what are really local affairs and the less democratic the exercise of power. In short, any revision of local government must be based upon a clear definition of the main objectives, not all of which are compatible.

Public interest in local government will vary directly with the extent of local authority powers and functions. Thus, if the present services are contracted it seems likely that interest in local affairs will also contract. Already there is apathy among the local electorate because it feels that the real power is not in the Town Hall but in Whitehall. Some degree of central control is essential, if only to ensure a minimum level of quality of service. Beyond this point central control is undesirable. It follows that local authorities should keep the services they now administer, including education and police, which can be regarded as 'national' services. Some argue that centralisation of these services could lead to more efficiency and lower costs; others argue the reverse. The basic issue is simply : what allocation of functions between Whitehall and local government would meet the citizens' needs most effectively and give him the chance, however small, of exercising some control over officials and others paid by and working for him? Few taxpayers or ratepayers today would say that 'Your obedient servant' who signs our official correspondence is either our servant or markedly obedient to our collective wishes. Rather we feel that we are doing what he decides we must do.

'Local democracy' versus 'efficiency'

There is an obvious conflict between 'local democracy', seen best in the smaller authority, and 'administrative efficiency', which nowadays requires the exercise of functions over wide areas with large resources. This issue is of growing importance. The social and economic problems confronting us in these islands, although apparently local, cannot always be dealt with locally. The obvious examples are local unemployment as in the north-west, or north-east, and the conurbation with its urban sprawl such as London, Birmingham, Manchester and elsewhere.

The first is now being tackled by the government on a regional basis. Inevitably *ad hoc* bodies will be created to link Whitehall more effectively with the local authorities within the region to ensure that their problems are seen as a whole rather than through the eyes of individual authorities. Undoubtedly one of the main advantages of local government is also its biggest defect. This is the jealous guardianship of powers and territory, especially evident in local reactions to the recommendations of the Local Government Commission on boundaries, and the efforts of the major cities to expand at the expense of adjacent authorities, or the conflict which arises when the main urban area of a County seeks County Borough status. The evidence submitted to public enquiries held by the Ministry of Housing and Local Government emphasises not so much the legalistic procedure, which tends to defer indefinitely any clear-cut action on urgent matters, but its own weakness. Every authority, so the Minister's Inspector is informed, is doing 'a magnificent job' for its inhabitants, whatever its size; it would be disastrous to the local inhabitants, to local agriculture, to local pride, to the efficiency of administrative functions, for the county and its minor authorities to allow as little as one or two per cent of its land to be transferred to the bulging city seeking space for its overspill and industrial development.

Equally apparent in such enquiries is the difficulty of assembling evidence upon which a decision might be made on social and economic grounds. There is a serious deficiency in the statistical information relating to our economy and social conditions because little data can be easily assembled for areas and regions that do not coincide with the Standard Regions used for most national statistics. The expanding population, the movement of industry and, above all, the increase in the use of the private car are key influences in urban and regional development. These problems cannot be sized up and solutions evolved to satisfy local authorities as at present constituted, or at least only for the very largest. What is needed is for Whitehall to create new regional areas within which the problems, social and economic, can be seen in the round. The first step must be to create statistical and information units which co-ordinate the data collected by the local authorities in the same way as the Central Statistical Office has co-ordinated the information supplied by the various departments of the government.

The government, through the work of the Local Government Commission, has already gone some way towards this objective, for example in the new plans for the north-east and on Tees-side. The recent review of the south-east illustrates both the nature of the problem and its magnitude. But there is also S.E. Lancashire, Merseyside, and the Midlands. If local boundaries are to be revised effectively and at the required pace the government will have to avoid giving way to political pressures from disaffected areas such as Rutland and the Welsh counties. The longer-term interests of the inhabitants are not best served by retaining the *status quo* but by devising a new administrative structure with some of the merits of the old and rather less of their disadvantages.

The structure of local authorities

The basic conundrum is simple enough to define. The larger the administrative unit the more remote from the elector is the seat of power. For effective local democracy the region is at the opposite end of the pole from the parish and, as its supporters would be the first to point out, local government should be local. A compromise is needed; it could be constructed by a form of two-tier administration, the upper in the region, the lower at the county and county borough. While the regional body would be concerned with longer-term issues such as economic development, urban renewal and overspill and the related problems of physical planning, such as water supplies, roads, etc., the minor authorities could concentrate on specific services with which the citizen comes into immediate personal contact, such as education, welfare services, refuse, sewage.

It will be argued that the transfer of key powers to the regional authority runs counter to the principle of democratic participation. There is no reason why the regional authority should not be popularly elected, as are the councils of the county boroughs and counties. The case for elected representatives from the major political parties to sit on the regional bodies would be more sensible than at present. In the present framework the party hack who is often elected to minor local office has not helped the public image of 'independent local government'. Regionalism diminishes the powers of the minor authorities, but the creation of vital regional government should offset the growing power of the executive at Whitehall. With such powerful and influential elected bodies as regional councils, there is every reason for believing that the electorate may turn out to vote with more enthusiasm than normally attends the average local election.

A new court of appeal – the Ombudsmen

When regional councils and executive bodies are created, regional Ombudsmen should be appointed with adequate staff to investigate complaints from members of the public about suspected abuse of power by regional officials. This would be a long overdue development, because the power of the individual British citizen *vis-a-vis* the executive in both central and local government has been steadily weakened since the end of the first World War.

Who wants to pay rates?

No other issue has so awakened public interest in local government than its cost to the taxpayer. On all sides, for reasons good and bad, the government is being urged to abandon the rating system, to increase Exchequer grants, to take over the cost of the national services such as education. The government clearly does not think the rating system is half as bad as do its most vocal critics. It is apparently convinced that when the Allen Committee reports on the extent of hardship arising from the rating system, most of the outcry will be found to be based upon the natural dislike of paying taxes which increase every year.

The rate tends to be regressive, that is, like indirect taxes it falls relatively more heavily upon the poorer and larger family than upon the better-off. But on the whole people occupy the type of property they can afford; the relation between the rate bill and the income of the head of the household is closer than the critics would suggest. Nevertheless, in view of the increased expenditure which local authorities must meet in the next decade some additional source of revenue must be found. It is idle to pretend that the rating system can be abandoned. How else does one propose to raise its current yield of over £900 million per annum of tax revenue? It could be done by increasing the standard rate of income tax to 10s., but no one who has studied the effects of post-war taxes and the spread of avoidance and evasion would regard such a proposal as realistic.

The loudest public clamour against the rates is merely based on the unspoken assumption that if taxes rather than rates bear the bulk of the cost of local services, someone else will bear the charge. This is a vain hope for most people. By increasing the Exchequer contribution to local authorities, or by taking over the entire cost of a major service, such as education, or a part of it such as teachers' salaries, all that would be achieved is a shift of the burden from ratepayers to taxpayers – mostly the same people ! Except for the very lowest and highest income groups the effects of replacing taxes for rates is not likely to be very noticeable. Whether a family benefits or gains will depend upon the type of house it occupies and its personal tax allowances and benefits. For the bulk of the occupied population no significant relief would be obtained from rates by the substitution of Exchequer finance or a take-over of education although they might assist the poorer retired people. On the other hand, any marked switch from rates to taxes would raise the already high marginal rates of national taxes and provoke just as much clamour and even more evasion.

Alternatives to local rates

The various alternatives such as site value rating might be considered as a means of raising some additional revenue from undeveloped land and agriculture, but it would hardly be sizeable. The simple truth is that if the average ratepayer or taxpayer wants to pay less to either Whitehall or the Town Hall, the only solution is to meet the cost of some of the services provided by the public sector directly out of his own pocket. 44 per cent of the gross national product is taken by the state in various forms of tax. Public insistence on better services and higher benefits means that the cost of public services must continue to rise. As Minister after Minister has pointed out, when criticised for the mounting expenditure of public authorities, 'expenditure depends on policy'. If we want to cut public expenditure and with it taxes and rates, the only solution is to change our policy towards defence, civil administration or the social services and other welfare benefits. This is the issue upon which the public should concentrate if it is really concerned with rising rate charges.

Paying for services directly

It is quite illogical that as private incomes rise the community should still rely upon a paternalistic state to provide services which the individual can pay for and, if so obtained, would ensure a wider choice and higher standard. Even within the most affluent society there may be a section of the community incapable of meeting the costs of daily life and the state must help them. But for the vast majority, there is no reason why other members of the public should be expected to subsidise without limit their children's education, their housing or leisure facilities. The real problem stems from the distorted sense of values which tries to justify a rent subsidy to a household that can afford to run a car; or a larger grant for higher education to boys and girls whose parents could make a much larger contribution to its cost. It is time the myth that the young men and women living on public funds at institutes of higher education were performing some sort of public service for the benefit of society was exploded once for all.

The ultimate problem of local government today is simple : what can the state do better than the individual; what can the individual do for himself without the aid of the state? Until the community is clear about the role it wishes to see the state and its executive organs perform, and what it is prepared to do for itself, it is difficult to arrive at a rational decision on the ultimate structure of local government in Britain.

In one way and another regionalism is here to stay. The appointment of a Secretary of State for Industry, Trade and Regional Development reveals the trend of events. Somehow or other the best features of local government must be retained and fitted into the new structure. The second half of this century has brought the need for physical and town planning on a larger scale than in the past. Urban renewal, i.e. the demolition of out-of-date town and city centres; a new network of roads and towns suited to the motor age; new towns to absorb the overspill of the old: these are now the most important functions of local authorities. They cannot be performed by the parish, the county borough or even the county. They need a larger regional unit to integrate the plans of the individual authorities.

In devising a new structure of local government, it is imperative to separate the personal services which the minor authorities are especially well suited to provide, such as welfare and education, from the physical planning powers relating to overspill and transport which can best be dealt with by the regional authority. Nor is there any reason why education, health or other local personal services should not contract in the years ahead if the public recognises that communal provision of standardised services is neither the most economic nor the most satisfactory method of meeting the differing wants of individuals with a rising standard of living.

In so far as he is a member of the community in which a measure of regional authority is needed, then some part of individual, local rights must be restricted for the benefit of the community at large. But this does not mean that the executive authority should ride rough-shod over individual rights; or ignore the human factor simply because the executive knows that the vast majority of citizens have neither the time nor resources to avail themselves of the ultimate defence against the misuse of executive powers, the courts. The misuse of power is no different, except perhaps in degree, whether it arises in the parish council or in the regional authority. To the extent that effective regional government would provide a counterweight to the dominance of Whitehall, it is to be welcomed. There is every reason for welcoming any reform of the administrative structure which may halt the inexorable drift towards the concentration of power which is so marked a feature of our industrialised and urbanised society. To the extent that industry and commerce as well as permanent officials are directly involved in making regionalism effective, it may be possible to achieve a balance of power between the different interests which will serve to ensure the rights of the individual.

Nevertheless, regionalism would lead to some weakening of the existing structure of the minor authorities, and it must be introduced with effective checks. Here the Ombudsman could prove to be the guardian of the rights of the individual. Only if some such measure is introduced before very long will it be possible for the intelligent citizen to feel satisfied that the growth of the powers of the state, whether central of local, may not ultimately be a potential threat to his own liberty of thought and action. Not least, regionalism, providing individual and local interests are taken into account, could make the machinery of government much more effective and efficient, and so contribute to the progress and dynamism of the national economy.

PART FOUR

STRATEGY FOR CHOICE

Necessity is the plea for every infringement of human freedom. It is the argument of tyrants; it is the creed of slaves.

William Pitt (1783)

. . . those who say that not reason but love should rule open the door to those who rule by hate.

Karl Popper (1945)

The worth of a State, in the long run, is the worth of the individuals composing it . . . A State which dwarfs its men, in order that they may be more docile instruments in its hands even for beneficial purposes, will find that with small men no great thing can really be accomplished . . .

John Stuart Mill (1859)

. . . the spontaneous interplay of social forces sometimes solves problems that no individual mind could consciously solve, or perhaps even perceive, and if they thereby create an ordered structure which increases the power of the individuals without having been designed by any one of them, they are superior to conscious action.

Friedrich von Hayek (1937)

JOHN CARMICHAEL

I was born at Christchurch, New Zealand, and graduated in economics at New Zealand University in 1938. I came to England in that year, joined Imperial Airways (later BOAC), served in the RAF and the Air Ministry during the war, returned to New Zealand in 1946 and worked with the NZ War History Branch in Wellington. Back in England in 1948, I had for three years an exclusive apprenticeship in the problems of economic growth as research assistant to S. Herbert Frankel, Professor of Colonial Economic Affairs at Oxford. After graduating at Oxford in 1953 I returned to the business world until 1962, when I wrote (with the Rev. H. S. Goodwin) *William Temple's Political Legacy*, published last year.

Although nominally about the political and economic ideas of the late Archbishop Temple, the book is concerned with current politico-economic problems. We were prepared to present our case for economic freedoms in the light of the archbishop's moral strictures on the 'capitalist' system. The central issue of the book was that of human limitations versus the planning/rationalist assumption of human omnipotence. It reasserted and demonstrated in relation to economics, man's profound fallibility (and the obvious existence of an 'invisible hand'). For these 'reactionary' ideas and for our lack of faith in state paternalism we were roundly abused by clerical reviewers, though the Dean of St Paul's expressed agreement with our general argument.

Anyone who feels out of his depth in economics has my sympathy. It is comforting to reflect that those who offer precise solutions are least likely to understand the problem. As we can no longer afford a divided world, neither can we afford economic policies protecting national vested interests. I suppose my own background makes this more obvious to me. I was born in New Zealand, my wife in Australia, my daughter in London. We are British, but I hope the finer distinctions do not matter.

15: THE MORALS OF MARKETS

JOHN CARMICHAEL *maintains that moral criticisms of the market economy have frequently been misdirected. He argues that only free men can act morally and that only a competitive economy gives men the choice and the chance of responsibility necessary for moral action. He therefore opposes state controlled economic policies and argues that the needs of the world – peace and economic growth – will be best achieved by individuals pursuing free choice under law.*

Hostility to an economic system resting on free markets has been based primarily on moral grounds. Today, it is also claimed that a planned economy is needed for maximum economic growth. But this is a recent innovation; until some years ago the productive superiority of the 'capitalist' system was not seriously disputed; intervention was demanded on 'non-economic' grounds for which an 'economic cost' was accepted. The usual charge against the system was, and remains, that instead of seeking the community's interest through cooperation it was based on self-interest through competition, favouring the strong and the rich at the expense of the weak and the poor. The critics have felt able to claim an exclusive concern for moral principles, to which supporters of the 'capitalist' system have seldom had an effective answer.

There is obvious truth in the charge that competition is or can be ruthless and unfair, and self-interest selfish. The whole truth is not so simple – indeed it is quite different. Hostility to the market economy, incited by the writings of such authors as J. K. Galbraith, Vance Packard and Richard

Hoggart, fundamentally misrepresents the system itself and confuses the moral issues.

The 'just price'

The morality of economic processes has long exercised theologians. The two main pillars of mediaeval theological economics were the doctrines of the Just Price and the Prohibition of Usury. Interpretation of the Just Price varied as economic development proceeded; but the principle remained that the price of an article should be fixed on moral grounds with due regard to the cost of labour and materials and to 'reasonable profits'; the vendor was not entitled to ask the utmost the purchaser would pay.

Today we understand better (or should do) the economic function of prices in relating supply to demand in competitive markets and the inadequacies of attempts to adjust them for moral or other purposes. Calvin in the 16th century (while not necessarily intending to do so) led the way to the rejection of price prohibitions, and to the acceptance of Luis Molina's conclusion that a price was morally justifiable if freely agreed between buyer and seller, provided neither was exploiting weakness or ignorance of the other.

This, with its implied safeguards for the economically weak, is a guiding principle to which all of us today should be able to subscribe. It requires, however, that we should correctly identify the weak and ill-informed and be sure we know how best to help them.

Self-interest

Criticisms of the market economy on moral grounds centre rightly on self-interest. But they have often misunderstood where the real moral issues lie. For how does anyone who is not a saint act other than in what he conceives, rightly or wrongly, to be his own interests? Is it suggested that opponents of the market economy do not pursue their own interests? To act in one's own interests is not necessarily to act selfishly. Self-interest is normally pursued in cooperation with, and with the aim of meeting the needs of, others.

In seeking his own interests a man will normally seek the highest welfare of his family and others; in this context he often acts unselfishly. So also in international affairs United States Aid to hasten Europe's recovery after the war was both self-interested and an act of unprecedented generosity.

The moral issue lies not in the pursuit of self-interest as such but in how that self-interest is conceived and pursued. And the requirement is that our interests should not be pursued in ways that injure others.

The 'competitive struggle'

The charge against competition is that it does injure others. This reflects one of the most fundamental and destructive of current misconceptions about the nature of economic activity. Instead of seeing trade as a process of *mutual* benefit, it is believed that someone's economic gain must be someone else's loss. Our tariff policies, for instance, are based not on an unequivocal recognition of the advantages of trade to both sides but on the assumption of a basic conflict in which we seek the maximum 'concessions' from others for the minimum 'sacrifices' of ourselves. While conscious of the dangers of a divided world, we regard our living standards as requiring protection from the competition of lower (and higher) wage countries. Where the urgent world need is for increasing integration through the removal of trade barriers, governments instead impose controls which, whatever their declared intention, confine economic activity as far as possible within the jurisdiction of the national planning authority. The object is national self-sufficiency instead of international integration.

Bertrand Russell has described competition as a doctrine 'promulgated by hard-headed economists for hard-headed reasons' who consequently failed to see that free competition could result only in monopoly if not war. It was not, he said, as if competition could deal with the problem of unemployment, and it was in any case far less important than it used to be because countries were now 'far more interdependent'. He therefore advised nations seeking prosperity to 'seek rather cooperation than competition with other nations'.

But how can increased world cooperation and interdependence come about except through competitive trade? And why should either side desire trade if it were not to its advantage? Indeed how can the most efficient distribution of productive resources be brought about *within* a country so as to use fully its productive and especially its human resources other than through competition? And even within the individual firm (or perhaps especially within the individual firm) competitive pressures remain the only known means of enforcing the constant changes needed for healthy and vigorous growth. The Labour Party rightly demands equality of opportunity, but equality of opportunity for the best jobs will be achieved only when employers are forced by competitive pressures to recruit on the basis of ability and can no longer afford the luxury of nepotism.

No doubt there have been occasions in the past when competition was literally 'cut-throat', when the Royal Navy was an instrument of British trade policy. But trade in the civilized world today is governed by a framework of laws, institutions and agreements designed to ensure 'fair' competition in Molina's sense. To the extent that competition today is price competition the 'throat-cutting' we inflict is on ourselves through inefficiency and trying to pay ourselves too much. On the other hand, although economic life calls for a high standard of competitive efficiency, it does not demand an intolerable effort from those unable to make it. A modern economy provides jobs to suit all temperaments, including almost complete security in central and local government employment; those who must undergo the main competitive strains are, like front-line troops, a minority. The moral aim, as well as economic, must be that no-one should gain or retain a job for which others are more suited, and only competition can ensure this result.

Do 'non-capitalist' systems *not* depend on competition? Or isn't it a fact of life entering into most of our activities, an essential spur to effort and efficiency? It can be particularly severe in education, and within firms (and government departments) for promotion. A vigorous society needs self-interest; it gives zest to life. Imagine, if possible, a game of football, from the point of view of both players and spectators (if any), in which neither side was striving to win. As with self-interest, of which competition is an instrument, the moral issue lies not in competition itself but in the way in which and the framework within which people compete.

Misconceptions

The current confusion between economic and 'non-economic' ends also reflects a moral confusion. Economic production (equated with material production) – at least when produced by the capitalist system – is regarded as morally inferior to 'non-economic' production; progress is regarded as lying in the extent to which we can abandon economic for 'non-economic' ends which are considered to justify *uneconomic* policies. The distinction is unreal; the extent to which we can afford 'non-economic' expenditure depends on the production of goods and services. The argument of Professor J. K. Galbraith's *Affluent Society*, that the production of private goods must be at the expense of public spending, that private affluence *causes* public squalor, is false. Public wealth derives from private wealth.

Provoked by Mr Enoch Powell, Sir Robert Shone, Director General of the National Economic Development Council, has dismissed 'the concept that the good of the whole is best achieved by individuals seeking their own maximum gain without regard to the broader national repercussions of their actions.' Today, he says, 'the players in the game are powerful enough to adjust the goal posts – or move the touchlines'; and he calls for 'a new economic morality'. Sir Robert states the problem, mis-states the liberal view, and draws the wrong conclusions. The problem as he indicates is that the players are fixing the game among themselves, without regard for consumers. It is already the government's clear duty to protect consumers; the assumption that a more powerful planning authority would do so more determinedly is naïve. The attractions of the system under which individuals seek their own gain are that, by requiring them to seek it in certain directions and by enforcing penalties on them if they fail, it *does* in fact work to the consumers' advantage.

Inequality and hardship

There is the serious charge that the 'capitalist' economy creates an unnecessary degree of insecurity and hardship, from which the working classes are the main sufferers. There is a case here to answer. But those genuinely concerned with the human suffering involved will be careful what answer they give. Part of the depression of the late 1920s and early 1930s can undoubtedly be attributed to an over orthodox and doctrinaire approach (by both Labour and Conservative Governments) to very exceptional circumstances. We now know that much of that hardship was unnecessary. But we continue to shy from the conclusion that economic security must still lie in a flexible economy in which there is necessarily some measure of unemployment if productive resources are to move into new and expanding industries. What is needed is *more* flexibility along with a recognition that people who suffer unemployment should be entitled to much more generous unemployment insurance payments. Not all unemployed, of course, are innocent victims of the system; but this should not be an obstacle to more realistic benefits for those who are. The increased costs should be far outweighed by the gains from increased flexibility.

There is another side to this problem. Anyone concerned with the corrupting effects of unemployment must not forget the frustrations arising within a job where, because of the absence of competitive pressures, abilities are wasted. At the same time the lack of flexibility in the economy and the built-in rigidities like non-transferable pensions funds make a change of job difficult. A good employer is not one who keeps on staff for whom he has no proper job and then gets rid of them in a bunch when competitive pressures make themselves felt.

Private versus public morals

One of the main obstacles to acceptance of the market economy is the difficulty of reconciling its proclaimed virtues with the known or suspected characters of some of its most successful practitioners. But let us be clear what its proclaimed virtues are. And let us not confuse private morals with commercial practice, or consider the problem peculiar to a commercial society. The essential claim is that a market economy is the most efficient system for creating the goods and services people want. To condemn a system because some of its leaders are not paragons of virtue not only shows a desire to equate moral worth with worldly wealth and success but misses the wood for a few trees. The extent to which society demands and is willing to pay for a businessman's services is no more determined by his social and moral virtues than is the success rightly accorded to outstanding writers, dramatists, composers, entertainers, sportsmen, etc. That he is a business leader suggests success in providing for public demands and in creating jobs. For the public and his employees this is what matters.

The moral issue posed by wealth and inequality of wealth within and between nations, and the 'growing gap' between rich and poor nations, is today widely regarded as our most dangerous world problem. Nevertheless I suggest that the moral issue again lies not in the possession of great and unequal wealth but in *how* that wealth is acquired and used. My own criterion for the redistribution of wealth would be, on both economic and moral grounds : does it help to raise living standards generally, or (by diverting wealth from capital investment to immediate consumption and by weakening the willingness of individuals to work and save) does it impede the raising of standards? Even if taxation in Britain today can be increased without harm to production, the danger is that the decision will be dictated by prejudice and envy. There can be neither moral nor economic virtue in a political redistribution of wealth which is not concerned with the size of the cake but simply to ensure that some people should not get more than others. What moral principle requires unequal work to be equally rewarded? And what deity is to decide which work is worth how much?

It is one of the most disturbing features of contemporary economic development that unions have often condoned, where they have not deliberately encouraged, practices inconsistent with a worker's best efforts (and therefore with his integrity) and which extort from the consumers the maximum return not for the best efforts but for the minimum work. Let it also be said, however, that they have been encouraged to do so. The chronic inflation which has been allowed to persist since the war has enabled the economically strong to exploit the consumer and the economically weak, whose interests it should be the government's duty to protect.

Intellectual vested interests

The most urgent moral issue in economics today is the misinterpretation of these issues. Aneurin Bevan once wrote[1] of the failure of the British Communist Party :

> an intellectual vested interest is in many ways the most stubborn of all.

But it is not only the Communist Party to whom this applies. The determined hostility to business profits, for instance, derives from the recognition that to admit the facts must be to undermine fatally the case against the market economy; in the opposition to which there is quite obviously a powerful political as well as intellectual vested interest.

Certainly there are difficulties. Nothing could be in more direct conflict with the current planning philosophy than the inference that, as Adam Smith claimed, some desirable end can emerge as an incidental and unintended by-product of the pursuit of self-interest. By equating the market economy with *laissez-faire* the aim has been to brand it as anarchistic and dominated by powerful interests. But this is a distortion. The market favoured by the classical economists

[1] 'Could Britain go Communist?', *Optima* (Journal of the Anglo-American Corporation of South Africa), June 1957.

did not work in a vacuum but within a framework of law and order. Its essence was not freedom for *producers* but competition amongst them to protect *consumers*, which the classical economists recognised would have to be forced on producers. The freedom of the market economy is abused, not by competition, but by the lack of it.

The world's over-riding political need is peace and the recognition of the fact of One World, with its clear implication that it is also one international economy from which trade barriers should be removed. The requirements for economic growth point in the same direction. While in one sense economic growth creates economic independence, it is at the same time a process of increasing integration and interdependence. The key is competitiveness in world markets. These over-riding objectives will not be obtained by economic policies in the 'national interest' but by leaving individuals free to pursue their own interests in cooperation with their fellow men. This might make things dull for politicians, civil servants and the intellectuals who advise them, but it opens up new and exciting prospects for the community as a whole. Misled by the equalitarian and authoritarian thinking the public sees international cooperation, economic growth and the improvement of social and moral standards as depending essentially on state action. But in essence these aims concern relationships between individuals, and they can only be successfully pursued by them. They cannot be imposed from above.

RALPH HARRIS

I was born in Tottenham in 1924 and survived council estates, elementary and grammar schools to reach Queens' College, Cambridge, where under Professors Robertson, Dennison and Prest, I read economics before the academic iron curtain temporarily rolled down on the Marshallian school. Having served in the RAF ranks before the end of the war, after living my early life among what were then properly called the 'working classes', I have never felt it necessary to romanticise or patronise most of my fellow men.

Since leaving Cambridge with a degree in economics, I have enjoyed teaching in a Scottish university, leader-writing for a Scottish paper and narrowly escaping being returned to parliament for a Scottish constituency. Since 1957 I have enjoyed even more going straight in helping establish the Institute of Economic Affairs as a small but expanding corner of independency, integrity and illumination in a world struggling everywhere against party political pleading.

Most of all I have enjoyed being married for 15 years and trying to read and write at home whenever my wife and our three children are not looking.

My appetite for miracles no longer inclines me towards grandiose political panaceas but is adequately diverted and satisfied (respectively) by membership of the Magic Circle and the Church of England.

16: A PLAN FOR COMPETITION

RALPH HARRIS *analyses the newest device for stimu-lating growth – The National Economic Development Council – embraced enthusiastically but uncritically by businessmen, economists and journalists in the fashion. He finds it has done more harm than good by distracting attention away from the institutional obstacles to eco-nomic growth. He concludes by outlining the alternative policy of competition as the stimulator of efficiency and rising living standards.*

SINCE the war too many British businessmen have suffered from too little vigour, imagination and adventure. The evidence is plainly seen in their widespread addiction to practices, often restrictive, which enable 'reasonable' profits to be made without discarding out-dated machines and methods of work or pioneering new techniques and markets. Governments and trade unions have shown a similar nos-talgia for the safety first of the 1930s despite the trans-formation in the opportunities for increased employment, standards of living and international trade. As though to make up for this flagging spirit of enterprise, many economic commentators have worked overtime to invent remedies.

Alas, the remedies did not usually go to the root of the trouble. When British exports were not enough to pay for imports, Mr Andrew Shonfield in the *Observer* urged ex-change control – without worrying too much for the moment about the upward pressures on costs that threatened to price our goods out of foreign markets. When subsequent spurts of inflation threatened our dwindling gold and dollar re-serves, Professor Alan Day and Mr Nicholas Kaldor held out the tempting solution of devaluation which would give us breathing space – during which we could presumably go on breathing while the fundamental causes of our poor economic performance would go on being ignored. When international comparisons suggested that European countries were increasing production faster than Britain, Mr Rees Mogg in the *Sunday Times* urged that the infallible remedy was more investment in machines – and then still more – without bothering too much about which machines and whether they would be efficiently used, or even asking why firms and whole industries neglected investment which should presumably have paid handsome dividends. When the evidence of the nationalised industries (including atomic energy) demonstrated that capital investment could be a wonderfully costly way of acquiring modern equipment that did not earn its keep, Mr John Vaizey and others directed attention to investment in human beings – as though a sudden expansion in university and management education could carry us to the top of Mr Harold Wilson's European league tables.

Meanwhile, the government itself shrank from a fundamental reform of taxes, tariffs, trade unions, and other restrictive elements so as to sharpen both incentives for the enterprising and penalties for the inefficient. Instead, in an uneasy effort to preserve full employment without full efficiency, it periodically allowed inflationary demands on the economy to build up dangerously before taking emergency action – usually by jerking up Bank rate, imposing taxes on consumer goods and restricting private credit in the hope of relieving the strain on the creaking economy. But because the action was delayed, it looked panicky and unconvincing, and because the government increased the high expenditure and borrowing in the public sector, the curb had to cut deeper into the private sector. The increases in purchase tax and restrictions on hire purchase disrupted the efficient forward planning of the enterprising industries producing cars, washing machines, television sets and other durable consumer goods, and raised prices with the predictable result of providing the shorter-sighted trade union leaders with the pretext for demanding more than compensating wage increases. When in 1958 Mr Peter Thorneycroft wanted to buttress his 7 per cent Bank rate with limitations of public expenditure, the Prime Minister, Mr Harold Macmillan preferred to take the resignation of all three Treasury ministers (including Mr Enoch Powell and Mr Nigel Birch) rather than hold back the sprawling public sector which henceforth began creeping up until it now accounts for not very much short of half the national income.

Small wonder that this one-sided, half-hearted application of monetary discipline failed in its purpose and brought the entire policy of trying to stop inflation into disrepute. When Mr Selwyn Lloyd's version of go-stop led to the ill-starred pay 'pause' in July, 1961 the make-shift character of the expedient became apparent. It was about this time that the economic witch doctors discovered a new magic remedy in French-style five-year planning which seemed to have yielded increased growth (blessed word) at twice the British rate, although admittedly it had not cured inflation (and may have aggravated it), witness the successive devaluations of the franc since 1945. Furthermore, what the French had achieved with the help of national planning, Dr Erhard's Germany had, as Jossleyn Hennessy shows elsewhere, surpassed by liberal 'planning' through competitive markets. With the enthusiastic encouragement of economists associated with the National Institute of Economic and Social Research and Political and Economic Planning, ministers and civil servants were swiftly initiated into the new fashion of growth *à la mode* and in September, 1961, Mr Selwyn Lloyd announced that leaders of industry, and trade unions were being invited to serve on a new National Economic Development Council (Neddy).

Once the Trades Union Congress gave its consent, Neddy lost no time in setting a target (May, 1962) for a 4 per cent annual rate of growth in gross domestic product over the period 1961–6. Remembering all the alarmist talk about the failure of the British economy, reflected so vividly in *Encounter*'s 'Suicide of a Nation' symposium (the 'smell of death' by Shanks, the 'crisis [and] short time that may be left to us' by Rees, the 'shoddiness an international scandal' by Shonfield), Neddy might well stand astonished at its own moderation in plumping for only 4 per cent. It was, after all, Mr Michael Shanks who thought 'stagnant society' a fitting label for the British economy after a decade in which it had grown by an average of 2 or 3 per cent a year and by up to 100 per cent or more in electronics, petro-chemicals, plastics, synthetic fibres, construction, machine tools, tractors and motor cars. Is 4 per cent the last word and is Neddy anyway the best instrument to keep standards of living thrusting ahead without the recurring evil of inflation which has almost halved the value of the pound since 1945? (This fall in the buying power of money has averaged $3\frac{1}{4}$ per cent a year which if the 'creeping inflationists' have their way is just sufficient to reduce the value of the pound to about two shillings over an average lifetime of 70 years.)

Neddy to the rescue

It was never clear what Neddy was supposed to *do*. In a sentence its terms of reference were to *examine* future plans for the public and private sectors, to *consider* the obstacles to the 4 per cent growth rate, and to *seek agreement* on ways of improving production and competitive efficiency. But was it to be an inspirer of confidence – to get less enterprising business men to lift up their eyes to a new vision of boom without bust? Or was it really a confidence trick whereby the government could pass the buck of responsibility for political decisions that might otherwise prove unpopular, particularly among the anti-growth Canutes on the Trades Union Congress led by Mr Frank Cousins? To any student of the royal commission technique, it looked awfully like the latter the moment the membership was announced. To six employers from the Federation of British Industries were superadded from the Trades Union Council exactly six nominees. When a brace of nationalised bosses, a trio of ministers and Lord Franks in person were thrown in, the likeness to a standard royal commission was striking. (I have since discovered that Neddy is voted funds as a commission).

Small wonder that most of Neddy's published statements have created something of the 7 day wonder of Radcliffe on money, Jenkins on company law, Pilkington on television, Guillebaud on railway wages, Jack on rural buses. Despite unrivalled access to leading companies, unions, authorities, and quite exceptional interest from leading journalists, broadcasters and all the rest who patiently follow in the wake of the intellectual fashion-setters, despite the potential public excitement created by the 1984 version of 'stagnation – bad', 'growth – good', despite almost inconceivable opportunities to transform not merely thinking but action, in short despite the shrewdest public relations campaign, what have we had? We have had a handful of reports, most of them mildly interesting, some usefully lifting the eyes of myopic business men to brighter horizons, but none sparkling much less galvanising. If we wanted acres of speculative statistics, we might have got them better from the NIESR. If we wanted a wide ranging discussion 'on the one hand . . . and on the other' there is PEP waiting competently to oblige. And if the Government wanted a sharply analytical series of studies of obstacles to growth it could have drawn on the Hobart Papers from the Institute of Economic Affairs – the first of which, published more than four years ago was, significantly, the classic by Professor B. S. Yamey on resale price maintenance. (The Editor will perhaps allow me to mention that other Hobart Papers have dealt with such impediments to efficiency and mobility as rent control, trade unions, taxation, company law, outdated welfare, farm subsidies, transport licensing, monopoly, tariffs – and, need I add, royal commissions and all that.) Instead of rigorous – and vigorous – economic analysis of the underlying human, technical, institutional prerequisites of growth and change in an open economy, the Neddy reports have been cautious, conventional and therefore rather boring lectures about some of the more obvious, immediate bottle-necks we must expect if we inflate the economy too noticeably. The less predictable flashes (wealth taxation) and omissions (restrictive labour practices and r.p.m.) confirm that Neddy's 'evenly balanced' Council will always concede more to the public posture of TUC-nominated block voters than to the business men who were appointed as individuals rather than as delegates of employers' organisations.

It is said that the early reports prepared by Sir Robert Shone's professional staff were better than the versions that got past the Council for publication. They surely must have been, or what is going on at what is grandly called 'The Office' whose staff at the last count had grown to more than 100? And later reports have begun to be hedged and trimmed in the light – or twilight – of what Neddy's professional staff judge can be got past the council.

Target practice

The only new element that Neddy has injected into the old arguments about economic policy has been the elaborate statistical five-year forecasts about the economy and its principal components, such as public and private sectors, consumption and investment, imports and exports. At first there was some mystification about where these figures came from and what they were supposed to mean. Were they projections of past trends more or less plus 4 per cent? If so, why the fuss and what was so uniquely right about past trends which, according to the critics of 'stagnation', were the confused outcome of an amateur muddle?

Perhaps rather rashly Neddy spokesmen began to talk of the forecasts as 'targets', which implied that if the economy didn't hit them it would be the fault of the economy, not an error of Neddy's highly professional figures. Alas, unkind memories stirred about earlier targets: the fuel gap, the adverse terms of trade calculations, the atomic energy forecasts and even population projections, all of which had proved so vulnerable to what might be called the target practice of reality. Worse still, two of the leading professionals in 'The Office' (none other than Sir Robert Shone its general director and Sir Donald MacDougall its economic director) had earlier gone on record with most meticulous sets of forecasts (on the steel and dollar 'shortages' respectively) which could hardly bear examination a year or two after they had been so confidently handed down from the most elevated statistical heights.

Neddy's forecasts turn out to be moving targets, and true to form, the latest report (March, 1964) shows that the professional statisticians have already started revising the figures. To begin with the 'targets' are shifted up and down by a few decimal places, but as with the old Economic Surveys more serious revision can confidently be expected.

Meanwhile, the *Economist* (previously an enthusiast for the whole hocus-pocus) writes :

> Forced by circumstances to revise its figures, NEDC will sacrifice anything to keep its 4 per cent growth rate for Britain sacred.

Whether or not we get 4 per cent growth, it will not necessarily be to the credit or blame of Neddy. A year after all the impressive consultations with 17 industries which seemed somehow implicated in the 'target', the NIESR conducted a survey among 126 firms employing one million people in the key metal-using industries, including engineering and vehicles. Three-quarters reported that they had taken no notice of the 4 per cent pep talk by Neddy and the Government, and of the remaining quarter many did not seem to grasp the question at all.

Commenting on this 'disappointing' finding, the director of the NIESR said of NEDC [1] :

> It will not be successful until industry is ready to commit itself to continuous growth.

Say this out loud to yourself three times and it becomes alternately obvious, alarming and meaningless. But then much the same mixed verdict would apply to most of the pronouncements on 'growth'.

The case against Neddy is, however, very much more serious than statistical legerdemain. My indictment is twofold. First, it has not done things it could have done, in particular it has distracted attention from the urgent need for more up-to-date facts and figures about the recent past and present which might enormously help business men to do their own forward planning better. We still need more official statistics – to improve Mr Macmillan's 'last year's Bradshaw' – and better company statistics – to satisfy the Jenkins Comittee and Harold Rose's Eaton Paper on fuller disclosure.

Secondly, Neddy could not hope to do most of the things that urgently need doing. Its three-fold terms of reference open up :

1. To examine ...
2. To consider ...
3. To seek agreement ...

Unlike Mr Shonfield and others who characteristically prefer the French version of 'democracy' to the British, I do not itch to arm Neddy with power to act over the head of parliament; but action in place of exhortation is badly needed, for example against trade union restrictions, tariffs, wasteful government expenditures, subsidies (or government contracts) to inefficient industries, rent restriction, burdensome taxation, and all forms of price-fixing, including the lunatic business of national, uniform wage fixing. But one has only to begin listing these more obvious *institutional* (rather than physical) obstacles to efficiency, economy and flexibilty, to grasp the plain fact that economic criteria conflict – indeed collide head on – with the basic political objective of not stirring up trouble. Mr Macmillan seemed to have hoped that Britain's entry into the Common Market would break down the Maginot line of economic restrictions for the Conservatives. But when that oblique approach failed, he was not ready with a 'do-it-yourself' kit to dismantle the tariffs and other barriers to efficiency. Perhaps the germ of Neddy was implanted in the flabby body politic not by the FBI's Brighton conference in 1960, nor by NIESR's enthusiastic propaganda for French planning in 1961, but by Mr Selwyn Lloyd's last despairing hope that a kind of royal commission on overall policy and things in general would somehow do the trick. Yet the true author of this latest twist to economic policy cannot be doubted by anyone who reads *The Middle Way* by Mr Harold Macmillan in 1938.

Unhappily, after trying 'to examine ... consider ... seek agreement ...' the Council of Neddy could not even agree on so well-established an impediment to economic progress as rpm. Nor is it by any means certain that the professional 'Office' would be anxious to persevere in helping the necessary re-formulation of a more competitive, self-disciplined economy that would leave the planners, coordinators, would-be controllers with a more modest, though still useful, part to play.

All neutrals now

Another reason for the bias of Neddy-type economists is that putting too much emphasis on competitive enterprise or consumer freedom of choice would run dangerously near acknowledging something that might loosely be called 'principles'. And this would smack of doctrinaire excess. Here we come to the most debilitating convention that explains why Neddy has run off the economic race-course; it is the fashion of 'objectivity'. All issues must now apparently be 'objectivised', which means roughly that 'responsible people' or rather 'people who want to be taken seriously' must try to avoid saying too much that may upset big business, will positively avoid thinking or saying anything whatsoever that could possibly upset big unions, and will never dream of looking for the cause of any problem in the existence of – dare I say it? – big government.

Thus to the widespread tendency to call for government intervention to deal with every imagined abuse – from trading stamps to the 'brain drain' – is added the rooted disinclination to relieve public authorities of 'historic functions' (i.e. every job politicians took on up to yesterday) even when they do them inefficiently and when competitive institutions could tackle them much more – shall we say – 'growthfully'. As Colin Clark, Arthur Seldon and E. G. West argue elsewhere there are wonderful openings in compulsory, universal state welfare to divest the politicians of responsibilities which they have mismanaged badly and which have led them to neglect other duties that government alone can discharge.

A classic example of 'objectivisation' carried to the brink of folly was the time-wasting efforts of the Neddy Council to beat out an incomes policy. Since the TUC nominees could not bring themselves publicly to accept the platitude that increased wage costs per unit of output have been for years the chief element in (though not necessarily cause of) persistent price increases, the search began for a formula that would check profits (without making them harder to earn), or tax them more severely (without presumably encouraging what might be called evasion through extravagance). After this hopeless academic exercise was exhausted (but not before it had won the 'responsible' blessing of the FBI), the Council 'objectively' turned its attention to methods of stopping firms increasing their prices. No time was wasted on such effective, standard methods as sharpening up competition, cutting taxes, reducing tariffs, checking monetary inflation. Instead another administrative formula was sought : for weeks those in the know must have rubbed their eyes as leading stalwarts of 'free enterprise' tried behind bolted doors to do a deal on wages, profits and prices with the leaders of sectional trade unionism under the imploring chairmanship of a Conservative Chancellor of the Exchequer. In the *Statist* (7 February, 1964) Professor Day lambasted the entire charade as 'irrelevant windowdressing' and concluded :

> The danger in these games is that the participants will get so involved that they take themselves too seriously.

The danger is not merely in prospect, but here and now. Nor is it only the participants but the audience, advisers, and even commentators who get taken in, or take one another in. Serious, or at least seriously-intentioned, writers in the *Financial Times*, *Observer* and the *Economist*, no less, committed themselves to the considered judgement that an incomes policy would be such a splendid idea that a way positively must be found to discover it.

It did not strike the economists who wrote in this vein (and was anyway against the 'public interest' to mention it) that the quest for an all-embracing wages-profits-prices pact, if it could overcome the administrative impracticabilities, would do immense harm in frustrating or distorting those very changes in relative prices (including the prices of labour and capital) that help allocate supplies and direct demand into faster-growing, lower-costing or higher-yielding avenues of employment and output. Luckily, the impossible defeated even the combined counsels of Neddy, and after months of fruitless effort, even the FBI admitted failure and resigned itself to looking nearer home :

> we think that in the short term progress is more likely to be made by concentrating upon raising productivity.

If institutions as well as individuals learn by mistakes, we may take heart that Neddy must be learning at an extraordinary rate. How long then before it shows some awareness that economic activity, particularly in a more rapidly developing economy, necessarily creates conflicts of interests – between new and established suppliers, between rising and declining regions, between unions, companies and groups of consumers. Here and there the state can intervene to adjudicate and perhaps ease the impact of change by (terminable) subsidies. But there must be a general, systematic method or discipline for resolving conflicts in a way that does not prevent the mobility of human and material resources to companies, industries, areas that can put them to the best use in producing not merely more statistical output but saleable goods and services. Broadly the choice of discipline is between letting competitive market forces operate more freely (the 'invisible hand' of Adam Smith who first taught the creative power of economic freedom) or instituting a much more rigorous system of central control (the 'heavy hand' of Thomas Balogh who never tires of calling for more powers for the planners). The more of either the less effective the other : if 'free enterprise' firms think they can look to the government for contracts or subsidies in difficult times, their incentive to be more competitive is impaired; likewise if a regime of extensive planning leaves pockets of competitive enterprise which make good profits and would attract resources away from the public sector, the planners will not easily rest until the 'saboteurs' are brought under 'responsible' control.

Alternative policies

Not surprisingly, we discover that there *are* after all not one but at least two contrasting ways of raising standards of living (democratic English for 'growth'). If we want to be sure that the outcome in volume and distribution of consumption and of leisure accords with the varying preferences of 36 million adult voters (and consumers) our method must be to widen the operation of competitive markets. As Professor (now Lord) Robbins once said, the market mechanism is a daily referendum with proportional representation for minorities. If that sounds old stuff, we might ponder Mr Enoch Powell's more contemporary analogy :

> the most wonderful working computer the world has ever known . . . into which are fed millions of facts, not only from all over this country but from all round the glope. The answers tumble out; it tells us what it is most advantageous to import or export; what can be produced economically and competitively and in what quantity and where. This wonderful silent mechanism is the market . . .

It is no refutation of this thesis for Sir Robert Shone to say that the market is imperfect and does not accord with some abstract textbook theory of perfect competition. Many of the avoidable imperfections are not merely man-made but government-imposed, like tariffs, subsidies, cost-plus contracts and less obvious protective devices; other imperfections like rpm, extensive ploughing back of profits, price leadership, closed shops, and similar business and labour restrictive practices have been condoned or encouraged by politicians, often irrespective of party. Finally there is the avoidable imperfection represented by the public sector which even where 'productive' is financed by a battery of taxes that must blunt (rather than sharpen) incentives and penalties across the private sector (see the essays by Mr Clark and Professor Wiseman). Furthermore, the public sector has become rigid, moving only upwards instead of varying to offset changes in the level of economic activity, with the little-noticed result that whenever the combined total sets up inflationary pressures (which is most of the time) the private sector is made to bear the main burden of adjustment through crude, short-term variations in HP controls, purchase tax, investment allowances, which disrupt forward planning and bring the management of the economy into the disrepute conjured up by the parrot-cry 'stop-go'.

After fundamental reform to recreate a more competitive, flexible economy, there will remain imperfections due to technical considerations and human resistance to abrupt change. Redundancy payments, retraining and assisted transfer can help reduce the elements of rigidity, but the main requirement is that all existing, established positions of power are disciplined by the threat of competition, just as Mr John Bloom challenged the heavyweight electrical firms and cheaper oil compelled the National Union of Mineworkers to allow Lord Robens to transform the nationalised coal industry. Here is growth through competition which looks a lot more healthy, honest and substantial than statistical fat induced by a mixture of fixing, faking and cajoling people to do other than what their business or trade union judgement of market opportunities would lead them to attempt.

Before turning our back on the liberal solution and drifting towards authoritarian expedients, we should grasp the central fact that the unstable intellectuals do not offer a middle way. Their episodic, unsystematic, ad hoc incursions almost always lead to a weakening of market forces and to a cumulative strengthening of the need for extensive state intervention. The eventual weakness and shallowness of this restless search for a non-liberal way was well displayed by

Sir Robert Shone in a recent speech to the Glasgow Chamber of Commerce. The new note came near the end :

> There has been considerable discussion and some tentative ideas about mechanisms – the teeth ! – for ensuring responsible behaviour. But sanctions, or legal pressure, are not of much avail unless there is a general climate of opinion making responsible action a normal attitude. We need, in effect, a new economic morality to cover the behaviour appropriate to the new conditions of modern economic life.

Talk about taking themselves too seriously ! The professional statistician begins to sound like an amateur preacher. Here we see the ultimate relapse of the would-be reformer – or revolutionary – who solves the crucial problem by simply stating the need. At least the Webbs knew that their secular religion would take a generation or two to establish, hence the Fabian 'inevitability of gradualness'. Yet here is Neddy planning to save us by 1966 and its Director General brooding on the need for 'a new economic morality'. Like the mule, poor Ned has neither pride of ancestry nor hope of progeny. In place of the automatic computer of competitive markets, it wants a hand (and mouth) operated economy, what might be called symbolically Shanks' pony.

Five-year plan for competition

If politicians shrink from the straightforward disbandment of Neddy or its exile to a distant depressed area (where it would bring lots of employment on standard Parkinson lines), 'The Office' might simply be given fresh instructions to chart the path back to an open competitive economy. The need is two-fold : fuller published information to enable competing companies to form better judgements of future customer requirements, and the modernisation of the legal and institutional framework to make the economy more competitive. We should not then need to talk of holding growth back to Neddy's modest 4 per cent.

Where Mr Michael Shanks proposes that the TUC be accepted as a partner in Government with a voice in forming social and economic policy in return for cooperation over an incomes policy, I should urge an early bold announcement of the following measures which as a concession to the intellectual fashion-mongers we could call a Ten-point Five-year PLAN. Implementation would start six months later when the victims had recovered from the shock, understood the government meant business and began to adapt themselves *in advance* to the onset of competition.

1. A reduction of government expenditure particularly on indiscriminate welfare and a cut in taxes particularly on companies and individuals, conceding £1000 million a year : tax back to Colin Clark's safe level of 25 per cent of GNP in five years.

2. A reduction of all protective tariffs by 20 per cent of the duty each year: free trade in five years, which would bring incalculable gains by directly lowering costs and prices and indirectly stimulating more efficient production and marketing.

3. Instead of burying trade union abuses beneath another royal commission, legislation should, outlaw the closed shop, intimidation and mass picketing; the logic of regional wage negotiations would then assert itself to the advantage of the self-depressed areas in employment and prosperity.

4. Restrictive practices of unions, professional bodies and other suppliers of services should be registered for review and prohibited where they cannot be shown to be essential for safety and efficiency.

5. Instead of judging business restrictive practices against escape clauses about the 'public interest', the '*per se*' rule discussed by Professor Jewkes should operate on American lines to rule out legal devices that restrict competition.

6. Patent protection should be reduced from 16 years to 5, with compulsory licensing thereafter to speed up adoption of new techniques and inventions.

7. Fuller disclosure by public and private companies

should be required and should be matched by improving the collection and prompt publication of official statistics to help improve the quality of business and political decisions in investment, techniques, employment, location, foreign trade, marketing and other policies.

8. The capital gains tax should be replaced by a differential tax on profits retained in a company which at present leads to the survival of the fattest.

9. Subsidies to private companies, nationalised industries and farming should be reduced by annual instalment to zero in five years.

10. Monetary policy, public expenditure and lower taxation would work together to prevent inflation; and tax inducements should be used to encourage redundancy, retraining and transfer schemes that would remove the hardship from unavoidable variations in the level of employment.

Although expressed briefly and perhaps dogmatically, this kind of economic policy has the merit of consistency and of combining the rapid advance of standards of living with the widening of individual freedom and responsibility. It has the further strength of drawing on the research and writings of many of the outstanding, independent economists of my lifetime, including such professional academics as Colin Clark, Milton Friedman, John Jewkes, Arthur Lewis, James Meade, Victor Morgan, Eric Nash, Lionel Robbins, Dennis Robertson, George Stigler, Basil Yamey, Friedrich Hayek and not least J. M. Keynes who urged his unpalatable revolution in national accounting as a means of bringing the 'Manchester system' back into its own. The stable foundations, good sense and firm grasp of realities that underlie this approach to an agenda for political leadership contrasts with the erratic, superficial, expedients of the week-end economic journalists who confuse their latest thoughts of the moment with new thinking.

JOSSLEYN HENNESSY

Before the war I was a member of the middle classes, but because I was educated at Charterhouse and New College, Oxford, and belong to a London Club, I have, since the war, apparently become a member of the privileged classes.

I have, in fact, had to work for my living all my life, and, useful as my old school tie has been in dazzling prospective employers, if I couldn't do the job, I was flung out: for instance, I was once in Lloyds Bank, but not after I had (inadvertently) locked up my manager in the strong room.

Thereafter, I launched *World Trade*, journal of the International Chamber of Commerce, Paris; travelled widely in Europe as chief Paris correspondent of the *News Chronicle*; was created Chevalier of the Legion of Honour; covered the Spanish civil war, where my dispatches upset Franco who offered a reward for my capture (I can't remember how much he thought I was worth). In 1939, I became Director of Public Relations to the Government of India; in 1942, I inaugurated the Indian Information Services in the USA. Then back to India to cover the transfer of power for the *Sunday Times*. From 1948 to 1953 I was in business in Calcutta. By then, I had (I thought) saved enough to retire, but I had not reckoned with the welfare state's continuous depreciation of the £, so in 1955 back to London to start a new career. Old school tie or not, nobody will take you on in the fifties, so my hobby, economics, became my livelihood. My working week is 56 hours: enquiry suggests that this is about the average for an Establishmentarian in good standing.

17: A BRITISH 'MIRACLE'?

JOSSLEYN HENNESSY *reviews the successes and failures of the economic 'miracles' in Germany, France and Italy and judges the extent to which an economic 'miracle' in Britain is possible to give effect to the policies outlined in other essays.*

POPULAR explanations of the French, Italian and German post-war 'miracles' are largely irrelevant or contradictory, or both. Confronted with Europe's fast growing national incomes, popular opinion in the UK alleges lower standards in the social services, longer working weeks, lower burdens of taxation and 'cheap' labour – 'hordes' of refugees in Germany and surplus agricultural workers in Italy. As France has not enjoyed such 'hordes', popular opinion substitutes 'planning' for 'cheap' labour as the secret of her growth.

None of these explanations stands up. The UK spends a substantially lower percentage of her national income on social services than these three countries. The difference is that in the UK the main impact falls on general taxation, while in Europe it falls on employers, who therefore have a powerful incentive to economise labour. Working hours are longer in the UK. The percentage of the national income taken in taxation is lower in the UK than in either France or Germany, the difference is that the percentages raised in income tax, and the maximum individual rates of tax, are lower in Europe, so that the incentives to personal effort are higher. Labour costs in Germany, France, Italy and the UK are within a few points of each other.

From status to contract

The truth is that Europe has no 'secrets' and there have been no 'miracles' – except in the eyes of those observers who cannot stomach the evidence : what has happened in Europe is that certain well-established economic principles, having been allowed free play, have produced the results outlined in the text books. At first sight the differences between the economies of France, Italy and Germany seem so great as to make comparisons useless. A closer look shows, however, that the outstanding factor common to them, is that since the war they have speeded up the process of moving from status to contract, which in this country reached its climax in the 19th century. The classical interpretation of the Industrial Revolution was that it hastened the disruption of a 'feudal' society based on inherited ascribed status and substituted contracts between man and man. A society governed by contract is competitive : it makes clear the connexion between personal effort and reward.

C. P. Kindleberger points out in his *Foreign Trade and the National Economy* that economic policy continuously faces the dilemma of whether to adapt to the dictates of the market and of efficiency – that is whether to strive to better ourselves by responding to consumers voting with their purses – and thereby inflict passing hardship on some occupational group, or to temper the wind to the shorn lamb and ward off economic adaptation, consequently undermining efficiency and retarding the multiplication of wealth.

The classic example is the contrast between the British and French responses to the fall in the price of wheat after 1875. In the UK the price collapse was allowed to dismantle agriculture as it had traditionally operated, to induce the transfer of a quarter of a million agricultural workers into other occupations. Whereas the percentage of the labour force in agriculture had been 15, in industry 43, in trade and transport almost 20, and in the professions nearly 7, by 1900 agriculturalists had shrunk to below 9 per cent, while workers in industry, trade and transport, and the professions had risen respectively to 46, 21 and nearly 10. This re-allocation of effort made for growth : national income *per head* (1913 prices) rose from £29 in 1875 to £47 in 1900. In France, on the other hand, the family farm was preserved by raising the tariff on wheat in 1881, 1892 and 1910, with the result that French agriculture stayed inefficient, highly labour intensive and without capital. This step was taken in the name of social stability. Modification of the traditional European structure did, of course, take place in the 19th century, but its slowness enabled the UK to forge ahead for many decades.

From defeat to realism

Europe's traumatic experiences between 1939 and 1945 – defeat, occupation, devastation – made Germans, French, Dutch, Italians and others ready to accept realistic economic remedies. They abandoned the protectionism that had kept interwar Europe stagnating. They insisted on competition and have been ready to allow the inefficient enterprise to disappear, thus releasing its capital and labour for more profitable use elsewhere. They took our place as leaders in change and growth.

The paradox of postwar Britain is that while popular opinion scorns contract and competition as inegalitarian, it simultaneously insists on the economic growth which can only come from a dynamic competitive society. Yet the trend has been away from contract back to status. Over broad areas of the economy, once the British worker is accepted as a union member, and once engaged in a job, it is his status, not the quality of his performance which entitles him to employment. The performance must, of course, be good enough not to flout loose customary standards, but to excel that minimum attracts sanctions from the organised up-holder of status – the union. The difficulty that an employer has in dismissing a unionised worker solely on the grounds of inefficiency emphasises status and *customary standards of work in established techniques*. The need to achieve the higher productivity of the constantly changing technologies that characterise a competitive society is virtually disregarded. All manual workers, more and more white collar workers, and professional people such as doctors, nurses or teachers, connect pay rises with an across-the-board wage or salary increase that they expect as routine from the next round of union-employer or union-government negotiations, in which the deciding factor is not increased productivity but the 'rise in the cost of living' that such practices render inevitable. In a contractual, competitive society, employers would reach a point at which, without increased productivity, wage rises would cease because prices had become too high to be passed on without falling profits.

I do not seek to imply that protectionism, monopoly and restrictive practices have been eliminated or that perfectly competitive societies have been created in postwar Europe, but it remains true that, *by comparison* with conditions in the UK, protection has been hit hard and competition given a tremendous boost. Whereas large areas of our economy have been rigidified, large areas of the economies of Germany, France and Italy have been loosened beyond recognition. Before the inauguration of the Common Market, French and Italian entrepeneurs and unions were as fearful as many of ours that competition would kill various national industries – particularly steel and automobiles. But the safeguards and 'waivers' written into the Rome Treaty to protect the weak have hardly been used. Today the UK stands out among the industrial nations as the world's highest tariff country, and suffers accordingly more than any other nation from the restrictive practices of employers and workers that can flourish only behind tariffs.

European investment: British misinvestment

Competition forces entrepreneurs to use their resources profitably or get out of business : it promotes investment. Protection allows resources to be used wastefully : it promotes misinvestment. Germany, France and Italy have had better growth rates because on average they have invested substantially more than the UK. This at first sight seems to contradict the view attributed to Colin Clark by his critics that growth does not depend on the volume of investment. But what *he* said in his classic Hobart Paper, *Growthmanship*, was that it is no use investing to produce more goods if nobody wants to buy the kinds of additional goods produced. This is not an argument against investment but against misinvestment. Colin Clark's views have been borne out by four subsequent investigations : by an English economist, Mr David Williams of Hull University; a Belgian, Dr A. Lamfalussy, Economic Adviser to the Banque de Bruxelles; a German, Dr Rolf Krengel of Berlin University; and an American management consultant, Mr W. Allen. The last-named has estimated that for each person required to produce one ton of steel in the USA three are needed in the UK; in aluminium the ratio is one to 2·5; in the maintenance engineering activities of the two chemical industries the ratio is one to four. In UK shipbuilding, he calculated that 40 per cent fewer workers could be used if labour were employed efficiently. It takes three to six times longer to build a house in the UK than it does in the USA. British builders take two to four times longer than Americans to build an office block. The sales prices per square foot of houses in the UK are only slightly lower than in the USA., although the wages of US construction workers are thrice ours.

One consequence of misinvestment is that UK income per head in 1962 was £425 compared with £860 in the USA. Even at the USA's present slow rate of growth, her national product rose in the three year's of President Kennedy's tenure of office by an amount equal to the whole of our national product. Germany's income per head is rapidly catching up with ours : in 1961, when the UK figure was £415, Germany's was £388. By 1962, Germany had jumped to £423. It is relevant to the argument that 'profits' has become a 'dirty' word in the UK. Significantly, the *Financial Times* (December 31, 1963) reported that seven leading German companies (Volkswagen, Daimler, Benz, Demag, Bayer, Thyssen, Mannesmann, Siemens) averaged net profits of 17 per cent in 1961, compared with under 5 per cent for seven leading UK companies (ICI, Elliott-Automation, Steward and Lloyds, BMC, Guest Keen, Vickers, AEI). 'Excessive' profits produce more national income than 'moderate' profits.

Under-employment in Britain

Full employment in Europe has meant the transfer of workers from contracting to expanding industries. Mr Allen argues that in the UK since the war there has been *under*-employment rather than full employment, and no shortage of labour. A high proportion of the labour force takes a large part of its wages not in money but in leisure, mostly enjoyed at the place of employment. Mr Williams's contention is that UK basic wages are too low, the working week too long, that, relative to the available manpower, capital equipment is insufficient, and that the existing capital equipment is under utilised because of the extensive under-employment of labour. International statistics support Mr Williams. Actual hours worked per week between 1952 and 1960 remained steady in France around 45 hours, in Germany they fell from 47·5 to 45·6, in the UK they remained 48 hours. Productivity between 1953–1961 rose in Germany by 44 per cent, in France by 61 per cent, and in the UK by 22 per cent. Hourly earnings in manufacturing rose in Germany by 58 per cent, in France by 83 per cent, and in the UK by 47 per cent.

European experience: France

Has France's growth rate been due to planning rather than to competition? When I put this question to M. Pierre Massé, France's planner in chief, he replied with disarming candour : 'I don't know! It's difficult to determine what part the Plan plays in *actual* development. But the results have been so good that one may suppose (*sic*) that the two have some (*sic*) connexion.' If France's chief planner pitches it no higher than that, there are not lacking realists in France to pitch it even lower as Vera Lutz shows in *Econo-*

mic Miracles.[1] French planning finds its warmest supporters among big firms, which fix among themselves the share that each will take of the expansion planned and its strongest critics among the Confederation of Small and Medium Enterprise, which see it as the spearhead of the movement away from a free market towards compulsion and centralisation.

It is clear from PEP's study *French Planning: Some Lessons for Britain* that in the Second Plan (1954–57), national income grew much more quickly than had been planned, at the cost of an excessively heavy investment effort, which forced up prices, thus impeding exports and creating a heavy demand for imports. Nor was the planned pattern of growth achieved. 'Non-productive' social investments in housing, health and education, greatly overshot the targets, while manufactures and the capital goods industries, particularly machine tools, lagged. This Plan reached its climax in two devaluation crises in 1957–58 and a period of austerity and recession. It demonstrated unbalanced growth rather than planned development.

The Third Plan (1958–61) coincided with France's entry into the Common Market, which initiated tariff reductions leading to an increasingly competitive economy to which foreign trade contributed a steadily rising part. Balance of payments equilibrium became imperative. From now on, France could less and less combine a high growth rate with slow expansion of exports and rapid inflation. *Today, France's problems are basically similar to ours and her planning experience throws more light on her past than on our future.*

The trouble with planners is that, by definition, they know better than anyone else (above all mere consumers) what the perfect allocation of scarce resources should be. French experience suggests, however, that they do not base their priorities on an objective assessment of needs (assuming, indeed, that such an assessment were possible) but on political considerations, and that the bureaucrat's classic attitude

[1] Published by I.E.A., 1964.

towards consumers' choice prevails. 'On the whole', report Mr and Mrs Hackett in *Economic Planning for France*, 'the French planners were, and are, sincerely perturbed by the direction taken by the spontaneous growth of demand in the mass consumption society which is rapidly appearing in France. The idea behind the French plan is substantially to increase consumption of collective goods and services.' This can only mean that the people pay more in taxes to meet the cost of items which the planners consider to be good for them, and that they are allowed to retain a smaller amount of their incomes to spend on what they consider to be good for themselves. *Timeo Planaos et dona ferentes.*

Italy

In 1948 Italy was one of the least industrialised countries of Europe, and suffered from permanent under-employment in a subsistence level agricultural sector. Between 1948 and 1960 she doubled her gross national product. Unemployment was reduced from 10 per cent to below 3 per cent. Industrial real wages rose 72 per cent and real income per head in the south 55 per cent. Growth at this pace can be maintained only by allowing profits to soar. Whatever the 'conspicuous consumption' indulged in by entrepreneurs, it was negligible compared with what they were re-investing, and the masses had their share in the rising prosperity. As Keynes pointed out in *Economic Consequences of the Peace*, referring to 19th century Europe as a whole, the vast investments in fixed capital – the new roads, railways, bridges, ports, factories, plants, machinery, etc. – which, 'to the great benefit of mankind', were built up before World War I could never have been accumulated out of 'fair' shares.

The inflation that began to undermine Italy's economy from 1962 arose because wage and salary earners were no longer content to enjoy a slowly rising share in a quickly rising national income. Under pressure of rising wages in 1963, demand for consumer goods in general rose 16 per cent, for cars 45 per cent, for consumer imports 24 per cent. This shift of money into the pockets of people who spent

rather than saved reduced the amount available for investment, so that the investment growth rate fell from 19 per
cent in 1960 to 7 per cent in 1963. Yet the needs of the
private and public sectors for new investment did not abate.
The government, for example, felt it would be politically
impossible to stop its annual development expenditure of
£100 million a year in the south, but it could continue only
by the forced savings of inflation.

Italy's experience poses a fundamental question for all
democracies. On the one hand, electorates are promised
annually increased investment on hospitals, schools, universities and other public aims. On the other, they insist on
annual rises in income in order to increase their current consumption. What democratic leaders need ceaselessly to pro-
claim – and demonstrate – is that the savings necessary for
expansion can come either : (1) by increasingly handing over
the control and allocation of resources to the state, with
consequent loss of freedom – personal, economic and political – ending ultimately in a Soviet society, or (2) by allowing free enterprise to preserve freedom by responding to
consumers' demand. Consumers must strike a balance between (a) motor cars or TV sets for current consumption,
and (b) allowing savings to be made for new hospitals or
schools. In the 1950s, wages and salaries were taking 72 per
cent of the UK's national income, profits 23 per cent, compared with about 40 per cent for profits before World War I.
It was out of that 40 per cent that the nation's vast existing
equipment in industry, railways, hospitals, schools, etc., had
been built up. For decades we have been content to live off
this inheritance, but now it is out of date. Whether we re-
equip ourselves by the methods of a free people or slide into
the state control, which the Italians and Germans threw off
with such remarkable economic results in 1948, depends on
whether our leaders, political and industrial, face us squarely
with the choice.

It is often suggested that at the root of our lack of economic purpose lies a social malady : class barriers and resent-
ments. Whereas the prestige accorded to businessmen in

France or Germany attracts the best talent into industry, monopoly by 'gentlemen' is alleged to frustrate our talent and to people Boards of Directors with 'guinea-pigs'. The public schools and Oxbridge are said to perpetuate class divisions and the cult of the 'amateur' by their alleged contempt of technological expertise and insistence that only 'all round' Arts men can have the 'broad view' necessary for higher command. The conclusion is that a social revolution is the necessary basis for economic advance.

There is nothing in this conclusion that is new, or exceptionally disturbing, or that need cause despair. Open a chapter of any history, of any country, in any century, and two points always emerge : (1) that every thoughtful citizen felt that he was living in 'an age of transition', that the period of his grandfather's generation was a golden era, whose problems were nostalgically simple compared to those of the present. (2) that, at all periods, economic advance has depended on the climate of opinion. Greek scientists knew about the steam engine, but no industrial revolution followed because the prevalent ideology esteemed farmers, soldiers and statesmen, and despised traders. A Polish inventor, who constructed a machine to weave cloth in the twelfth century, was hanged for this threat to the established order. But social revolution may be achieved only by bloodshed if the forces of tradition are strong enough to block change. The central analysis that all such pessimists miss is that, historically, *social evolution has most successfully avoided bloodshed, and economic advance has been least painful, because quickest, wherever competition has been most free.* An example: between 1846 and 1850, when Britain's population was 19 million and factory workers numbered 600,000, the railways, unhampered by a stage coach workers' trades union 'fief', created 600,000 *new* jobs. There is nothing new in the Beeching report : at the age of 51, William Chaplin, a leading stage coach proprietor, sold his 70 coaches and 4,500 horses on routes where railways were being built and invested the proceeds – in railways. He died chairman of the London and South Western. There were plenty of sympathisers with

the 30,000 odd coachmen, guards, turnpike men, innkeepers
and ostlers, whose livelihoods were at stake. But had they
had their way, the period of adaptation, instead of being
short and painful, would have been long drawn out and
anguishing, with the risk that other countries might have
launched the new technology ahead of us.

Competition: a 'rat race'?

Professor Milton Friedman in *Capitalism and Freedom*
points out that 'competition' suffers from the confusion between its popular use and the economist's technical use. In
ordinary talk, competition means personal rivalry with one
individual seeking to outdo his known competitor. To economists, competition means the opposite. There is no personal
rivalry in the market place. The wheat farmer in a free
market does not feel himself in personal rivalry with, or
threatened by, his neighbour, who is, in fact, in economic
language, his competitor. The essence of a competitive market is that it is *impersonal*. No one participant can determine
the terms on which other participants shall have access to
goods or jobs. All take prices as established in the market and
no individual can have more than a negligible influence on
price, although all participants together determine price by
the combined effect of their separate decisions. Monopoly
exists when an individual, an enterprise, or a trade union, is
allowed sufficient control over a product or service to determine significantly the terms on which other individuals shall
have access to it. Monopoly comes closer to the popular
concept of a 'rat race', because it does involve conflict and
personal rivalry. Of course, competition is rarely, if ever,
perfect, but the better the efforts to approximate to it, the
speedier do economic changes promote economic growth *and*
social evolution, and the nearer the approximation to social
justice.

Throughout history, the powers and privileges of castes
and ruling classes have depended, ultimately, on their control of wealth. No society – including the USSR and the
USA – has ever been entirely classless, but the more competi-

tive a society the wider can wealth be spread, the greater is social mobility, and the nearer the approach to classlessness. Monopoly, private or state, leads to totalitarian government. So Competition is essential for a healthy democracy.

Germany's experience

Most of *Encounter*'s contributors appear to accept this argument but imply that opinion in Britain today is such as to make competition an impossible counsel of perfection. The masses, however, do not think up ideologies for themselves. New ideas emanate from individuals, writers, intellectuals. They supersede prevailing ideas if they are forcefully preached and if experience substantiates them. In this age of mass electorates, national leaders have a greater duty than ever before to explain their ideas until they are accepted or rejected – *in short to practise leadership*. Nor is this necessarily a slow process, as we can see from postwar Germany's experience. When Erhard came to power in 1948, the prevailing view was that nation-wide devastation could be tackled only by national planning, that the problems of recovery were so vast that they were far beyond the scope of individual enterprise to solve, that the millions of unemployed could only be put to work by Keynesian schemes of credit creation to establish full employment. If Erhard had acquiesced in the contemporary orthodoxy, and accepted the timid advice of Anglo-American occupation generals, an élite of key administrators and planners would have borne the responsibility of organising the German people for recovery and would be in power today. But what Erhard and his advisers wanted was to *enlist the energies of the people to organise themselves* for a recovery that would not be imposed from above but would give each participant first a sense of purpose and thereafter of personal achievement. The German opposition denounced competition as a 'rat race'.

Erhard and his advisers faced this ideological challenge. Day in, day out, they proclaimed that the more competitive a society the more entrepreneurs and workers are compelled to use the least costly combination of resources. It is in their interests and in the interests of society to do so. To use resources wastefully or to slack on the job is obviously in the interests of neither. On the one hand, entrepreneurs seeking to make higher profits and avoid losses, and on the other suppliers of resources, including employees, seeking higher monetary rewards, bring about the changes in the allocation of resources, and therefore in the composition of the output, which society is demanding. Free enterprise conceives society as a spontaneous combustion, which not only sorts out comparative aptitudes and technical advantages, but is a means of utilising and enlarging a heritage of knowledge incapable of being grasped as a whole by any individual. Progress (whether in industry or in education) lies not in enforcing preconceived aims or plans based on the limited experience of experts, but in the emergence, through the interplay of the attempts of millions of individuals to meet the demands of society, of social ideas as yet unconceived. In all this the state has its role : to uphold the equality of all before the law, to aid the poor, the helpless and the unemployed, to provide free education from primary school to university — but in such ways as to cure helplessness, not to increase or perpetuate it. The true welfare state, as Erhard proclaimed time and again, teaches people how to stand on their own feet, not to live with their hands in each others' pockets.

It is no paradox, but a statement of fact, borne out by the headlines in any popular contemporary daily, that the less competition there is the more intense the sense of social injustice. It is easy to see why. Where competition prevails, prices, wages and salaries are determined objectively by impersonal forces. The more competition is diminished, the more powerful become monopolies in industry, in trade unions, and in the professions. Prices, wages and salaries become more and more divorced from the impersonal market, more and more controlled by subjective assessments of 'fairness', which lead to 'leapfrogging' rivalries between union and union, profession and profession, as now the postmen 'lag' behind the electricians, now the doctors behind the consultants.

The worst 'free for all' society is the egalitarian state, because it fosters on a nation-wide scale the appetite for acquiring as much as possible – in education, health, pensions, etc. – for nothing. Acquisition by personal effort is a contribution to the community. Acquisition by electoral bribes is not. Far from providing social incentives, the idea of 'fair' shares spreads social poison – envy. What *is* the 'fair' share of a stenographer, coal miner, policeman, managing director, nurse, bricklayer or skilled factory worker? Who can persuade the individual stenographer, coal miner, etc., that the share allocated to him by a National Job Evaluation Commission is 'fair'? The implication behind this concept is a slow-moving, traditional society, based on status.

The Europeans accepted the need to tighten the link between effort and reward. The implication is a changing society responding to man's needs. Ideal social justice is no more attainable than ideal happiness, but as long as the currency is kept stable to uphold society's real valuations, there will be a constant approximation towards social justice.

Wanted: courageous leaders

Does all this mean that Britain faces a glorious past? It is up to us. We have, in fact, made a start. The government has done a good deal to mobilise the forces of competition. The process began with the dash for freedom from physical rationing and from excessive demand inflation during the chancellorship of Mr Butler in 1951 to 1955. It has continued with the scrapping of virtually all physical controls on imports, the establishment of the restrictive practices court, Dr Beeching's drive to adapt the railways to contemporary needs, and new measures to deal with monopolies and resale price maintenance.

Existing measures to promote competition have gone nothing like far enough. We need more information in company accounts, unilateral tariff cuts, an end to subsidies to, or protective duties on, agriculture, fuel, aircraft, bus and taxi services, etc. — a really tough crack down on monopolies, restrictive practices and resale prices maintenance, and we must seek to join the European Economic Community. The basic difference has been that whereas Europe's leaders in politics, industry and the trade unions, particularly in Germany, have had the courage of their convictions, ours have not.

ENOCH POWELL

I have had three lives.

In my first existence I studied classics at King Edward's, Birmingham (my birthplace) and Trinity College, Cambridge; became a fellow of my College in 1934 and Professor of Greek at Sydney University in 1938. While waiting for the war to come, I wrote half a dozen books on Herodotus and Thucydides, including a dictionary; also some poetry.

My second life began in 1939 when I joined the Royal Warwickshire Regiment in the ranks. Promotion to lance-corporal was the tallest hurdle I ever cleared; but after that I went on to be a lieutenant-colonel in the Middle East and a brigadier in India – all chairborne. By the time peace came, I had picked for my third life politics.

Three years in the Conservative Research Department, a forlorn-hope by-election, and then MP for Wolverhampton South-West by a margin of 691 votes in 1950. For two-thirds of my nearly fifteen years in Parliament I have been a backbencher; but I served a year in the Ministry of Housing and helped Duncan Sandys to plan the Rent Act, and another at the Treasury in 1957 under Peter Thorneycroft, with whom and Nigel Birch I resigned on an issue of government spending. Later I was Minister of Health from 1960 to 1963, and in the Cabinet for the last fifteen months of that time.

My wife, who married me in 1952, has put up with all this – and with two daughters.

In 1960 I wrote *Saving in a Free Society* for the Institute of Economic Affairs, where I see I said:

> 'I happen to believe that when a society's economic life ceases to be shaped by the interaction of the free decisions of individuals, freedom is in a fair way to disappear from other sides of its existence as well. The terms 'free economy' and 'free society' are to me interchangeable.'

In 1964 I still believe that, though some people seem to think it tactless to repeat it just now.

18: IS IT POLITICALLY
PRACTICABLE?

ENOCH POWELL *argues that the economic pessimists lack historical perspective, suffer from hypochondria and underestimate the extent to which the economy
can be influenced by the opinions held by members of
society. He sees nothing inevitable in the recent tendencies to increase state authority, but believes we are at
liberty to consider alternative policies. He considers that
the method of allowing people more freedom in their individual lives can be more productive than state authority
because it draws on more human capacities and that its
political practicability turns on overcoming prejudices
which have been allowed to harden against the market
economy.*

THE great difficulty which besets all introspective diagnosis
and prescription for national ills is that of historical
perspective. The starting point is so often a false assumption.
We are aware of our own present doubts, discontents, uncertainties, dejections. Those of former generations are either
unknown to us altogether, or known only partially and then
at the cost of much study. Because the details and moods
of the past are lost or unknown, we assume that the past
was simple and uncomplicated, and we people the empty
spaces on its canvas with figures as confident, purposeful and
self-assured as we feel ourselves to be the reverse, endowing
them with a foresight and vision which is really our own
hindsight. Having done this, we demand what ails us that
our generation is so different and so degenerate.

If those who complain that Parliament is losing its authority and its influence would take the pains to enquire, they

would find that at no time for which there are records has that complaint not been heard. If they would immerse themselves in the writing and discussion of 1863 – or 1463 – they would be startled by the same lamentations over the impending suicide and 'the short time left to us'.

Historical projections can mislead

History, it is true, does, with the aid of distance and much simplification, undertake to compare and contrast the state and mood of different nations, and of the same nation at different eras. These comparisons may tell us the bald facts about comparative size, power and wealth. If they are large and crude enough, we can project them into the present : there is no great difficulty about comparing in very broad terms Britain's military strength or wealth now and one or two generations ago, either absolutely or in relation to other nations. If anyone likes, he can join up these points and call the resultant line a trend. But even these crude material measurements need to be taken over substantial periods of time, and when you have got them their significance may be highly debatable.[1] The recent passion for watching indices of exports or industrial production month by month and writing them into international 'league-tables' is the habit of a hypochondriac taking his pulse and temperature every five minutes and going into a tizzy over every rise or fall. Far less are we in any position to detect, and

[1] One of the tables in 'Suicide of a Nation?' *Encounter*, July 1963, is a nice clear graph showing the change in the shares of West Germany, France, Italy and Britain in world trade in the ten years to 1962 as percentages. West Germany's rose from 10 per cent to 20 per cent, Italy's from 4 per cent to 6 per cent, France's fell from 10 per cent to 9 per cent, and Britain's from 22 per cent to 15 per cent. In the third of a century to 1937, Britain's had fallen from 32 per cent to 22 per cent, France's from 16 per cent to 6½ per cent, while Germany's began and finished at 22 per cent and Italy's remained at 3½ per cent. If world trade were a football league or Lent race this would be a 'bad show' – except for Germany. As it is, might one ask what on earth a percentage share of total world trade, or these figures in particular, are supposed to prove about the prosperity, progress, or wellbeing of a country?

dogmatise on, trends and changes in national psychology, where both the factual material and the means of measurement are absent.

The myth of the Ages of Gold and Iron (the contrast between a glorious past and a decadent present), and the twin myth of the Isles of the Blest (the contrast between other lands where all is well and our own where everything is wrong) – these myths have been and no doubt always will be embraced in every age and clime. They belong to humanity's stage properties for dramatising its lot. There is no need to be surprised or indignant when they turn up again in our own time and country – in the pages of *Encounter*, for instance.

Is Britain decadent?

In itself the universal addiction is probably pretty harmless. The harm starts when it is used and exploited to furnish the philosophy of a political change and to provide the means to accomplish it. Though the fears of the hypochondriac are without physical foundation, hypochondria itself is a real and harmful state, and you do a man harm if you inculcate, encourage or confirm it in him. His own vigour and confidence and effectiveness are impaired and he becomes an easier prey to quackery, imposture and fraud.

The opinions which the members of a society hold about it and about themselves as members of it have a close relationship with its wellbeing and happiness and with its future course. What precisely that relationship may be – whether of cause and effect and, if so, which is cause and which effect, or whether the one is a manifestation and accompaniment of the other – is as problematic as the relationship between the mental and physical states of an individual. Nor do we know how far, if at all, those opinions can be influenced and altered by deliberate intent – this leads us into the conundrum of free will and determinism. All political activity, however, in the widest sense of the word 'political', assumes, and must assume (just as all decision-making assumes free-will), that those opinions can be influenced, and that in turn they influence the fate and fortune of a nation in space and time. This is why politics is always more than an infinitely complex and exciting game played for high stakes. It is a continuing fight for the mind of a nation.

For the last dozen years the output of a sizable number of writers and thinkers has been dedicated to the thesis of the decadence of Britain. No argument or statistic has been neglected which would tend to show Britain as losing the relative position it formerly occupied and falling behind in what is represented as a race or contest with other nations. True, there are a number of embarrassing inconsistencies.

If Britain is decadent, the virtues which it has lost and which need to be restored to it must have been present in an earlier age : if it has fallen behind other countries, it must formerly have been ahead of them. But that former age is none other than the 'bad old days' which are the indispensable stock-in-trade of every denigrator of the present : their business ought not to be with past Golden Ages but with future Utopias. Again, these other countries held up to our shame as paragons of progress and success have a variety of political and social systems of which no-one could say that similarity to the system recommended by the critics is a striking common characteristic.

This is awkward; but no matter. At whatever cost in logic and consistency, the theme of national decadence and failure must be hammered in, for the sake of what follows. When the victim is rendered sufficiently suggestible, the revelation is produced, the order is pronounced, and – if the technique, familiar to military interrogators and communist brain-washers, works – he will do what he is told. In its simplest form the complete thesis is this : the nation has failed, it has neither the energy nor the enterprise nor the insight to keep pace with other nations in the modern world; therefore it must be 'taken over' by those who do have these qualities, who will exercise on its behalf all the economic and social decisions that matter.

The coolness and the arrogance of the proposition are breathtaking. There has been no attempt at modest concealment. This is tactically sound : history has plenty of examples to show that impudent claims have the best chance of acceptance if they are boldly and unblushingly announced. The development of land, the erection of major buildings, the investment of capital, the direction of savings, the objects of consumer expenditure, in short every type of decision which shapes the future of the economy (and more than the economy) is to be determined by government : it is written, it is spoken, 'he that hath ears to hear, let him hear'. And if anyone should presume to ask, 'But why is all this necessary?', the answer is ready-made in that hypochondriac fear, turned by dint of repetition into unassailable fact : 'Because you failed, because your own decisions were wrong, because "the attitude of the average Englishman must prove suicidal", therefore your destiny must be taken out of your hands and placed in better keeping.'

Pessimism repudiated

My fellow essayists in this collection are a varied lot. They are not only concerned with different aspects of the nation's life; they also differ perceptibly in mood, method, and approach. But one thing they have transparently in common. They repudiate instinctively as well as intellectually the judgement of Britain as a nation doomed to decadence, and they reject the interpretation of our recent past and our present which would lead to that conclusion.

What unites all these essayists and indeed all those – I believe them to be a clear majority of the nation – who reject the pessimistic thesis is a conviction of the unexplored and unlimited potentialities which lie within these fifty millions of people and their islands. The possibilities of that future are as much beyond our power to define as the reality of the present exceeds the imagination of our forefathers. Neither the vision nor the knowledge of any individual or group of individuals, however talented, with whatever powers and resources equipped, can make a worthy estimate of the scope of these possibilities or of the directions in which they extend. Nothing less than the knowledge and insights and efforts of the whole nation can suffice to work out its future.

From this conviction follows the practical thesis which all the essayists in this book are elaborating from their respective points of view : in its economic life and in its social life the future course of the nation ought to be shaped by the choices of its members to the utmost extent that is possible in a modern state. In the economic sphere the capitalist system of competition and free enterprise is the only form of organization yet devised which enables a nation to do just that.

What is 'politically possible'?

This is the theme which my fellow essayists explore. In doing so, they not only argue against possible future limitations of the mechanism of free choice; some of them also consider the case for restoring it to areas from which it has been excluded or into which it has not yet been introduced. Such an exercise immediately challenges the question : 'Is it politically practicable?' Readers who share the basic thesis of this book may follow the arguments with sympathy and even enthusiasm, yet feel that what is called 'the trend' has set so firmly in the opposite direction that it is politically impracticable to halt, let alone reverse, it.

Before attempting to answer the question, be it first observed that statements and proposals which are not 'politically practicable' are not necessarily for that reason worthless. It would be an intolerable limitation on freedom of discussion if the pursuit of an argument or a train of reasoning had to halt on the line which was judged — judged, incidentally, by whom? — to mark the extent of the 'politically practicable'. Those whose business it is to think, to study and to criticise have a positive duty to follow the *Logos* where it leads them; it is the business of others (or of the same people in another capacity) to speculate on what might be 'politically practicable', and how, at any particular moment of time.

What is 'politically practicable' is not a constant; it changes, not necessarily predictably and sometimes swiftly,

while the validity of the arguments and principles remains.
Indeed, the enunciation of 'politically impracticable'
thoughts and proposals has itself often made things 'politically practicable' which were not so before. It is hardly too
much to claim that most of the political acts of one generation would have been regarded as 'politically impracticable'
in the previous one. Politics would be caged like a squirrel if
political thought were confined to what is 'politically practicable'.

First of all, then, let us examine this alleged 'trend' towards the reduction of choice and the extension of state
control which is supposed to be 'inevitable'. A senior civil
servant whom I knew had the rule of deleting the word
'inevitable' wherever it occurred in any draft or brief. It is
wonderful how salutary the exercise is. There are very few
trends whose continuation is inherently inevitable by some
natural law : it is advisable to wait till after the event before
hailing them as 'inevitable'. To do so in advance is just ex-
trapolator's folly. How easy it would be to make a fortune on
the Stock Exchange out of 'inevitable trends'; but alas, in
human affairs trends have a habit of pausing, stopping or
even reversing. Therefore even if there were an observable
trend in the direction alleged in recent years or decades, it
would need to be proved, and could not be simply asserted,
that it must 'inevitably' continue.

No trend to state control

I deny, however, that such a trend is in fact at all clearly
or unambiguously observable. On the contrary, during the
greater part of the last twelve years in this country the trend
has been the opposite way. In the early part of the 1950s
markets in food, in commodities and in land were restored,
the apparatus of physical controls was dismantled, and –
most significant of all, perhaps – savings were gradually
allowed to command their market price by a return to rates
of interest reflecting the balance of supply and demand for
capital and credit. The same trend continued in the later
1950s : the distortions of the housing market were reduced

though not eliminated; restrictions on the external movement of money and capital were simplified or removed;
restrictive trade practices were brought under attack; free
trade was established with the EFTA countries and attempted with the countries of the Common Market. Even in
the most recent phrase, during which it could be argued that
regional plans, NEDDY and NICKY, and such other developments represent a shift in the opposite direction, policies designed to improve the internal and external market
have continued to be pursued : witness the legislation on
resale price maintenance, and the moves to reduce or eliminate restrictions on international trade. Only during the last
few years has the proportion of the national product determined by public expenditure ceased to fall and begun to
rise again.

These facts are, at the very least, inconsistent with the
theory of a steady trend in Great Britain away from a free
economy. The indications abroad are equally ambiguous. It
would be a strangely biased observer who would describe the
Western European countries as having shown a constant tendency towards *dirigisme* in the 1950s and 1960s. If France
could be pleaded in support of the proposition, Germany
and Italy could equally be cited against; only in very recent
years, perhaps under the influence of Common Market institutions, have the arguments for a planned economy begun to
be loud in the European countries which have most con-
spicuously practised competitive freedom. At the same time,
from behind the Iron Curtain, come more and more frequent
intimations that the Socialist Republics are beginning shyly
to experiment with the benefits of dispersed decision.

In short, the alleged 'trend' itself, let alone its 'inevitability', is not an objective phenomenon, but the product of
wishful (or fearful) seeing. If it is not 'politically practicable'
to prevent the area in which the mechanism of free choice
operates from being further limited or to enlarge it in old
or new directions, the reason is not the fact of an 'inevitable
trend'. It is 'politically practicable' as soon as, and as far as,
people are prepared to will it; and there lies the crux.

To make men love their institutions was discerned by Disraeli as the essence of the statesman's task. It must be admitted that in respect to the institutions of the free economy the task has not been discharged in Britain with any conspicuous degree of success. One of the strangest ironies is the coldness, suspicion and even hostility with which the British in the mid-twentieth century regard the mechanism to which they owe, if nothing else, a material affluence that has increased up to the present time at an accelerating pace. Like other ironies, this one is susceptible of historical explanation; but I am not concerned here with the causes, only with the current phenomena. What is it that surrounds capitalism here, but not (for instance) in America, with an aura of disapproval?

The ideas with which it is associated in Britain are inhumanity, ruthlessness and unfairness. Now, the Briton prides himself upon being humane, kindly and above all fair. Call a thing 'unfair' and, for an Englishman, all further argument about it, or even examination of it, is at once at an end. The political practicability of maintaining or extending the area of free choice and dispersed decision depends on dissociating it from the ideas of inhumanity and unfairness, and associating it with the contrary notions of humanity and fairness.

Misunderstandings about 'capitalism' and markets

It is here that the public relations of capitalism have been found wanting; yet there is no inherent reason why. Success depends upon the inculcation of a few, essentially simple propositions, which people can test for themselves by common sense. Here are some of the principal ones.

1. A market need not be perfect in order to be superior to no market at all. All competition in the real world is imperfect[1] but, however imperfect it is, it will still tend to a

---

[1] It is arguable that theoretical perfect competition is self-stultifying, and that only when imperfect is it dynamic (F. A. Hayek, *Individualism and Economic Order*, 1949).

more effective employment of resources than would be achieved in its absence.

2. The benefits of capitalism can be reaped even in an economy of which some parts are managed on a different principle. For example, if part of a nation's industry is in state ownership, the market will still secure the best return on the productive resources which are left available to the rest. It is false to contend that capitalism must be applied everywhere or not at all.

3. There is no inconsistency between capitalism and community action for social or political ends. For example, a capitalist state can also be a welfare state; indeed, other things being equal, a state which is capitalist can provide more welfare than one that is not. (This is what Dr Erhard tried to express with typically German clumsiness and accuracy by the expression *Sozialmarktwirtschaft*.)

4. If capitalism is a mechanism, it is not a 'soulless' mechanism. It is the means of giving weight and effect to individual choices and preferences, and securing some power of self-expression to every member of the community. Respect for humanity and tolerance for the individual are implicit in the capitalist system as in no other : it is the planned economy which insults people – by producing, for instance, consumption goods that they do not want.

5. There can be no worse unfairness than to deny people the chance to put whatever assets they have to what they judge the best use. The market is the fairest standard, impartial and impersonal, treating like things alike, which is the essence of justice.

Education in free economy

Once dispel the emotional aura of inhumanity and unfairness, and a powerful emotive idea is ready to be brought into play on the other side : freedom. The dislike of being dictated to is as profound a British characteristic as the addiction to fair play. Superior knowledge, and superior knowledge localised at a geographical centre, is the assumption inseparable from *dirigisme* and a planned economy. It is an assumption calculated to attract the maximum unpopularity.

'Political practicability', then, will be proportionate to the success of the free economy's public relations in establishing basic propositions of this kind in people's minds. In calculating the consequences, account must be taken of the fact of political inertia. The effective presumption is always against the attempt to alter what the Romans, if they had spoken their own language worse, would have called the *status quo*. The degree of conviction necessary to prevent further erosion of the area of the free economy is likely to be much less than would be required to extend it at the expense of existing habits and institutions. People will summon up the will to scrap or alter what they are already used to accepting only if they are strongly impressed with its inconveniences and disadvantages, and not merely with the theoretical superiority of some alternative.

The wider and deeper the implications of the free economy are explored and probed, the better. The bolder and more radical the proposals for extending it, the more we shall appreciate its benefits. Politically, the practical strategy is first to secure the existing frontiers and then move over to the offensive as the numbers and strength of the free economy's adherents from time to time permit.

GUIDE TO WRITERS CITED

Abel-Smith, Brian, Reader in Social Administration, London School of Economics

Albu, Austen, Member of Parliament

Allen, R. G. D., Professor of Statistics, University of London

Allen, William W., American management consultant

Balogh, Thomas, Economist at Oxford University

Benn, Anthony Wedgewood, Member of Parliament

Bevan, Aneurin, Late Member of Parlaiment

Beveridge, Lord, Late economist and public servant

Buchanan, Colin, Professor of Transport, University of London

Buchanan, J. M., Professor of Economics, University of Virginia

Caine, Sir Sydney, Director of London School of Economics

Calvin, John, 16th-century religious reformer

Chapman, Brian, Professor of Government, University of Manchester

Clark, Colin, Director of Agricultural Economic Research Institute, University of Oxford

Coase, R. H., Professor of Economics, University of Virginia

Cohen, Baron, Chairman of Council on Prices, Productivity and Incomes (1957–9)

Crosland, C. A. R., Member of Parliament

Crossman, R. H. S., Member of Parliament

Dancy, John, Headmaster of Marlborough College

Davies, Ernest, Former Member of Parliament

Day, Alan, Professor of Economics, London School of Economics

Erhard, Ludwig, Chancellor of West Germany

Fleming, Lord, Chairman of the Committee on the Public Schools and the General Education System, 1944

Fogarty, Michael, Professor of Industrial Relations, University College of South Wales and Monmouthshire

Friedman, Milton, Professor of Economics, University of Chicago

Gaitskell, Hugh, Late Member of Parliament

Galbraith, J. K., Professor of Economics, University of Harvard

Geddes, Charles, Member of General Council of Trades Union Congress

George, Henry, 19th-century advocate of single tax on land

Gibbon, Edward, Author of *Decline and Fall of the Roman Empire*

Guillebaud, C. W., Cambridge economist

Hagenbuch, Walter, Economist at Canterbury University

Hall, Peter, Lecturer in Geography, University of London

Hall, Sir Robert, Formerly economic adviser to HM Government

Hayek, Friedrich von, Economic and social philosopher

Hennessy, Jossleyn, Economic journalist

Hicks, Sir John and Lady, Oxford economists

Hibbs, John, Economist with British Railways

Hoggart, Richard, Professor of Literature, University of Birmingham

Home, Sir Alec Douglas, Member of Parliament

Hughes, Donald, Headmaster of Rydal School

Ilersic, A. R., Lecturer in Social Statistics, University of London

Jack, D. T., Professor of Economics, University of Durham

Jenkins, Lord, Chairman of the Committee on Company Law (1962)

Jewkes, John, Professor of Economic Organisation, University of Oxford

Jewkes, Mrs Sylvia, Wife of John Jewkes

Keynes, Lord, Late Economist

Kindleburger, C. P., Professor of Economics at the Massachtussetts Institute of Technology

Koestler, Arthur, Author

Krengel, Rolf, Professor of Economics at a Berlin (W) research institute

Lamfalussy, A., Economic Adviser to a Belgian bank

Lees, D. S., Reader in Economics, University of Keele

Lincoln, Abraham, Late President of the United States

Lincoln, John Abraham, Writer on trade unions

Little, Ian, Oxford economist

Lutz, Vera, Economist

MacDougall, Sir Donald, Economic Director of the National Economic Development Council

Macmillan, Harold, Member of Parliament

Maine, Sir Henry, 19th-century jurist

Molina, Luis, 16th-century economist

Packard, Vance, American journalist

Peacock, A. T., Professor of Economics, York University

Pigou, A. C., Late Cambridge Economist

Pilkington, Sir Harry, Businessman

Popper, Karl R., Professor of Logic and Scientific Method, University of London

Powell, Enoch, Member of Parliament

Prest, A. R., Professor of Economics, University of Manchester

Rees, Goronwy, Writer

Richardson, Gordon, Accountant

Riesman, David, American writer

Robbins, Lord, Economist

Rose, Harold, Reader in Industrial Finance, London School of Economics

Rostas, W. B., Economist

Russell, Bertrand, Philosopher

Sargeant, J. R., Lecturer in Economics, University of Oxford

Sawers, David, Economist

Schacht, Hjalmar, Former German Finance Minister

Seale, John, Physician

Seldon, Arthur, Editorial Director, Institute of Economic Affairs

Shanks, Michael, Economic journalist

Shone, Sir Robert, Director General of National Economic Development Council

Shonfield, Andrew, Director of Studies at Royal Institute International Affairs

Slesser, Sir Henry, Former Solicitor-General

Smith, Adam, 18th-century economist

Strachey, John, Late economic writer and Member of Parliament

Titmuss, R. M., Professor of Social Administration at the London School of Economics

Tocqueville, A. de, 19th-century political philosopher

Townsend, Peter, Professor of Sociology, University of Essex

Turvey, R., Economist

Vaizey, John, Oxford Economist

Verdon-Smith, Sir Reginald, Businessman

Wakeford, John, Sociologist

Wiles, P. J. D., Professor of Economics, University of California

Williams, Raymond, Lecturer in English, Cambridge University

Wiseman, Jack, Professor of Applied Economics, University of York

Woodcock, George, General Secretary, Trades Union Congress

Young, Mrs Elizabeth (Lady Kennet), Writer